One Acre
and
Security

how to live off the earth without ruining it

Illustrated by

Arthur J. Anderson

One Acre and Security

Bradford Angier

STACKPOLE BOOKS

ONE ACRE AND SECURITY

Copyright ©1972 by
Bradford Angier
Published by
STACKPOLE BOOKS
Cameron and Kelker Streets
Harrisburg, Pa. 17105

27960

Printed in U.S.A.

Library of Congress Cataloging in Publication Data

Angier, Bradford.
    One acre and security—how to live off the earth without ruining it.

    1. Farm management—U. S.   2.   Country life
—U. S.   3.   Outdoor life.   I.   Title.
S561.A574   630   72-179608
ISBN 0-8117-1161-7

To
our friends of years
and right trusty partners
BETTY BROWN and
LT. COL. FREDERICK W. BROWN
the author dedicates this book as a small
tribute to their patience, faithfulness,
and unswerving loyalty, with the earnest
hope that time may but knit us even closer

OTHER BOOKS BY BRADFORD ANGIER

HOW TO LIVE IN THE WOODS ON PENNIES A DAY

GOURMET COOKING FOR FREE

THE ART AND SCIENCE OF TAKING TO THE WOODS
(with C.B. Colby)

A STAR TO THE NORTH
(with Barbara Corcoran)

HOME MEDICAL HANDBOOK
(with E. Russel Kodet, M.D.)

MORE FREE-FOR-THE-EATING WILD FOODS

BEING YOUR OWN WILDERNESS DOCTOR
(with E. Russel Kodet, M.D.)

THE GHOST OF SPIRIT RIVER
(with Jeanne Dixon)

SKILLS FOR TAMING THE WILDS

FREE FOR THE EATING

HOME IN YOUR PACK

MISTER RIFLEMAN
(with Colonel Townsend Whelen)

WE LIKE IT WILD

WILDERNESS COOKERY

HOW TO GO LIVE IN THE WOODS ON $10 A WEEK

ON YOUR OWN IN THE WILDERNESS
(with Colonel Townsend Whelen)

LIVING OFF THE COUNTRY

HOW TO BUILD YOUR HOME IN THE WOODS

AT HOME IN THE WOODS

Contents

CHAPTER ONE

Country Living
Near the Cities

ARE you one of the millions who are working harder than you want, at things you don't like to do, in order to afford the sort of existence you don't care to live?

Then how about moving to some secluded acre, perhaps within a few miles of your present home but still away from the rat race and the traffic jitters, where you can live to a healthy extent from the land itself? You may even be able to get by at first on just a half-acre, perhaps using your earnings to expand later to a more profitable two or three acres.

Probably we've never had a generation of people in the United States that was more tense, more high-strung. Every night in this country the public consumes 19 million sleeping pills. As for aspirin, Americans gulp down 11 million pounds a year. Given our present population, this comes out to about 50 headaches apiece per annum. Why not make your move now to escape the anxious sleeping-pill and aspirin mobs?

Aspirins and sleeping pills are not going to cure America's tensions although they may help temporarily. To get at the real source of our anxieties we must find serenity within ourselves.

11

There is an Edwin Markham poem that reminds us that energy and power are related to calm control. "At the heart of the cyclone tearing the sky," Markham wrote, "is a place of central calm." That is to say, a cyclone derives its power from an inner tranquility. In this tense and harried cyclonic world of ours, it is vital that we learn how to live robust and relaxed lives peacefully in the center of outer frenzy. How?

Man's Need for Open Skies

Scientists are mindful that nature intended human beings to spend most of their hours beneath open skies. With appetites sharpened by outdoor living, they should eat plain food. They should live at their natural God-given pace, unoppressed by the artificial tension and scurry of man-made civilization.

Yet the mass of city men, stalking their food at the city market instead of in the green fields and cool woods, put up with existences of quiet desperation. They make themselves sick in their cheerless hysteria to lay up something against a sick day. Their incessant anxiety and strain is a well-nigh incurable form of disease. When they aren't feverishly wondering how to get away from the city, they're cursing the chains that drag them back.

Most of what the government doesn't take, they spend in trying to keep up with the other fellow. How many families do you know who will be needlessly poor all their lives because they must live in a house or apartment like their neighbors? Before it became unfashionable, comfortable homes were built on this continent almost entirely of such materials as nature furnishes ready to hand. Incidentally, this book tells how.

How sensible is it to spend the best part of life earning money in order to enjoy a questionable liberty during the least valuable years? Not everyone may fully heed the call of the open places, of course, but many who think themselves shackled to civilized tasks are held back only by such needlessly inhibiting factors as habit, inertia, environment, doubt, resignation, lack of confidence, and often a general misunderstanding of man's makeup.

The truth is, *Homo sapiens* was bred for the fields, plains, deserts, canyons, and mountains. He gets along in his steaming asphalt jungle after a fashion. But is it the normal and healthy life? Ask any family doctor, plagued as he is by long lists of complaints—symptoms of nothing so much as man's instinctive rebellion against the race to polluted destruction into which he has pressed himself. Deep down underneath it may well be this very revolt that is driving him more and more toward those atomic weapons of annihilation that can plunge those of us who survive back to the cave, with its roasting brace of rabbits sputtering above a simple little blaze in front.

But you can enjoy that rabbit now, plus the profits from a few hutches of this rapidly reproducing animal. Or there are guinea pigs, a small flock of sheep, a few hogs that can live largely on your own garden and table scraps, your own dairy cow, goats, chickens, ducks, geese, and a lot more, plus thrifty hives of bees both profitably to occupy your time and to provide delicious living-off-the-land meals.

Many a modern worker, tied to a wage or salary and penned in the city or seam-bursting suburb by the daily grind whereby he ekes out bare support for himself and his family, has been awaiting the opportunity to escape to the uncrowded places where he can take charge of his own life and live it in a happy, decent, and invigorating way.

But can he cope with country life? Can he subsist off the land? Is he still strong enough to strike off on his own? Can he put up his own house? Can he feed everyone the year around from the family garden? How can he earn extra money regularly? These are among the thousand questions that beset every refugee from the rat race in his search for the good life.

This book is written for just such individuals, who want to move not to the distant wilderness but just far enough away from the smog and the screaming traffic to be where meat will be theirs for the raising, fish for the catching, fruit and vegetables for the picking, fuel for the cutting, home for the satisfaction of building, and open land for the surprisingly few dollars that will set them free to settle on it—breathing cleaner air for a change, beholden to none, doing what they want to do most and giving it their best.

If one advances confidently in the direction of his dreams and endeavors to lead the sort of life he has imagined, assured Henry

Thoreau, he will meet with success unexpected in common hours.

"If you have built castles in the air, your work need not be lost. That is where they should be. Now put the foundations under them."

Country Living Near the Cities

Building a home is not as difficult as many people think, and you don't have to go to the wilderness to do it. It's possible to build a log cabin just far enough from urbanized areas to get away from the smog and the traffic jitters and yet close enough to the cities to keep the comforts of civilization accessible.

Why not build such a cabin even if, right now, you can get to it only during vacations and weekends? At the very least, it will be more satisfying than burning up the highways, with a day here and an hour there.

Picking Your Acre

How can you pick your ideal escape niche? Weekend searches of the countryside within easy driving distance of your home or business may turn the trick. Following the advertisements, scanning maps, consulting a real estate expert, and talking to friends who may have been there may be of considerable assistance, too.

Detailed information can be secured from the government tourist offices that are situated in all state and provincial capitals. You may pass along your problems to the Departments of Agriculture and the Interior in Washington, D.C., or to the affable Canadian Government Travel Bureau in Ottawa, Ontario, pinpointing your requirements perhaps and asking for names and addresses where you may obtain more specialized information.

Adjectives will be necessarily discounted. Conclusions will be drawn from temperature charts, rainfall tables, wildlife surveys, forestry reports, contour maps, graphs of frost-free periods, botanical lists, population figures, and other such definite factors.

Making Sure of Land Title

When you buy land anywhere, be sure that you are getting clear title and, unless the property is on a public road, a definite right-of-way to it. Friendly professional advice in the matter should be considered. The help of a competent and unbiased lawyer, usually for a small overall fee, may be good insurance.

As you probably already know, the common procedure when purchasing land is first to reach a verbal agreement, then to put its terms on paper. This becomes binding once it is signed by both seller and buyer. The vendor undertakes to deliver a definite piece of property at a certain time. The purchaser, who ordinarily makes a small payment on the spot as evidence of good faith, promises to accept delivery on that day and to pay as agreed.

The waiting period between the time of the agreement and the actual sale gives both parties time in which to get any necessary affairs in order. The purchaser owes it to himself to examine the title and to verify the boundaries. An actual survey, payment for which should be a matter of agreement, may be in order.

The reason for searching the title is to make sure it is held undisputedly by the seller and that, unless otherwise specified, it is free of encumbrances. These may include building restrictions such as zoning codes and easements, which are privileges given some outside party, as, for example, a right-of-way accorded a power company or municipality.

A local lawyer will generally be glad to investigate the title for a small fee and, unless a title company is operating in the vicinity, it is ordinarily advisable to secure such assistance. Aid may also be obtained in some instances from local registry boards, from a local bank (especially if a mortgage is being applied for there), and occasionally from one's own real estate agent.

The deed to secure if possible is the warranty type. The terms of this make the seller and his heirs liable to defend the title to date of sale from any claims or litigation. A quitclaim deed, the other common variety, is self-explanatory. The seller merely signs over to the new owner any and all rights he may have in the real estate. It is often a wise precaution whenever possible, fees being so minimal, to insure the title with a title guarantee insurance company.

If a bank loan is arranged for the property, the bank for its own protection will assure itself of all necessary details. The bank in this instance ordinarily acts for a set fee, perhaps divided between seller and buyer, as escrow holder. It retains the purchase money, in other words, until all terms of the written agreement between buyer and seller are fulfilled to its satisfaction, relieving both of burdensome technical details.

Once the deed has been transferred to the new owner, the latter should affix any necessary documentary tax stamps and for his own protection record the transaction in the local land office.

Vacation Homes on National Forest Land

There are those for whom remoteness is one of the most desirable factors. They want to laugh in the farther places—where meat is free for the hunting, fish for the casting, wild fruits and vegetables for the gathering, fuel for the cutting, and a cheery log cabin for the fun of building. But that's another book, Stackpole's and my *How to Live in the Woods on Pennies a Day*.

Many people, on the other hand, do not want to live away from the city or the suburbs all year round but would like a vacation home fairly far removed from urbanized areas and yet with neighbors not too far away. A residence on national forest land may be the answer. Such a home will provide an annual vacation at minimum yearly expense.

Some 19,000 private homes already nestle in our national forests, and there is room for a few more. Your best bet, though, is the possibility of taking over such improvements from private owners who are disposing of them for one reason or another. Real estate offices in the general area in which you are interested can give the current picture. Should you find a site in this manner, it is suggested that before purchase you get in touch with the District Ranger in that region to determine the status of the particular special-use permit.

Recreation-residence lots within approved sites in the national forests, administered by the Forest Service Division of the U.S. Department of Agriculture, are established for recreation occupancy. The use of such lots is authorized by special-use permits which set forth the conditions of occupancy and require payment of a small annual fee usually ranging between $50 to $200 per year, depending on the location, and subject to adjustment every five years. The homes, in addition, are subject to state and county taxes. Each Forest Supervisor issues and administers the special-use permits on his forest and has the records of the sites, their locations, specific requirements relating to construction and maintenance, and the annual fee.

An average lot is approximately half an acre in size. This is of sufficient size to permit one vacation residence with adequate screening from adjacent lots. Isolated lots are not sanctioned. Homes are planned in colonies as this reduces vandalism, lessens development costs for permittees, and pares the administrative costs for the government. A recreation home is for the enjoyment of the permittee, his family, and friends. It may not be used as a year-long residence or for commercial purposes, and is, therefore, pretty much restricted to vacation use. Building standards must be met and maintained, and building plans must be approved by the District Ranger.

While no new recreation residence sites are being planned at the moment, a few lots do still remain in already established tracts in three of the western Forest Service regions. For up-to-the-minute information on them write:

Recreation Management and Land Use Branch
Division of Recreation and Lands
Forest Service
Missoula, Montana 59801

Special Land Use
Forest Service, Region 6
P.O. Box 3623
Portland, Oregon 97208

Division of Recreation and Lands
Forest Service
334 25th Street
Ogden, Utah 84401

If you avail yourself of such a site, you will be encouraged to join recognized summer-home associations in areas where these have been formed. Community improvements, such as water systems and roads, are sometimes constructed and maintained by such an association, the individual being assessed for these services. Where these facilities have been constructed by the Forest Service, an amortization charge is added to the land rental fee to recover the government's investment.

Permits specify that construction start within a reasonable time and that homes be located as staked by the Forest Service. Summer homes must be well constructed and of a design appropriate to the forest environment. Natural forest conditions must be preserved to the fullest reasonable extent, with tree and shrub-clearing being held to a minimum.

Restrictions on Homes in Canada's National Parks

Canada's present policy regarding residents in its national parks has become restrictive. "Business and commercial enterprises are allowed in the parks to provide services needed by visitors, and only those residents who must live in the park because of their duties are permitted to occupy property," John I. Nicol, Director of the National and Historic Parks Branch, told me in Ottawa. "The existing leases for summer cottages are still valid, but our intent is to gradually remove them. This will take some years, of course, but we plan to have only those who can fulfill the work requirement living in the parks."

CHAPTER TWO

Building Your Own Home in the Country

NOTHING can equal the sheer satisfaction, as well as the substantial money savings, of building your own home. This can be a picturesque and practical log cabin, high, incidentally, in resale value. Or would you prefer a space-saving, modern A-frame? Then there are the prefabricated houses, now turned out by dozens of quality firms, which have come a long way in recent years and which with some models you can put up yourself in a week.

In any event, you're zeroed in on the get-away-from-it-all beam. Harried weekends spent baby-sitting with neglected city lawns, drafty windows, leaky faucets, blocked gutters, and corroded pipes are no longer your idea of relaxation. Neither is bundling up the family and kenneling the pets for a two-week dash to beach or mountains.

The inner-you hungers for a spot in the sun where the body will be free to unwind, the mind to dream, and the spirit to repose—far from today's rat race. For example, everyone talks about building a log cabin in the country, but few ever get around to doing it.

This is too bad in many ways, for log cabin living besides being ultra-economical is, as I can personally attest, a delightful experience that's absolutely unique.

Cabin building itself is very simple. The job takes a brief period of relatively hard work and a certain amount of muscle, but requires no particular skill. Best of all, it proceeds with satisfying rapidity.

Any reasonably able-bodied youth or man can put up a comfortable cabin by himself. If he has a wife and perhaps children to help, the construction will go all the faster. You don't even have to swing an ax if you don't want. All the necessary cutting and trimming can be done with a saw, with occasional assists from chisel and hammer.

Log construction has been called costly. Yet one small cabin near ours was put up by one man in three days for less than two dollars. Recently I installed new windows in our own log home for the price of the glass alone. Trappers, prospectors, and lumberjacks have a bundle of ways of making stoves at no expense other than that of the pipe. Log cabins, in other words, are still possible for rich and poor, strong and weak, and skilled and inept alike.

A gasoline-pressure lamp may become your lighting plant, a pair of pails the water system. There may be other inconveniences, too. Well, perhaps city friends will look upon them as that. But as I can substantiate from thirty years of country living after my own escape from big cities—Boston and New York, to be exact—they are freedoms, too. If stoves roar with your own wood, high fuel costs and labor-management troubles are something to plague the other fellow. And if you don't have running water, there's no concern about monthly bills and freezing pipes. You can go fishing instead.

How Much Skill is Needed?

Play golf? Then you should be able to swing an ax with the best of them. However, don't let your log-cabin dreams falter just because you are not an apt axman. The happy fact is that today no ax whatsoever is required for the building of a log home.

Logs can be neatly notched into place with a saw. Or you can help the work along with a chisel and mallet. The fact remains, however, that ax-made joints are considerably less difficult than you'd suppose. The timberjack who slashes them into place by eye alone, though, is something for Hollywood. In real life you measure and mark everything with considerable care, and it's then not hard to follow the lines. Perhaps you'll make the big scoops with a freely swinging ax, then do the fine work by shortening both handle and arc. Or maybe you'll prefer a hatchet.

But if you can swing a hammer and ply a saw, you're capable of putting up a warm and presentable log cabin. The job is not exacting, particularly as leaving a space up to two inches wide between the logs will actually assist in the future caulking and chinking, the simple ways by which the wilderness home is tightened and insulated. Building a snug, beautiful, and sturdy log cabin is actually less complicated than putting up a satisfactory frame dwelling.

How To Sharpen an Ax

No matter what tools you use—saw, chisel, knife, or ax—keep them sharp. A major reason why many an individual distrusts his axmanship, as a matter of fact, is that the woodpile weapon to which he's accustomed is duller than a butterknife.

W.D. Randall, Jr., P.O. Box 1988, Orlando, Florida 32802, citrus-grove owner whose hobby is making by hand the best knives in the world, recommends the following common-sense ax-sharpening procedures:

"Use an 8 or 10-inch mill file and a full stroke towards the edge, holding the ax in a vise if one is handy. Do the same amount of work on both sides of the edge until you can not see any shiny-appearing dullness.

"If a feather-edge shows, remove it with light strokes, filing at a high angle to the edge. A professional will use a round ax hone to remove any such feather-edges and to attain true sharpness. For usual purposes, however, this is not needed. However, if the ax was made and sharpened properly in the first place, you can keep it keen by using only a hone. These usually have two sides, one for removing the initial dullness and the other for finishing the edge.

"If an ax is extremely dull and has perhaps been chipped by accident or abuse, you can speed up the work by using a grinding wheel to get the tool into shape. The thing to beware of is too much heat. A fine-grit wheel generates more heat than a coarse one. Unless the metal starts to discolor, though, you have not built up too much warmth.

"A double-bitted ax, used by professional woodsmen, will have one blade sharpened for cutting and the other for splitting. For cutting, the edge bevel, which from the side appears crescent-shaped, should be deeper back from the edge and thinner for keen cutting. The splitting blade should have a thicker bevel, with the sharpening crescent only about a half-inch deep from the edge. The sportsman's and amateur home-builder's ax is generally single-bladed and smaller than a timberjack would use, with its edge a compromise between cutting and splitting."

The Fine Art of Seasoning Logs

Like everything else, the hardest part of log cabin building lies in getting started. Once you've overcome this initial inertia and have the land cleared and ready, you'll be well under way. Frame houses may begin with readying the foundations. With log construction, however, it's best to fell the necessary trees at the first. Then they can be drying while the rest of the basic work proceeds.

The seasoned log, like the preshrunk fabric, is insurance against later work. This does not mean that undried timber is not used every day. The problems aggravated by subsequent shrinkage are just greater, that's all. Greater and more prolonged chinking efforts will be necessary, and until things get dried out inside, the first few days after you light the stove are apt to be pretty steamy.

Logs, like people, become progressively leaner while they are dehydrating. Their lengths remain the same.

Once you drop a tree, it starts to dry. Preferable to letting the log just lie on the damp ground, though, where its bottom may start to rot and the whole unevenly seasoned stick may be infected with insects, is to set it at least one foot above the earth on skids, which can be merely two logs laid at right angles at either end of the pile.

The logs should be well separated, with no parts touching, so that all portions of each will reap the advantage of good ventilation. Unless you're in a hurry, they'll do best in the shade for at least the first couple of months. If you've stacked them in the open, handy to the building site, you will still be able to keep off enough of the direct sunlight by covering the heap with a layer of evergreen boughs about six inches thick.

It will still be advisable to turn the logs every one or two months. A quarter-turn each time will result in sounder and truer sticks than if you give them half-turns, although it is not necessary to be that exacting. On the other hand, the closer attention you pay to particulars, the wider margin you'll have for error.

In any event, logs so handled will, if they are dropped shortly after the first hard frost, be ready for ordinary building purposes the next spring. A full year's seasoning will be even better.

Seasoning on the Stump

Prospectors, trappers, and other professional outdoorsmen frequently cannot wait for logs to dry and so use green sticks as soon as they fell them. Ordinarily, though, they seek a few sound, standing dead trees for ridgepole, purlins, and other key spots. Such wood has seasoned on the stump.

Fire-killed stands furnish many of these, and no matter how deeply you venture into the country, a forest blaze has probably preceded you. Such trees, therefore, can often be found in unfortunate quantities that, peeled if necessary and then perhaps scrubbed with sand if you are particular, present hard white surfaces.

Best Time for Felling Trees

Building logs can be cut and used at any time. However, there are certain rules-of-thumb that will prove advantageous to follow whenever possible, again allowing yourself the greatest margin for error. For example, winter felling is preferable. In most localities logs season better when brought down in cold weather, put up on skids, and peeled when the bark loosens in the spring. Danger of insect damage is also at its minimum during this time of the year. Where there's snow, this serves as a protective cushion for the thundering timber.

How to Fell a Tree with Ax or Saw

There's no trick to felling trees, by the way. Even the greenest tenderfoot will be able to drop tall trees safely in the general direction he wishes if he will follow the very simple principles here detailed and illustrated. Wind, incline, weight, and surrounding objects must be taken into consideration, but that's only a matter of common sense and can be accomplished easily enough by eye.

A small safety notch is first cut to minimize any possibility of the butt's kicking back or the trunk's splitting. Below this, on the opposite side of the tree where the timber is to fall, a wide notch is cut. When this nick is about three-fifths through, a few strokes at the first cut should send the tree crashing.

As you can see from the illustration, the two notches are so placed that the wood remaining forms a natural hinge. This hinge governs the direction of the fall and lessens the danger that the butt may thrust backwards. However, you should still have a safe place picked out, a clear line of retreat assured, and you should hasten there when the tree starts its final creaking.

A saw is used in a similar way. There's first the brief cut, a deep slit opposite and below on the side you want the forest giant to fall, and finally the subsequent deepening of the first incision. An ax or a wedge, often a wooden one cut on the spot, may have to be driven into the lower indentation to free the saw. There are instances, too, when the upper cut will bind and will call for such wedging. In fact, particularly stubborn trees are sometimes eventually dropped in the desired direction by the driving in of a wedge or wedges in the top slit.

The right kind of saw resolves felling and cutting into a relative pastime. The ultimate, of course, is the modern power saw. One of these will drastically shorten even the brief time required to build the usual log cabin, then will provide an annual fuel supply with a minimum of effort. The sharp thinness of a Swede saw helps it to slice through both green and seasoned wood with a minimum of exertion. Its lightness makes it easy to manipulate horizontally and in other odd positions. On the other hand, these qualities do conspire on occasion to make the Swede saw twist and bind.

Many pick the heavier, more rigid crosscut saw for this reason. Both can be plied by either one or two individuals. The crosscut is

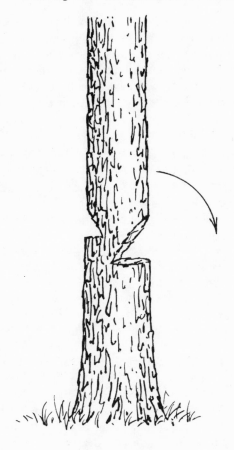

How to Fell a Tree

of especial merit in log-cabin building for making the straight cuts necessary for window and door openings. Besides being surer and steadier than the temperamental Swede saw, it can be inserted in a wall in the space made by removing a portion of one log as you build.

The Swede saw will neither accomplish this feat, nor can it be used for following a guide board once the distance between blade and handle has been spanned. The handle, of course, then gets in the way; and when the steel is twisted to allow for this incursion, it quickly strays off the straight line.

If you are going to do much cutting, perhaps you can buy a Swede saw and borrow a crosscut. The one-man version of the latter tool, on which an additional handle can be clamped in a moment, will suffice for all but the biggest jobs.

How To Choose Firewood

A lasting supply of firewood for the home is a more pressing consideration than nearby building logs. When the latter have been brought to the site, the matter will be concluded. Woodpile replenishing is an endless chore.

Country woodpiles will generally furnish information as to the likeliest local fuels. Heat-producing power is usually proportional to weight, to give a rule of thumb. Hardwoods in general furnish comparatively steady fires and lasting coals. The resinous softwoods, habitually noisy and short-lived, provide excellent kindling. Pine, often standing fire-killed stuff, is nevertheless the principal fuel of many a community.

Two pounds of dry wood of any nonresinous species contain about as much heating value as a pound of good coal. Figuring in tons and cords, a ton of anthracite has the equivalent value of a cord of heavy wood, one and one-half cords of medium-weight wood, or two cords of light wood. The following table is an approximation of the number of cords of seasoned wood of various kinds needed to give the same amount of heat as a ton of coal, on the basis of eighty cubic feet of wood with a moisture content of some 15 to 20 percent.

1 cord	hickory oak beech birch hard maple	ash elm locust cherry longleaf	= 1 ton coal
1½ cords	shortleaf pine western hemlock red gum	Douglas fir sycamore soft maple	= 1 ton coal

2 cords	cedar	cypress	= 1 ton coal
	redwood	basswood	
	poplar	spruce	
	catalpa	white pine	

Resin gives twice as much heat as wood, weight for weight. Therefore, such woods as the pines and firs have more heating potentiality per ton than nonresinous woods. The resinous woods in the table, incidentally, are considered as having the average 15 percent of resin.

The fuel value of wood depends in many cases not only on its heating power, of course, but also upon such qualities as easy ignition, rapid burning, minimum of ash, freedom from smoke, and uniformity of heat. The softwoods burn more readily than the hardwoods, as a rule. The pines give a quicker, hotter fire and are consumed in a shorter time than birch, whereas birch gives a more intense flame than the very steadily burning oak.

"Every man looks at his woodpile with a kind of affection," Thoreau noted. "I love to have mine before my window, and the more chips the better to remind me of my pleasing work. How much more interesting an event is that man's supper who has just been forth in the snow to hunt the fuel to cook it with."

Safe Axmanship

A practical way to avoid mishaps with an ax is always to work with a wide safety margin, sacrificing power and speed if need be for self-protection.

Experts often handle an ax so that the only safety margin lies in their supreme skill. A sound axiom to follow is not to be that sort of an expert. Be prepared to have the blade glance off a knot and be standing so that this will make no difference. Make certain to clear away any brush, including overhead limbs, that may deflect the blade rather than depend on your sure swing for insurance. Don't fall into the habit of steadying a billet with hand or foot while splitting it. Try always to foresee all possible accidents, then to proceed so that even if they should occur, no injury will result.

As a matter of fact, axes are considerably less dangerous than even such a very common substance as glass. Any shortcomings lie not with the ax but with the individual.

Cutting Logs Efficiently

"Beaver-cutter" is the disparaging name given to the greenhorn who fells a tree or bisects a log by hacking at it from all sides—like a beaver, which, despite the opinion to the contrary, actually does not know in which direction his timber will topple.

It will save time if the notches are wide enough at the onset. When the log to be divided is on the ground, for example, each of the necessary two notches should be as wide as the diameter of the stick at that particular part. Two such **V**s, cut on opposite sides of the log so that their points meet in the middle, will separate the log most economically.

Sawhorses

The simplest of the sawhorses used in log work is two poles driven into the ground to form an **X**. A chunk of wood jammed through the lower gap in this primitive contrivance will steady it. The poles are often wired together in the middle for additional support. Two such sawhorses located conveniently side by side will save a lot of stooping and maneuvering.

A handy portable sawhorse of the same original type can be made by boring and cutting a hole in two heavy slabs, their flat sides crossed and nailed into an **X**, and inserting a long pole which is then spiked into place.

Especially if you're working pretty much alone, you'll find that you can supplement this labor-saver by boring small holes about two feet apart along the top of this slanting pole. Then a particularly heavy log can be levered up the gradual incline with a minimum of muscle and held, whenever you want to get a new purchase, by a peg inserted behind it at easy stages.

Making a Saw Guide

If you intend your log home to have squared ends, you'll save time by providing some sort of simple guide to direct the saw. This

Handy Portable Sawhorse

may be two square plank ends spiked together in a right-angled **V** that can be inverted across each log end to guide the saw.

With the usual rectangular log cabin, you'll need two groups of wall logs, each of different lengths. When the dwelling is not large, a single variation for each set will do the trick—in each instance, two of the above broad **V**s connected on one side by a plank of the desired length, as indicated by the drawing.

Another elementary arrangement especially adaptable to poles is a long trough, open at one or both ends, made of three planks joined together at right angles in an open rectangle. The inside of this should be large enough, of course, to hold the particular building sticks.

Let's say you want a home a cozy eighteen by twelve feet, with corner posts taking the place of notches. Then build your trough eighteen feet long, taking pains to make it square. The sticks for

Two Vs Connected on One Side by Plank

the longer side can be slid into the trough, moved so that the best portion of each will be utilized, and then sawed accurately and swiftly to measure with each end of the contrivance guiding the saw.

A precisely measured and squared twelve feet from one end of this same box, a saw cut can be made that will direct the blade in the manufacture of the shorter wall sticks. Numerous other improvisations of this mitre-box principle can be devised extemporaneously to fit the task at hand.

Mitre Boxes For Logs

A mitre box large enough to accommodate logs can be fashioned in a few minutes with three pieces of board or preferably plank, as indicated by the drawing. It may be three or four feet long. All edges, of course, must be straight and parallel.

After the box has been nailed or screwed together, draw a straight line at right angles across the bottom and then follow this up both sides and across the edges of the two boards at the top. A saw cut following this line should then be carefully made down through both sides to the base. Then when a stick is held tightly against one of the sides, the slit will guide the saw blade in cutting a square end.

This mitre box will similarly act as a guide for other cuts made at specified angles. The bevel can be cut in the sides of the box with, for instance, a sample rafter's being used as a guide. Then all other rafters can be readily sawed to that standard, which in log cabin work will be the important thing. As we'll consider later, it will make little difference if the roof of your log home has a 40-degree instead of a 45-degree pitch just so long as the identical angle is followed throughout.

It is simple enough, incidentally, to make a slit in your mitre box that will guide the saw blade on an exact 45-degree pitch. As shown in the drawing, measure along one bottom side a distance equal to the width of the box. Using your try square, draw a vertical line from one end of this measurement up that side. Then, extending the opposite end of the measurement to the other side of the box in a

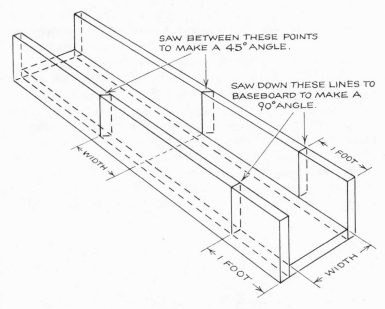

SAW BETWEEN THESE POINTS
TO MAKE A 45° ANGLE.

SAW DOWN THESE LINES TO
BASEBOARD TO MAKE A
90° ANGLE.

WIDTH

I FOOT

I FOOT

WIDTH

How to Saw Angles with a Mitre Box

straight line across the bottom, prolong that line up the opposite side. A saw cut connecting these two points on the top of the box will form a guide for the sawing of precise 45-degree angles.

The Protective Value of Living Trees

"In wildness," said Thoreau, "is the preservation of the world."

When you're readying your land for building, remember that a living barrier of trees and bush is nature's protection from storm, pollution, and boisterous wind. On the other hand, dead or threatening growth should be taken out of the way before construction is commenced. Such towering trees as black poplars, whose energy is expended in climbing toward the sun, are among the prime offenders in the matter of unexpectedly tumbling limbs. Natives will be able to help you with advice about which trees to save and which to relegate to the woodpile.

But don't forget, trees help supply the oxygen we need to breathe. Yearly each acre of young trees can give off enough oxygen to keep eighteen people alive. Organic plant life as a whole produces 60 percent of the world's newly released oxygen. Too, trees help keep our air supply fresh by using up carbon dioxide which engines and factories emit and which we ourselves exhale.

Trees use their hairy leaf surfaces to trap and filter out ash, dust, and pollen carried in the air. Trees dilute gaseous pollutants in the atmosphere as they release oxygen. As a matter of fact, trees can actually be used to indicate air-pollution levels of sulphur dioxide. Trees comfortably lower air temperature by enlisting the sun's energy to evaporate water in the leaves, at the same time providing shelter for birds and wildlife and even for us when we're caught in a shower.

Trees cut noise pollution by acting as barriers to sound. Each 100-foot width of trees can absorb about 6 to 8 decibels of sound intensity. Tree leaves, decaying, replace minerals in the soil and thus enrich it. Tree roots hold the earth and keep silt from washing into streams. In addition to all this, trees salve the psyche with pleasing shapes and patterns, fragrant blossoms, and seasonal warmths of color. And they lavish upon us a constant supply of products—logs and lumber, cellulose for paper and fibers, as well as delicious nuts, sugars, oils, and fruits.

Selecting the Logs

The usual log cabin seldom contains more than fifty or sixty logs. The available timber should be picked over very carefully, therefore, and only the best of it used. Care in selection will be very much worth the trouble, immediately in the building and later in function and beauty.

Logs from six to twelve inches in average diameter are a good general size. If a stick is seven inches through at one end and nine inches thick at the other, its average diameter, of course, is an estimable eight inches.

The larger timbers are eminently satisfactory, particularly for the more pretentious dwellings. Their weight, however, makes them harder to handle, and it may take a crew to do the job. The same consideration is manifest in length, which, especially for novice woodsmen working alone, may well be limited to about twenty-five feet.

The less taper there is to the logs, the easier and more satisfactory will be the work. The timbers will be alternated throughout, of course, to compensate for the pyramidical effect caused by this gradual diminution of thickness. Walls can be kept reasonably level throughout, that is, by laying one tier clockwise, butts to tops. The next tier will then run counterclockwise, tops to butts.

The easiest way to visualize this is to lay four wooden kitchen matches together in the smallest possible rectangle with the tops all on one side. The effect will be fanlike. But arrange them so that the butts and tops alternate, and you'll have a reasonably even figure.

If where you're settling you can pick the building logs from a grove where they grow tall and thick, you may be able to assemble a surprisingly uniform set. In any event, if you can get on skids some fifty to sixty logs that are very much like one another, the task of keeping the rising cabin walls plumb and level will be considerably lessened.

But don't worry if the circumferences of the logs vary. Uniformity is fortunately not necessary in home building. In fact, there are those who don't care too much for its resulting appearance, which may then have a sort of commercial slickness. When thicknesses vary considerably, you can even capitalize on this shortcoming by building unusually graceful walls that are stoutest at the base and which diminish gradually as they climb.

Building With Poles

Only small poles may be available where you are going to live. You're still in business! In fact, the construction will be even easier. The main difficulty with pole construction is that later chinking may be difficult; but there are ways around this quandary, as we'll consider later.

Pole construction is simple. The frame is put up first. The poles, sawed to a common length, are toenailed between flattened sills and plates.

This palisade style is actually so comely and effective that full-size logs are sometimes set upright in the same manner. Some especially attractive log cabins combine both motifs. The sticks are laid horizontally throughout, for example, except for vertical panels and windows, doors, and gables.

Best Woods

It pays to pick the soundest and straightest trees that are handy. The evergreen conifers as a whole furnish the most popular building logs through North America. Cedar, spruce, pine, balsam, tamarack, fir, redwood, and hemlock all are excellent.

Some other woods—for instance, oak and chestnut—have to be seasoned and then hewn into shape if the country home is not to resemble latticework.

Cottonwood, buckeye, willow, aspen, basswood, and other such quickly deteriorating trees are not practical. If you have no choice in the matter, be sure that there are high and well-ventilated underpinnings to protect them from dampness.

Cedar, in many instances the best all-around choice, is also especially advantageous for pillars, furniture, and general decoration. Too, it provides ground-embedded posts that are hard to beat. Cypress has similar durable robustness. So does redwood, chestnut, locust, and Osage orange.

Iron oak resists ground decay and is a prime foundation and post wood. So, when you can find it large enough, is juniper. Birch, although too susceptible to rot to be used as cabin logs even when it grows straight enough, is universally prized for built-ins and for furniture because of its adaptability and beauty.

Advantages of Peeling Logs

Peeled logs weather better, last longer, deter everlastingly tunneling insects, and assure a cleaner and brighter home. The only things in favor of unpeeled logs are less initial work and more rusticity, although a few trees including the cedar are reasonably functional with the bark left on.

How To Peel Logs

Bark peels easily from most trees when the sap rises in the spring. The way to go about the peeling is first to hew or shave a thin strip of bark from the log along its complete length. The bark can then be readily pried off in great rolls by inserting something such as a spud between bark and trunk.

A spud? This is merely a long-handled wooden chisel. You can whittle your own from a length of hardwood in a few minutes. Individual likes vary, so there are no established dimensions. A convenient size for barking is a slim wedge-shaped head, about three inches wide, at the end of a two-foot handle.

Trees peeled when the sap is dormant must be drawshaved, hewn with an ax, or otherwise laboriously stripped. Such logs as the soft pine have to be so handled throughout the year.

Preserving Logs from Insect Damage

Beetles, borers, and their sharp-fanged brethren are a cause of both damage and annoyance in some areas, especially if the log or slab is left unpeeled. Some on-the-spot inquiries will tell you what to expect.

A sound rule in insect-infested regions is to drop the trees after the first heavy frost if possible and to get them at once up off the ground in well-ventilated positions on substantial skids, then to see that each stick is turned periodically as previously considered.

On the other hand, such durable species as cedar, redwood, juniper, and cypress are usually immune even though summer-felled. A precaution to follow even with these, however, is to cut off the tops immediately and to put the usable lengths up on skids, apart from one another, where they should be turned at least three times at weekly intervals. It's good insurance to use such naturally resistant woods whenever possible in insect-plagued localities.

Arranging the Logs

Your home will go up more speedily, happily, and satisfactorily if all logs are divided into separate piles before any are used. The straightest, soundest, and sturdiest will be set aside for the ridgepole.

Piled near it will be such thoughtfully picked sticks as the sills, joints, and purlins.

If the materials are not too hard to come by, a number of extra sticks should be at hand. Then if an error is committed, you will be able to reach nonchalantly for an alternate and relegate the first one composedly to the woodpile.

"Shall we," asked Thoreau, "forever resign the pleasure of construction to the carpenter?"

How To Visualize Your Future Home

The usual cabin is small enough so that it's practical to join four stakes with string of the correct lengths and move these around your prospective property until you find the ideal spot.

Allot plenty of time to your looking and recheck the site morning, noon, and evening. Look at the spot from all angles, both inside and out, and ask yourself all the important questions about sunlight, view, shade, wind, prevailing breezes, safety, accessibility, and drainage. If the answers are not satisfactory, it will be a simple matter at this stage to move the stakes and test other possibilities until the most advantageous site is located.

The Foundation

You've got your land; logs are straight and sound. Stakes and string, moved until the best of all locations has been found, mark where the new home is to rise. In pioneer days the women of the household would have been preparing a feast for the neighbors due to congregate for the log-raising bee. In fact, there are localities such as ours where this pleasant old custom still survives.

The foundation of your log cabin can be as simple as you want to make it. However, it should be level and solid throughout if the work is not to be unduly prolonged.

Four cornerstones, embedded with their flat surfaces uppermost, will be sufficient in dry climates where the ground is firm and the dwelling small. None need be larger than what you can move and set up by yourself. Pits filled with rocks can be improvised as bases for such supporting cornerstones where the earth is soft.

Two flat stones at each corner are greatly preferable. The reason is that moisture ascends single stones and rots the wood. But if one slab is laid atop another above the ground and not cemented, the top stone acts as a buffer which prevents dampness from rising by capillary attraction to decay the sills. Such a precaution is essential in wet climates.

Log homes should be supported at each corner and, too, at about every six feet. Therefore, a cabin some twelve feet wide and eighteen feet long, to use a common example, needs one additional prop at the center of each short span. Two more bolsters should be spaced equidistant beneath each long side.

How To Mark the Corners

A stake at each four corners will do to mark small homes with simple foundations, inasmuch as squaring and leveling will be largely accomplished by trial and error. As far as that goes, the tapering nature of logs makes work with them in any sort of structure more a matter of compromise and approximation than the precise measuring that is possible with milled timber.

A stake or any other marker set directly at the corners will, it is obvious, have to be moved when any sort of a foundation is laid there. When you go beyond the simplest form of base, therefore, you can save time by resorting to a marking method that will continue to indicate angles and levels as the work progresses.

The simplest way to go about this will be to extend each foundation line. This can be accomplished by driving in additional stakes about a half-dozen feet beyond each end of each line. These are first trued. Then the levels are marked by a nail driven into the working side of each of the eight pegs. Weighted cords strung across these nails will intersect to show the foundation corners. The closer you come to accuracy, the wider margin for error you'll enjoy later on.

The corners can be made exactly true with the aid of a try square or any other right angle, perhaps the cover of this book. Whenever any two diagonally opposite corners are determined to be right angles, as you know, the entire rectangle will be proved square.

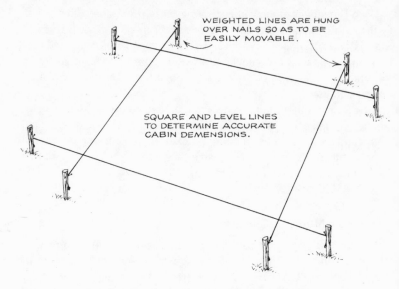

Extending and Marking Corners of Foundations

Start at the corner nearest the ground, make sure that nail is set at the desired height, and then bring the other seven nails in turn to that common level. The use of a carpenter's level, or even a long, slim, tea-filled bottle in which an air bubble can be centered, will make this task relatively easy.

Sills

When your foundations are ready, you'll want to get the four bottom logs into position. Inasmuch as the entire weight will rest on them, they should be surpassed in strength and straightness only by the ridgepole and based as solidly as possible on the foundation. It is frequently best for this reason to flatten them somewhat at points of contact by using saw, chisel and mallet, plane, adz, or ax.

When you're building with notches, lift either the two short or the two long logs into position first. Then roll up the other two logs. These will set half a log higher than the first logs. This you'll accomplish by notching them, as we'll take up in a moment. These four bottom logs should be solid, square, and of nearly equal height at the corners. When you've got them ready, spike them together.

With certain types of corners, all four basic logs will lie at approximately the same height. Junctures in this instance are strongly and easily made by half-laps as shown in the accompanying drawing. The whole procedure is so simple that, if you want, you can accomplish it with sixteen saw cuts, eight vertical and eight horizontal.

Checking Plumb and Level

Use the inside measurements when building a log home. Keep the insides of the walls plumb; that is, straight up and down. One way to do this is by spiking guide boards upright inside the four corners. Check these with a plumb line to make sure they're perfectly vertical. A string with a pebble at its end will do for this. Or if such guides are going to be in the way, keep checking with the plumb line as you proceed.

The logs should be kept as level as possible as each tier rises into place. They will then furnish a reasonably level base for the

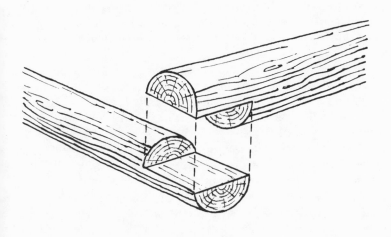

Half-Laps

roof, door, and windows. These levels are very easily regulated by the deepness of the various notches.

It's not necessary to knock yourself out in this matter of getting everything straight and level. When you're dealing with logs, you can only approximate these ideals at best. But especially as the logs can functionally be as much as two inches apart wherever you want, it's just as easy to keep everything fairly true and thus to allow yourself the widest possible margin for error. You'll end up with a more substantial and better-looking home, and there will be less work when you get around to putting in shelves and cabinets.

Log walls, which ordinarily can be raised in a very few days, are complete in themselves. You won't have to bother with studs, girts, shores, braces, and a dozen other complications. When these walls are caulked and chinked, which as later explained can be accomplished if necessary within two days at no expense other than perhaps the cost of some nails, all weatherproofing and insulating will be finished. So will be all necessary interior decorating.

Corner Posts

The quickest and easiest, although not the most substantial way, to build log cabin walls is by spiking sawed logs to corner posts. This method is also the most economical, inasmuch as the full length of each stick is utilized.

When milled stock is available, a simple way to prepare the frames for square corners is by nailing two planks together at right angles. Four sets should be made, each a safe few inches taller than the walls will probably rise inasmuch as it will be easier to trim them than to lengthen them.

Posts to reinforce these frames can be made by flattening two sides of four small logs until each resembles an elongated quarter of pie. Such posts can be used by themselves, of course.

The corners, whatever they are to be, are spiked into position. The wall logs are sawed to measure on the ground, rolled into place between the corner supports, and each spiked at least twice at each end. One fastener alone too often becomes a pivot on which the stick will roll. It will usually save time to prepare these two sets

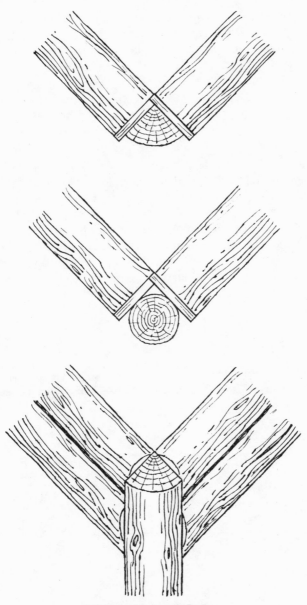

Building with Corner Posts

of logs in quantity, using one of the methods suggested earlier to secure standard lengths and square ends.

For a rough but quickly built cabin with corner posts, especially handy when you're working with ax alone, see the self-explanatory drawing.

Notches

Until you've actually notched in a corner, this is the part of log-home building that will probably loom up as the stumbling block. Actually, as you'll discover, corner work is simple in the extreme.

The main reason is that log walls are not built to fit with any of the tightness of frame buildings. As a matter of fact, as we've already stressed, you'll end up with a warmer and tighter cabin if you see to it that the wall logs remain up to two inches apart. This

Quick Temporary Cabin-building with Corner Posts

will provide a plenitude of space in which to maneuver while notching to keep the logs level, and it will make the later chinking considerably easier and more effective.

Either of the two notches suggested below will give you a better cabin than if you had used corner posts. There are other notches, of course, just as there are other overall techniques and shortcuts—as detailed in my complete book on log work, *How to Build Your Home in the Woods,* with its some 140 on-the-spot illustrations by Vena, available from me for $7.00 by mail in Cambria, California 93428, or at Hudson Hope, British Columbia, Canada. But just the material in this volume should suffice.

No ax, as we've already said, is needed for notching a log. They can be sawed, gouged, chiseled, or even whittled into shape. The job isn't limited to fictional experts who take a quick Hollywood squint, nod to any onlookers, and then proceed to hew a flawless joint with a few swift strokes. In real life, one measures and marks where the joint is to go, then follows the guidelines.

If all this is new to you, why not saw some straight saplings into short lengths, then experiment with a jackknife until you have a sound working knowledge of exactly how your corners are going to fit together.

The general procedure in wall building is to get the log into position. Move it until it is resting on its straightest length. Then make sure that the better of the other two sides is on the interior. Now you're ready for your notch.

The Saddle Notch   This is a quickly made notch. It is both good-looking and professional-appearing, and it's functional in that no cut is left upturned to gather moisture. The drawing, showing the first log being fitted over the sills, is pretty much self-explanatory. Succeeding notches are made in similar fashion.

As the walls go up, first of all you measure. The notch at its widest will, of course, ideally be open just enough to cup the log below. The notch's depth, also governed by the log over which it is to fit, will be a little less than half the diameter of the working stick itself.

Each log should be notched so that it will lie fairly level. Suppose that the still unnotched log is an inch high on one end? Then one solution will be to cut the notch on that end one inch deeper than that on the opposite side. All this is simplified by the fact that you have a

Saddle Notch

couple of inches to play around with. Wall logs may be functionally laid that far apart at their widest gaps.

Especially when you're beginning, it usually takes a few tries before everything fits to satisfaction. You make your notches, roll the log into place, mark where perhaps a little more hewing is needed, roll the log off, make the cuts, and try again. When the corners are tight, spike them.

The Tenon Corner   This type of corner can be very easily cut with a saw. It is fashioned by flattening the top and bottom ends of each log so that the resulting tongues fit squarely upon one another. Each of the tongues will generally be a little more than half as wide as the log end in which it is made. Leveling and measuring are the same as with all corner construction.

The drawing practically explains itself. Each tongue can be fashioned with two vertical and two horizontal cuts. A swiftly working Swede saw or a heavier but truer crosscut will make all of these. Or you can saw down the two vertical marks, then quickly split out each slab in gradual bites with chisel and mallet. A power saw is fastest and easiest of all.

Raising the Logs

The handiest way to lift logs is with a block and tackle, usually available for the borrowing in most backwoods areas. Very often this is suspended from a portable tripod, made on the spot by lashing the tops of three sturdy poles together. Leaning pole skids into place from the highest part of the wall to the ground will ease the raising of the logs even more.

Windows and Doors

When there is no shortage of logs, the quickest procedure is to build solid walls and then saw-cut the necessary openings. When you come to the top of the future aperture, just frame it inside and out with perpendicular boards, carefully measured and squared. Then saw-cut the top log inside these guiding supports. Later you can insert a crosscut saw in these openings and complete the work.

Although the bottom logs themselves can be flattened to provide their own door- and windowsills, there will be less water damage if you insert separate sills extending several inches beyond the frame.

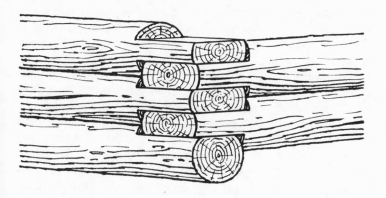

Tenon Corner

Doors should be built on the spot and should be solid and massive. A practical door can be inexpensively constructed, for instance, of two thicknesses of slabs or planks with waterproof building paper between. The exterior layer should be put on vertically so that there will be no horizontal cracks to trap moisture. Spike everything firmly.

The Roof

Once the walls are up and the openings made, ordinarily the next procedure is to put on the roof and make it waterproof. Log construction is rugged, and most cabin roofs are small. Except in very heavy snow country, a steep roof is unnecessary.

One of the most helpful and at the same time comely features that can be incorporated in a log home to avoid decay in walls, foundations, and around windows and doors is a wide roof overhang. Good projection of eaves and rack of gables will eliminate much storm water that otherwise would flow over the walls. Broad gables also provide additional protected storage and working space.

A projection of not less than two feet is recommended. Incidentally, roof-supporting members, whether poles or sawn lumber, should not ordinarily project beyond the eaves or they'll be unduly susceptible to decay.

A gable roof with a 25 percent pitch is generally excellent. To determine this slant, measure between the two side walls. Say the distance is ten feet. Then the top of the ridgepole should be roughly five feet higher than the tops of the side walls.

With some five or six short logs, build the two sides of the cabin up to the necessary height. Then center the crowning ridgepole.

You'll next need purlins. These are the straight, slender logs the same length as the ridgepole. The handiest way to put them up is to cut off the end of each short gable log just enough to allow the purlin to be positioned atop the log below.

The stepped-up purlins should follow the slant of the roof in such a way that they will support boards or poles laid from the ridgepole over the top of the side walls. When all the fitting has been done, spike everything down.

The pole roof is the most beautiful of cabin roofs, something

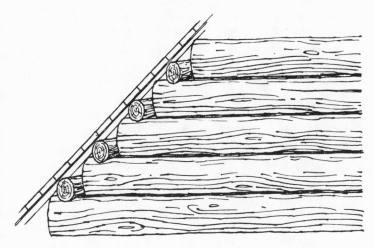

Purlins Set in Steps

you'll appreciate when you're day-dreaming up at it from inside the coziness of your country abode. For this type of roof you'll need a quantity of peeled poles, long enough so that they'll butt together atop the ridge and then reach down to the eaves. These sticks can be prepared all at once on the ground. Butts and tops will be alternated, of course, when they are spiked into place.

Cover the top of this pole roof with building paper. Spike on flattened poles or two-by-fours some two feet apart, parallel to the ridge. Fill in between these with dry sphagnum moss, readily and freely available by the sackful over thousands of miles of countryside. Nail on boards, then cover with waterproof roll roofing of whatever color you prefer. Voilà! A warm roof.

If you don't want to bother with poles, lumber can be used throughout instead.

In really frigid weather in the northern states you can tell a poor roof from a good roof at a glance. The inadequately insulated roof not only soon becomes bare and icy, but you'll be able to make out heat waves shimmering up through it. Look around and see who have warm roofs. Then ask how they made them.

One fast way to insulate a board roof is by providing a dead-air chamber. Cover the initial layer of boards, nailed to the ridgepole and purlins, with heavy roofing paper. Spike poles or two-by-fours along the edges and parallel to the ridge, about three feet apart. Nail on another layer of boards. Cover this with waterproof roofing, following the directions accompanying the product.

There are innumerable solutions to the roof problem. You can split out your own shakes, for instance. Sod roofs and dirt roofs are still common, but dirt is apt to sift down from these roofs into mulligans and other uncovered cooking. Both the described roofs are trim and clean.

The Floor

The floor usually goes on only after the protective roof is in place. Easiest way to provide for this? Spike top-flattened poles, or milled two-by-fours with their narrow sides up, the length of the two longest bottom logs. Make sure they are level and parallel. Lay similar poles of milled stock, narrow sides again uppermost, from wall to wall across these about a foot apart. Spike these joists solidly.

If you are not able to obtain seasoned flooring, perhaps as Thoreau did from another structure you're tearing down for its materials, it will be better not to nail it permanently until the second year.

Most of the drafts in log homes swirl in around the feet. You can guard against such cold by banking the home each fall before freezeup. You may also find it worthwhile to put in a double floor at the start, laying this at right angles to the first and with heavy waterproof building paper between. The covered surfaces can, of course, be left rough, a procedure which often saves time and money.

Caulking and Chinking

The walls will be completed as soon as they are caulked and chinked. Many wilderness builders take care of the former by stringing sphagnum moss, or, if preferred, purchased oakum, liberally between logs and in all joints as the construction proceeds.

The chinking is often an annual affair of mixing a thick mud, slapping and pressing it into cracks, and then smoothing it with a flat stick or a small trowel. The numerous mixtures for such chinking become subjects of considerable neighborhood interest, being heatedly discussed and debated through the years. Some earths stay in place better than others, particularly if you drive lines of small nails upright in the cracks for anchors. This procedure is almost mandatory for pole construction.

Plasters of cheap flour, salt, and water are common in some areas. The toughest and most harmonizing chinking I've ever seen was made by mixing sawdust from the job with melted sheet glue, obtainable inexpensively in bulk from hardware and general stores and from theatrical suppliers. That I've used has been very inflammable; so melt it with care in a container set in water over a small outdoor fire. This chinking does tend to dry and crack, however.

You can do a functional permanent job at more expense than the other methods with spar varnish, linseed oil, and mineral wool of the sort that is sold in batting form for insulation. Varnish is brushed between the logs. Before it dries, rock wool is tamped into place with a spud or with the end of a board about ⅜ inch thick and 6 inches wide. Varnish or linseed oil is applied to the exposed surface of the rock wool by sweeping the brush over the surface quickly to avoid deep penetration of the liquid.

The rock wool, preferably brown although perhaps white inside the building, adheres tenaciously to the logs. It has sufficient elasticity to compensate for ordinary wood shrinkage except where the logs twist badly. Even where it has broken loose because of such twisting, it can easily be tamped back into place. Our experience of the past two years is that insects are not inclined to attack chinking of this kind, although squirrels and other rodents like to pull it out for their nests.

The tightest and best-appearing joints can be obtained, of course, by cutting deep grooves accurately in the top and bottom surfaces of each wall log and inserting a spline. But this is a lot of work. A simpler although still arduous variation is just cutting a groove in one side of the log and inserting some expanding insulation in this.

Care should be taken in avoiding the formation of crevices in

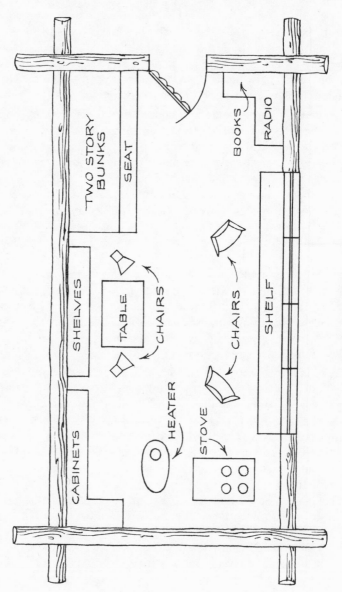

One-Room Cabin Layout

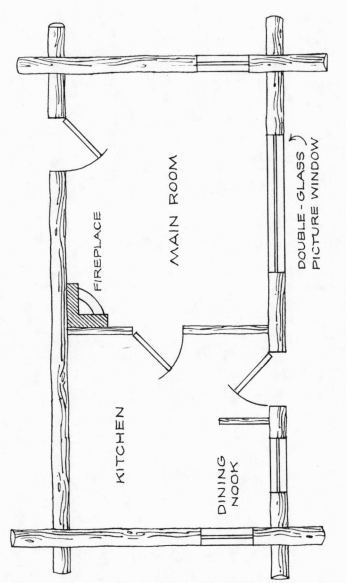

MAIN ROOM

FIREPLACE

KITCHEN

DINING NOOK

DOUBLE-GLASS PICTURE WINDOW

Two-Room Cabin Layout

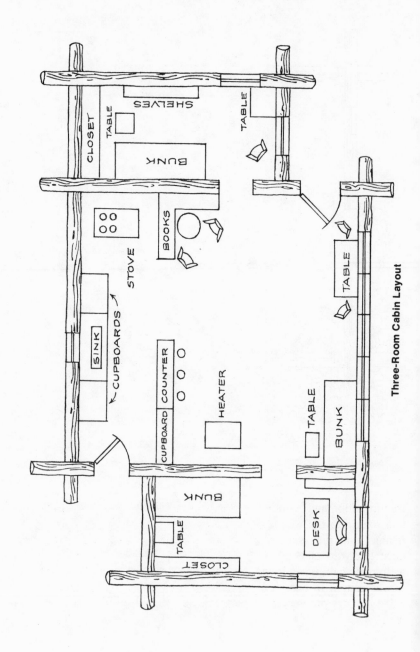

Three-Room Cabin Layout

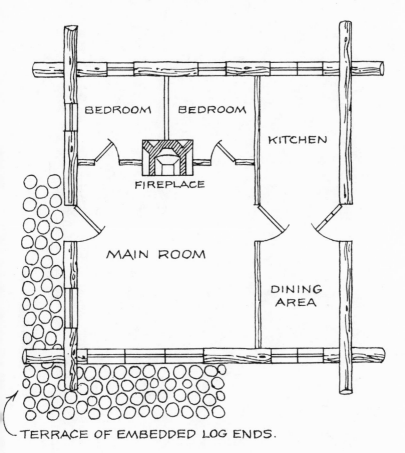

Four-Room Cabin Layout

framing door and window openings, where water can accumulate and soak into the wood. Fittings should be made as tight as practicable, and they should be supplemented by caulking at places most likely to take up water. Storm water does little damage in well-made cabins, as it will run off quickly. However, if the moisture is caught in crevices, joints, and checks, it will soak into the wood and dry out very slowly. Decay can easily start in these damp areas.

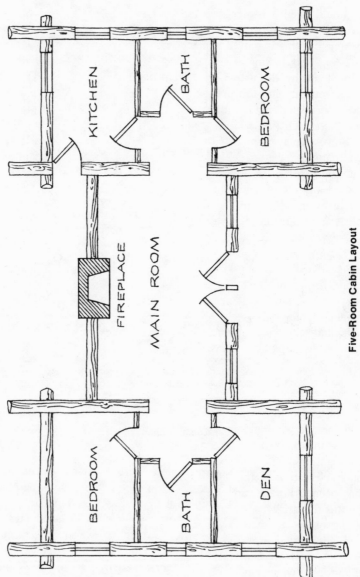

Five-Room Cabin Layout

Furnishings

You'll need a heater and a cook stove with a good oven. An oven of sorts can be purchased and fitted onto the stovepipe of the heater, but this is only a makeshift arrangement if you plan much roasting and baking. Fireplaces are not practical in homes occupied during the winter in cold climates, although if you want them you can find full details for a number of different types and their corresponding chimneys in my *How to Build Your Home in the Woods*. Or find a Franklin stove.

Stoves are available from mail order houses, although sometimes you can get a better deal locally. Satisfactory second-hand stoves may very often be bought on the spot, and in fact we've never owned any other. The same is true of heaters, some of which are made by local countrymen from oil drums and give off cheerily blistering heat year after year.

Any ordinary wooden bunk makes a fine bed if you've an air or foam mattress to go with it. You may like to buy an easy chair apiece, such as the inexpensive and harmonizing wickerware from Hong Kong, and to build others. The only thing to remember is that when chairs and tables are used together, the difference in height is commonly twelve inches. These, shelves, functional cabinets, and other such appurtenances for the log home will probably turn out to be more fun than work.

A-Frames

These two illustrated A-frame cabins can be built by three or four people who have reasonable ability in the use of tools. Someone with a knowledge of concrete work may be required to place the footings. The frame itself should present no problems, nor should erection of the end walls, roof, and interior partitions. It has been assumed that electricity will be available at the site to permit the use of power tools and to provide for lighting, heating, and cooking.

Each cabin is provided with a modern kitchen that contains a refrigerator, sink, range, and adequate cabinet space. Provision is made for a water heater under one corner of the floor cabinet arrangement.

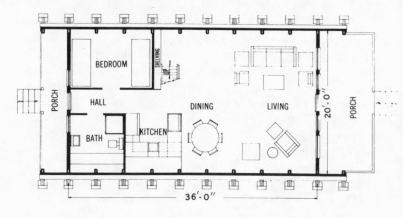

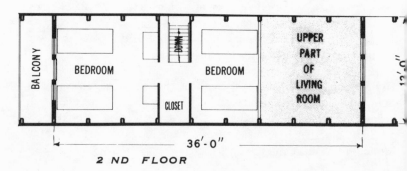

2 ND FLOOR

Plans for 36-foot A-frame Cabin

The bathroom contains a lavatory, toilet, and shower. A storage locker for linens is also provided here. The water supply could come from a well or spring. The piping, where exposed to the outside air, should be properly insulated and provided with drain valves so that all water can be drained from the system if the home is perhaps temporarily vacated during winter weather.

The 36-foot cabin contains three bedrooms, one on the first floor and two on the second floor. The front bedroom on the second floor is a balcony which overlooks the two-story living room. If sleeping space for more than six individuals is required, cots can be placed in the living room.

Cutaway View of 36-foot A-frame Cabin

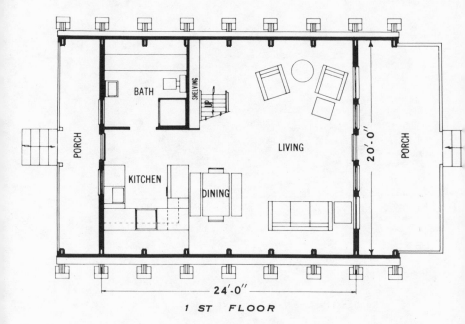

BATH

SHELVING

UP

PORCH

KITCHEN

DINING

LIVING

PORCH

20'-0"

24'-0"

1 ST FLOOR

BALCONY

BEDROOM

DOWN

CLOSET

BEDROOM

BALCONY

12'-0"

24'-0"

2 ND FLOOR

Plans for 24-foot A-frame Cabin

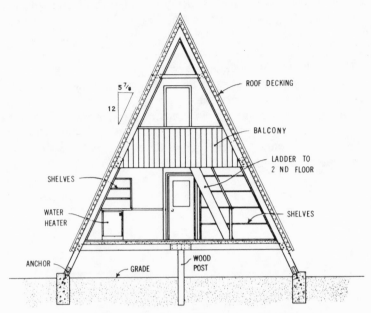

5 $\frac{7}{8}$

12

ROOF DECKING

BALCONY

LADDER TO
2 ND FLOOR

SHELVES

WATER
HEATER

SHELVES

ANCHOR

GRADE

WOOD
POST

Sectional View from Living Room Toward Rear

The 24-foot cabin contains two bedrooms, both on the second floor. The living-dining area is smaller than in the 36-foot home, and the living room is only one story high.

Ventilation in both homes is good, the windows at each end providing excellent circulation of air.

Storage shelving is indicated adjacent to the ship's ladder that leads to the second floor.

If a fireplace is desired, then a prefabricated unit can be easily installed. Wood may be stored under the cabin for use during cold weather or for cooking.

It is noted on the working drawings of the smaller home that the size of the rear bedroom can be increased by extending the second floor to include the rear balcony. The second floor can also be extended at the front of the cabin if desired. If this is done, the door shown on the plan should be replaced by a double-hung window.

The sectional view from the living room toward the rear gives some ideas for constructing the A-frame. After the footings have been placed, the lower half of the frame may be erected and the rough flooring nailed in place at the first and second-floor levels. The second floor can be used as a work platform while the upper half of the frame is put in place.

The roof sheathing should then be put on, followed by the finished roofing. The end walls may then be framed and completed and finally the interior partitions.

For added protection in cold climates the space under the first floor and in the end walls should be insulated. Additional insulation may be installed on the underside of the roof sheathing between the frames if the climate requires.

CHAPTER THREE

The ABC's of
Organic Gardening

WHEN our pioneer ancestors first planted their thrifty
gardens in this New World, the virgin soil was rich with an average
4 percent of humus—the brownish and black organic material
formed by the partial decomposition of vegetable and animal
matter in and on the ground. Although even this beneficence of
humus was slightly below the optimum 5 percent, the present figure nationally is closer to a disturbing 1.5 percent.

Today's resulting hard, compacted ground shuts off too much
of its necessary air and water, so that instead of forming an ideal
50 percent of the breathing, drinking whole these are now down to
about 30 percent. On the other hand, the inorganic mineral content, ideally 45 percent, is up to an alarming 68.5 percent, partly
because of the residue of chemical fertilizers and sprays.

Luckily, you can rejuvenate poor soil on your own at little expense beyond tender loving care. Just put back the humus in the
form perhaps of compost, mulch, manure, or if you have the time
by the so-called green manure provided by some such crop as
vetch, by the incidentally highly edible clover, or by one of the

pod-bearing plants such as beans or peas which you duly turn under.

From Soil Test to Soil Treatment

If you'd like to be really scientific, have your soil tested free of charge by a U.S. Department of Agriculture agent or a nearby college laboratory, or do it yourself with one of the simple home kits on the market.

With the latter, merely drop a bit of your soil sample into a test tube and add, according to accompanying instructions, the proper chemicals. Then it's just a matter of comparing the resulting hue with the provided color chart. You'll thus discover just how your prospective garden plot stands in such essentials as nitrogen, potassium, phosphorus, and acid-alkaline balance. With this knowledge, you can make any necessary corrections simply, cheaply, and intelligently.

Suppose your ground needs nitrogen? Manure, often free for the carting, is a rich natural source. So is the activated and digested sludge often available from sewage processing plants. If you've more money than time, dried manure is readily procurable in the stores, as are cottonseed and other vegetable meals like those from soybeans and flaxseed, blood meal or dried blood, and bone meal.

Potassium, so necessary for strong plants that will resist heat, cold, and disease? Wood ashes, protected from the rain until used, are a free rich source, that from hardwoods being nearly twice as efficacious as softwood residue. Perhaps a nearby manufacturer will let you have such potassium in the form of waste products like peanut shells, cocoa bean hulls, and even wool waste.

The various seaweeds are rich in potash as well as trace elements necessary to human life. Greensand, procured from undersea mineral deposits, is a fine supplier of potassium as well as some lime, phosphorus, and trace elements. Granite dust, sometimes called ground rock potash, is another naturally occurring substance replete with the element potassium.

Phosphorus deficiency is held by the experts to be the leading factor in too scanty crops. An excellent natural source is powdered rock phosphate. Another natural supply almost as rich is colloidal phosphate. Or you can use fish wastes, dried blood, activated sludge, guano, or even garbage. Humus and manure combine to make such natural phosphates more rapidly and regularly available to your plants.

As for the acid-alkali balance, this is essential as too much imbalance either way will check the release of both major and minor plant foods. If anything, a slightly acid content is preferable. The majority of vegetables, fruits, field crops, and flowers thrive best in ground that is slightly acid to neutral; that is, soil having a pH level of about 6.5 to 7.

Organic matter is the best additive for either a markedly acid or alkaline soil inasmuch as its tendency is to neutralize both excesses while acting as a buffer against unfavorable pH levels during the time this process is continuing. To counteract highly acid conditions, use natural ground limestone, bone meal (which is the modern relative of pulverized buffalo skeletons), wood ashes, crushed mussel or oyster shells, and the like. For alkaline earths, cottonseed meal, acid peat moss, basic slag, sawdust, wood chips, leaf mold, and such will help.

How to Make Compost

The combination soil conditioner-fertilizer of the successful organic gardener is compost. If you can produce a steady supply of this humus-enriching key to gardening success, the odds are a hundred to one that your garden will be healthy, robust, and happily productive. And it's all so easy.

Most practical is a compost pile roughly five feet high, five feet wide, and of whatever length you can easily maintain. If you have found a permanent haven of happiness, you may wish to provide for a continuous compost heap. What you use for this will depend, of course, on the site. An open-ended rectangle or two of uncemented building blocks may be the answer. Or you can furnish yourself with a fenced-in-area, making this portable if you want by using four loosely screened sides that hook together.

Making compost is an easily arranged process. It's true that the rapid conversion of a mass of undecomposed organic materials into life-maintaining fertilizer is one of nature's miracles; yet the

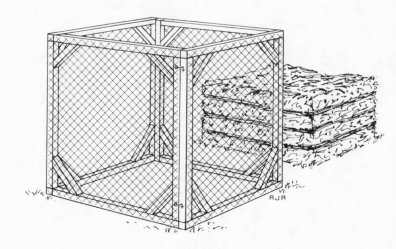

Compost Heap and Portable Frame

elementary steps by which you yourself can bring this about are simple and remarkably easy to follow.

Essentially, the basic formula provides for the heaping or piling of certain natural ingredients in layers or in mixed proportions, seeing to it that they get the needed air and water, and, perhaps halfway through the process, forking the mass over so that the previously outer materials can have their turn at being in contact with the heat and bacterial action of the mound's center.

If you'd like to escape the work of forking, just buy a supply of earthworms from one of the advertising concerns that ship them inexpensively. In fact, you may even decide to start up in this sideline yourself by following the instructions in Chapter 6.

First, provide a base for the compost heap by putting down a layer of grass clippings, dead plants, weeds, crop wastes, leaves, or the like. Next comes a two-inch layer of manure or some other nitrogen-rich material such as bone meal, cottonseed meal, sewage sludge, or blood meal. Soybean meal will be even more effective. Cover, in turn, by a sprinkling of topsoil and pulverized limestone

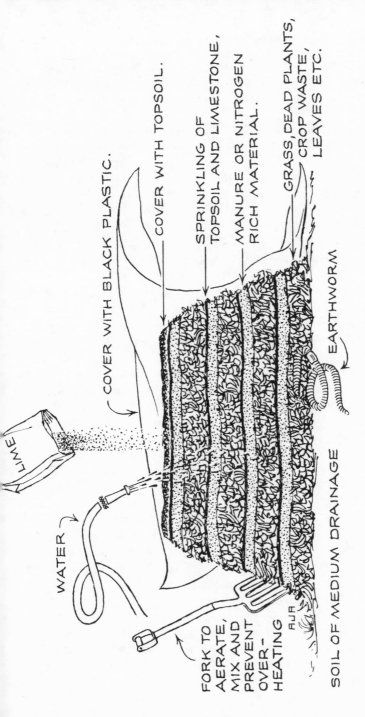

COVER WITH BLACK PLASTIC.

COVER WITH TOPSOIL.

SPRINKLING OF TOPSOIL AND LIMESTONE.

MANURE OR NITROGEN RICH MATERIAL.

GRASS, DEAD PLANTS, CROP WASTE, LEAVES ETC.

LIME

WATER

EARTHWORM

FORK TO AERATE, MIX AND PREVENT OVER-HEATING

SOIL OF MEDIUM DRAINAGE

Components of a Compost Heap

or hardwood ashes not over ⅛ inch thick. Never use sand as a substitute. Wet down each layer. The layers are repeated up to a
height of about five feet. Cover with a two-inch layer of topsoil.
That's all.

At the end, you may find it handy to seal the mound by covering
it with black plastic, weighed down along its edges by stones or
sticks. This will do away with odors and insects, hold in the water
and heat, reduce turning to a minimum, and speed everything so
that you'll have finished compost in two to three months.

You can also work in layers of garbage—fruit and vegetable
scraps, fish bits, coffee grounds, tea leaves, table scraps, bones,
moldy bread, and the like. Too, the neighborhood store will likely
be glad to give you cartons of produce that has started to spoil or
that has become too old to retail. Use these, too.

You can also have layers of pine needles. Seaweed works very
well. So does sawdust, often available at sawmills for the hauling.
If you are making your own wine, here's the place for the discarded skins, pulp, and seeds. In fact, commercial wineries usually
have more grape residue than they can use to fertilize their own
vineyards. Then there are spent hops from breweries. Riding
stables will often let you have their shovelings of manure and
straw, perfect for composting. With enough of these free for the
taking, there's no need to spend money on so-called bacterial
compost activators.

After two or three weeks, it's a good idea to turn the pile, if
only to check on its dampness and on the degree of decay. If it
seems too dry, wet it down again. The pile should be moist but not
soggy. If the middle of the heap has not decayed well, you may
need more manure or other nitrogen-replete material. Fork over
everything until what was formerly the top and sides becomes the
center. Then recover with the plastic, if you are using a cover.

Earthworms will probably have found their way to the heap.
The more there are, the quicker the pile will work. In fact, it will
pay to buy a batch.

That's all there is to it. This process can be continued for as
long as you have a garden. And what a garden it should be! Such
compost, incidentally, is surprisingly heavy, a cubic yard weighing
approximately half a ton.

Applying Compost

Ideally, the compost should be put into the garden about two months before you plant. Perhaps using a spading fork, loosen the ground. Then mix the compost into the top four inches of soil. For best results with vegetable and flower gardens, first put the compost through a half-inch sieve, returning the heavier portions to the compost heap.

Just a half-inch of compost can do a lot of good. But if you want really dramatic effects, use from one to three inches. After four or five years of such enrichments your garden will become one of the marvels of the community.

Compost can be applied once or twice a year, thus stimulating nature's never-ending cycle. The amount you use will depend, of course, on the original fertility of the plot. You can't add too much. For instance, a single tomato seedling planted in a compost heap may produce 100 pounds of vitamin-filled, mineral-rich tomatoes.

Mulch

Mulch will protect your carefully won garden soil, conserve moisture, retard weeds, protect the ground against temperature extremes, discourage erosion, stop the formation of a hard crust, cushion the ripening produce and keep it clean, and eventually, when organic, decay to improve soil fertility and structure.

Mulch is merely a layer of material, preferably organic, that is spread over the soil. Decaying hay, or even dead grass harvested free from a next-door field, is excellent. Cocoa bean hulls not only smell nice and look lush, but, upon disintegrating, add potassium, nitrogen, and phosphorus to the plot.

Pine needles are fine, and so is seaweed. Dead leaves will serve. So will grass clippings, ground corncobs, sawdust, and the hulls of various seeds and nuts. Although they lend nothing to the richness of the ground, roll roofing, aluminum foil, or even newspapers will do.

When your garden is properly mulched, one deep watering a

week will do. You won't have to weed. Neither will you need to cultivate.

How much mulch? When your crops are to be in the ground throughout the greater part of the summer, use enough mulch to stop weed growth. Actually, this will be a matter of personal experimentation, using the materials most freely at hand.

You'll find that a thin layer of well-shredded plant materials will be more effective than unshredded loose substance, a good argument for something like a rotary power mower if you want to invest that much capital in the yard. Such substances as leaves and corn stalks in particular should either be shredded or combined with some such light material as straw to keep them from becoming soggy masses. In such a mixture, unshredded leaves may be effectively spread a foot deep for the winter.

To give you an idea, a five-inch covering of sawdust will keep back weeds as effectively as eight inches of the moldy bales of hay, spoiled insofar as cattle are concerned, that are sometimes inexpensively available. Incidentally, to offset sawdust's lack of nitrogen, you may wish to add some extra manure to the soil before mulching. Like similar carbon-heavy materials, sawdust will ofttimes turn plants yellow if used by itself. But it is a good organic substance that, decomposing, eventually enriches the soil after it's served its purpose as a mulch.

The lightness and bulk of ground corncobs, another highly recommended mulch, help prevent a hard crust's forming on the surface of your garden spot and, incidentally, may do away with any black spots on your roses. It should be spread at least an inch deep on vegetable and fruit gardens. If you're having lawn difficulties, by the way, try spreading a half-inch of this mulch on the troublesome greenery twice a year.

A 1½- to 2-inch covering of salt hay, if any wavers freely where you live, provides the best mulch for strawberries. Or use a 2- to 4-inch depth of pine needles. Blueberries, on the other hand, prefer some six to eight inches of sawdust. Cranberries and raspberries like wood shavings as well as other acid mulches such as pine needles, sawdust, and salt hay. Two or three inches of commercially prepared shredded pine bark, pleasing to the scent for several weeks and thereafter darkly attractive to the eyes, will increase he acidity of the soil to a minor degree but does not noticeably build up the need for added nitrogen.

If mulches are hard to come by locally, you can always put down your accumulations of old magazines and newspapers, but only after the ground is well soaked. Then help along the appearance by covering them with something such as pine needles or grass clippings. Being organic, the paper will slowly and steadily add humus to the ground.

Even manure makes an excellent mulch if you cover it with something such as a clean footing of spoiled hay or straw. The odor quickly disappears, and the eventual decomposition is abundantly complete. Then there are those bright semiprecious pebbles and stones from beaches. Laid permanently around a tree, for instance, such a rocky mulch discourages weeds and rodents, helps retain moisture, and serves as a temperature regulator.

Plastic and aluminum-foil mulches are best for the plants that grow best in warm soils. Foil, such as the 100-foot rolls available in supermarkets, not only can nearly quadruple corn production, but its reflecting qualities repel troublesome aphids. Foil, too, repels bean beetles, a fact which explains in part the doubling of crops of this legume. Although apple maggot flies are lured by reds, green plastic attracts practically none.

Potatoes, on the other hand, grow better with something such as a hay mulch or a pale green plastic that will reflect the heat. Heat-absorbing black plastic is particularly effective on crops such as crisp head lettuce and sweet potatoes.

A handy time to apply mulch is during planting. Mulching should be continued year after year as a part of the gardening cycle. Your vegetables will be larger, richer in vitamins and minerals, and far tastier. Your flowers will be sweet, huge, and astounding.

Using All Available Space In Planting

From here on, you're on your own except that it will pay to buy the seeds most productive for the locality; while, until your experiments have proved otherwise, it's only reasonable to follow the directions on the packets.

For beauty as well as production, try not to waste an inch of your carefully prepared garden areas. Concord grapes can twine over the posts that hold your clothesline. More grapes, as well as pole beans, can be planted along a fence or the otherwise unguarded perimeter of your property. Here is the place, too, for fruit trees. Asparagus will prosper along the outside edges of your flower beds. Onions will like it under the drip lines of the trees.

Double and sometimes triple rows can often be put where but one is the common practice. Try reducing the amount of space between plants, too. Corn, for instance, will often grow luxuriantly only six inches apart. If you have hens, you might plant mulberry and maple trees in their yards. Don't forget the decorative pear tree, dwarf varieties of which can even be trained to grow flat against house, garage, or garden shed.

Space a problem? Then buy one of the pyramid beds of aluminum sheet metal, set up in series of circular tiers starting with one six feet in diameter, that will accommodate forty plants in a ten-foot-square area while still allowing for footpaths. Or build a similar one yourself, squaring the design perhaps and using twelve-inch-wide planks.

Using Plants To Repel Insects

Gardens prepared along the sound natural lines just considered will be less apt to be troubled by diseases and troublesome insects than they would be otherwise. Furthermore, it is often possible to help matters along by planting the varieties that are shown in the catalogs and on their packets as being immune or only slightly susceptible to local problems.

Suppose, however, unlikely, there are still signs of disease and insect injury in your garden? Then you can still combat them by natural means.

A few nearby clumps of chives, for instance, will chase aphids from roses. Not only that, but the purple blossoms are attractive by themselves. As for the young leaves, they're delectable chopped up in soups, salads, sauces, and cheese dishes.

Chive's cousin, garlic, is not only a savory crop by itself, but it will keep peach borers from killing your trees when the garlic cloves are separated and planted apart at least one-half inch deep, roots downward of course, as close to the trunks as possible.

Sowing marigolds in your bean rows will keep them from being eaten up by Mexican bean beetles. Nearby potato plants, too, will keep these Mexican beetles from attacking your beans. And if you are having difficulties with potato bugs, just plant horseradish among the potato rows.

Horseradish? This familiar plant, whose young stalks and leaves cook up into tasty greens, can really satisfy those who like to add character to their steaks, chops, and roasts. The part of the perennial used for this is the long, whitish root. For a sauce that will really start those taste buds thrilling, grate three tablespoons of freshly dug root. Combine with ⅛ teaspoon salt and a similar volume of paprika. Mix with ½ stick of fresh butter, maybe from that cow you're keeping.

Beds of the brightly attractive and tangily edible nasturtiums between vegetables and fruit trees repel aphids. Asparagus beetles? Just plant tomatoes near the asparagus shoots. Basil, coriander, and anise are particularly effective against many insect pests, too.

You don't even have to buy those poisonous ant repellents to keep ants out of your home. Mint, spearmint, and tansy planted around the walls will keep them away, too. Flies don't like the mints, either; and if you're wondering how to use such edibles in your kitchen and medicine chest, just look at one of the old-time herbals. Tansy has long been used in home remedies for a host of ills. Squash and pumpkin leaves, crushed and rubbed on the backs and heads of cattle or pets, are natural fly repellents.

Asters, marigolds, chrysanthemums, and their relations, are distasteful to insects. So are coreopsis and cosmos, even geraniums, those delightful tidbits for deer. So you can well have color in addition to protection among your vegetable beds. The weed-suppressing French marigolds, tagetes, will save potatoes affected with verticillium wilt. Wireworms and potato eelworms don't like them, either.

If the black, sucking little chinch bugs turn up in your corn patch, plant something such as quickly growing and highly edible sowbeans as a ground cover, as these destructive pests don't like shade. The reliable and showy marigolds discourage cucumber beetles. A companion crop of chives or garlic will help guard your lettuce from plant lice. The sentinel for tomatoes, as well as eggplants and peppers, is basil. The nasturtium does the job for squash, especially when planted at the same time.

The final method for controlling pests is the maintenance of healthy plants. Vigorous flowers and vegetables, like healthy individuals, have the strength to ward off insects and disease. Develop a good soil. That's the most important thing.

CHAPTER FOUR

Making Money with the Ancient Art of Herb Culture

HUNDREDS of people across the country with one or two acres of land at their disposal, or even with only a half-acre, have achieved security growing herbs, notes N. P. Nichols in his interesting booklet, *Profitable Herb Growing,* obtainable for $1 from the Nichols Garden Nursery, Albany, Oregon 97321. He gives a number of examples.

For instance, Sheldon and Hariette Widmer, when they retired to a small Indiana farm, determined it would be fun to raise herbs. The hobby grew into a successful business, and today their Cherry Hill Herbs are nationally famous. Starting earlier, Roy E. Anderson was given a dozen chive plants by his mother when he was a schoolboy; now, growing and marketing 35 acres of this herb, he is the largest raiser of chives in the country.

Then there's a Miss Arnold who in 1939 bought a single horehound plant at a Providence, Rhode Island flower show and now produces 3000 pounds of this dried herb alone, plus scores of other varieties. Patricia Winter, whose start was equally humble, at this writing grows fifteen acres of herbs and employs a dozen workers at the height of the season.

How does it work? Well, Mr. Nichols recently found that a 25¢ package of sweet basil, selling in the supermarkets, contained approximately ¼ ounce of the herb. A single basil plant will produce four times this amount of the dried herb. Considering that 15,000 plants can be grown on an acre, two or three acres should provide plenty of land to operate a well-paying herb farm.

Packaging

Packaging is easy. You can put about ¼ ounce each of your herbs in small transparent plastic bags and seal these neatly with a hot iron. Fifty of these alluring little sacks can be stapled, ten in a row, on a twelve-by-eighteen-inch display card. Head this boldly with some catch phrase, perhaps FRESH MAINE-GROWN (or whatever) HERBS MAKE YOUR FOOD TASTE BETTER. Another profit-stimulating procedure is to insert a few tempting recipes for the particular herb, perhaps mimeographed to save time, in each packet. For variety, to make your products move faster in the store, each row may contain a different herb.

Retailing Arrangements

The herbs will retail at, say, 25¢ a packet. The merchant will need to net one-third or perhaps 40 percent on the sales. That is, such a card will retail at $12.50. When the store requires 40 percent, such a display will be wholesaled to the merchant for $7.50.

Even if you devote only an acre of ground to herbs, you should be able to raise enough to fill at least 1,000 of these display cards. Once the herbs are dried and placed on display racks, this means a gross return to you of $7,500 an acre. Actually, inasmuch as each fifty-packet display card requires less than one pound of herbs, the figure will be better than this. With expenses running about one-third, that will leave you with a yearly profit of at least $5000 an acre.

Your likeliest prospects will include the supermarkets, ordinary grocery stores, health food establishments, specialty shops, and in fact any enterprise that sells food. An optimum time to talk to the manager is in the morning, incidentally, when he is less apt to be rushed.

Sales Arguments

Sales arguments? The fact that your herbs are locally grown means they're fresh and full of flavor. Therefore, discovering that their stauncher taste means that they go farther, the economy-minded housewife is more apt to become a repeat buyer. Then there's the fact that the transparent packets are attention-getting and purchase-inducing, while their being lightly stapled to a display card from which they can be easily detached makes them a prime self-service item.

Emphasize, too, that you'll give the merchant regular service, making sure that there will always be an attractively and adequately fitted card on display. It'll pay you to pick up cards not completely sold, crediting the store with the packets remaining and transferring these to fresh cards when you get home so that you'll incur almost no loss on the transaction. In fact, when a buyer is difficult to convince, you can guarantee him the privilege of returning any unsold portions for a cash refund if he comes to the opinion, however unlikely, that the herbs do not move fast enough to warrant his stocking them.

Herb Teas

With herbs presently getting so much publicity, you'll be able to take a free ride with your own products. Perhaps, for instance, you'll wish to push herb teas with all their benefits and attractions. Herbs used in brewing these include: lemon thyme, lemon balm, yarrow, catnip, sweet woodruff, chamomile, pennyroyal, sage, and sweet marjoram. To be more attractive, the dessicated leaves should be left as whole as possible. If you like to experiment, try brewing various combinations and maybe you'll come up with an original best-seller.

Be careful with your labeling and do not use such a word as "cure," although yarrow is useful for clearing up catarrh and for cleansing the kidneys, anise for coughs and upset stomachs, catnip as a sedative and for feverish colds, sage for inducing perspiration that may help break up a cold, the various mints for a complex of complaints ranging from diarrhea to nausea, and so on. Once more you can utilize a display card and transparent packets large enough to hold at least four ounces of your product, plus the intriguing directions.

Herb Vinegar

Then there are the various herb vinegars which you can concoct very easily by picking the herbs you use fresh, bruising them as with a rolling pin and a bread board, and then strewing them in an uncovered cask or crock. Next heat some bland cider or wine vinegar, bought inexpensively in bulk, to the boiling point, and pour it over the herbs. Now cover tightly, put out of the way in a corner of the kitchen, and stir every other day. About two weeks usually turns the trick, although you should be sampling every day, as too much steeping may bring out flavors that are unpleasantly strong.

When your herb vinegar has exactly the right piquant tang, strain it through several thicknesses of cheesecloth until it is clear. Seal it in attractive bottles which you can buy wholesale, perhaps at the drugstore to start with. And be sure to label it with a provocative, distinctive design. The better stores, as well as keenly competitive eating places, will be your customers. Until they are sold, store the filled bottles in a cool, dark place, perhaps a cellar or the back of a garage.

The herb heading the popularity list for such vinegar is French tarragon, followed by dill, sweet marjoram, sweet basil, and the many mints. Again, perhaps you can create something original.

For tarragon vinegar, to give you an idea, pick the green leaves on a dry day, just before the plant flowers. Dry these, then put in a wide-mouthed earthenware crock and cover them with a good-quality vinegar, filling the jar. Let steep fourteen days and then strain through cheesecloth or a flannel bag. Or, tasting as you proceed, you may agree with some connoisseurs that the best tarragon vinegar should be steeped two months.

Sweet basil vinegar is prepared in precisely the same manner.

For burnet vinegar, nearly fill a wide-mouthed bottle with the fresh green leaves of this herb, cover them with vinegar, and let everything steep for two weeks. Then strain off the vinegar, wash the bottle, put in a fresh supply of burnet leaves, pour the same vinegar over them, and let it infuse a fortnight longer. Strain the combination again, and the liquid with its cucumber flavor will be ready for use.

For green mint vinegar to be used with iced tea and colorful fruit punches, as well as being the basis of mint sauce for use with lamb and mutton and sparingly in the oil dressing for lettuce and cress salads, first bring a quart of pure cider vinegar to a bubble. Add one cup of granulated sugar, plus two cups crammed with fresh spearmint leaves and young stem tips. Simmer five minutes, stirring and crushing. Then strain, bottle, and seal hot in glass jars.

Potted Herbs

The various herbs can be transferred into pots for winter use and these sold through stores to housewives who'd like the beauty and utility of a fresh herb growing in their own kitchens. Chives and parsley are particularly hearty. Potted thyme, sweet marjoram, chervil, and sage will also be especially practical for such merchandise.

Powdered Mixed Herbs

Try your own recipes for soups, omelets, and stuffings. Then mix what you find to be the proper proportions and cork tightly in bottles with labels showing their use. These labels will attract more attention if, seasonally, they are headlined for such interesting uses as: the Thanksgiving turkey, the Christmas turkey, the Yuletide goose, Christmas pig, Saint Michael's goose on September 29, Fourth of July duck, and Christmas sausage.

For the goose, pig, and duck, sage and onion will predominate. Other sweet herbs such as thyme, chervil, and sweet marjoram may be added. The onion for the duck, incidentally, must first be parboiled. Thyme and sage predominate in pork sausage.

Chicken, which you should include, may be stuffed with chives, parsley, sweet marjoram, thyme, and a bit of sage and basil. Sage, summer savory, sweet marjoram, thyme, parsley, and chervil will point up the savoriness of turkey.

Tarragon is particularly tasty in fish sauces, spearmint in lamb sauce, basil in tomato dishes, and winter savory with stringbeans. For use with omelettes, bottle thyme, chives, tarragon, marjoram, and a dusting of chervil. For ground meats, an answer is marjoram, winter savory with half as much basil, thyme, and the reliable tarragon.

The following blend will do things for poultry stuffing: two teaspoons apiece of sage, parsley, and celery; and one teaspoon each of savory, marjoram, and thyme. This amount of mixed herbs will take care of two quarts of dry bread crumbs, one small chopped onion, salt and pepper to taste, ¼ cup butter, and a well-beaten egg.

Soup Bags for Flavoring

Make small cheesecloth bags about two inches square and fill them with a bouquet of dried herbs. For example, the quantity given in the following receipt for flavoring beef stock and meat gravies will fill three such bags, rendering each sufficiently potent to season two quarts of liquid. The bags are dropped into the simmering soup toward the end of the cooking period and left not more than one hour.

For the above sample recipe, mix a teaspoonful each of the leaves and stems of dried parsley, thyme, and marjoram; ¼ teaspoon apiece of dried bay leaf, and the leaves and flowers of both dried savory and dried basil; plus two teaspoons of dried celery. The latter may be in the form of leaf and stem tips or the grated root of the herb.

Herb Jellies

The ways you can handily make money with herbs will be limited only by your imagination and ingenuity. For example, there are the brightly colored herb jellies, so simple to make. As far as the market for them goes, just thumb through the home magazines during the holiday season and see the number of advertisers caught up in the whirl of merchandising fancy jams and jellies. Perhaps your best initial chances of success will be to specialize in just several varieties of herb jellies and to make them better than anyone else. Once you gain experience and your markets expand, so can your selection.

Mint, for instance, has a tasty affinity for cider vinegar, sweet marjoram for lemon juice, sweet savory for grapefruit juice, thyme for the preceding two juices mixed, sage for cider vinegar, and rosemary for orange.

Herb Candies

Then there are the herb candies which, when you make them at home, should be different from mass-produced sweets such as chocolate peppermints. There's candied angelica, wrapped sesame sweets, hard-sugar herb candy, and attractively candied flowers and leaves.

For candied mint leaves, pick your prettiest leaves of spearmint or peppermint and make sure they are dry and clean. Dip both sides in whipped egg white, thinned by a half-teaspoonful of water. Then, holding them by the stems, coat them immediately by immersing them in granulated sugar. Lay apart on waxed paper to dry, after which they can be packed in boxes. These will remain green and sugary for a year. One way of serving them is on the saucer with a steaming cup of tea.

Herbs for Wreaths

Herbs may be woven in the evergreen Christmas wreaths. Thyme, for instance, if cut back immediately after flowering will produce winter shoots for this use. Rosemary, thyme, rue, hyssop, lavender, and the like may be layered, a process discussed in Chapter 12 with grapevines, employing the long woody stems on the outside of the bushes and covering these with earth. They soon root and by fall produce strong growth with verdant foliage through December.

The ancients have given to some of the herbs special significance—marjoram for happiness, rosemary for remembrance, thyme for valor, and gray sage for long life and immortality.

Specialty Uses for Herbs

Then there's the use of herbs for incense. The leaves of southernwood are among those that will pleasantly scent a room when strewn over the coals of a damped fire.

Herb breads and pastries are enjoying an expanding market. Once you begin supplying customers, attracted to your wares with small classified ads, with such a product as crusty fennel bread, you'll find they'll also ask about such additional wares as herb cookies and cakes. Likely the overall demand will soon exceed your supply.

Take some samples of a tasty herb potato salad to your local store or supermarket, and it's not unlikely that you'll come home with enough orders to develop into a prize sideline business. One formula? Several hours before you make what will be roughly a quart of salad, stir a teaspoon apiece of basil, summer savory, and marjoram into a cup of boiled dressing or mayonnaise. Slice a medium-size onion into enough cider vinegar to remove its sharpness. Slice four cold boiled potatoes into a large cool bowl and add the onion, two sliced hard-boiled eggs, and salad dressing. Salt and pepper to taste, dusting on a bit of celery salt for extra flavor. Mix well, strew with paprika and parsley flakes for color, and refrigerate.

You can also sell herb plants and seeds and, as considered in Chapter 5, the honey from bees, which will forage avidly for nectar from growing rosemary, sage, hyssop, thyme, and in fact practically every variety of thriving herb.

Then there are aromatic herbs for the bath, such as chamomile herb hair rinse, fancy herb pillows that are such favorites at souvenir and gift shops, lavender packets for drawer and closets, and even the incessantly selling catnip mice and catnip pillows which can ride along with the hundreds of millions of dollars of pet supplies sold in the United States every year.

As the Chinese say, to walk a mile you must take the first step. To produce an acre of herbs you must plant that first seed.

How to Grow and Use Popular Herbs

There's magic in the very names of herbs—basil, lavender, chives, dill, sage, marjoram, summer savory, rosemary, thyme, and even parsley. Not only will these grow in abundance outdoors in your own personal garden plot, but during the winter months they'll thrive in the house, their aromatic greenness bringing springlike verdure to a southern window.

Caraway Caraway, for instance, likes a sunny, dry situation. It is a hardy herb, and on this continent it fruits well, especially in the northern contiguous United States and southern Canada. The piquant seeds ripen in June and early July, at which time they should be bottled to preserve their flavor. Incidentally, an oil is sometimes

Caraway

extracted from these and used internally for colic. More commonly, though, the seeds are used to flavor bread, biscuits, and cheeses, and, encased in sugar, to liven cake and cookie frostings. The tender shoots and young leaves are sometimes used in salads, while even the slender tap root is prized for its delicious flavor.

Chives

Chives Chives are simplest and easiest to grow of all the herbs. The round, slender, hollow tubes that are the leaves thrust up easily soon after you sow the seeds, preferably in the early spring, half an inch deep in mellow, well-drained soil. They should be eventually clipped with scissors, by the way, although if you don't mind the onionlike aroma they impart to the hands, you can easily nip off a few for salads and soups with the thumbnail. Plants can be started by dividing the clump and setting out the tiny bulbs.

Attractive little bushes, perhaps a foot high, are formed by the chives, which produce subtle blooms with a lavender cast. Therefore, they're particularly useful and ornamental as a winter pot plant.

The delicate, delightful flavor of chives is so appealing to almost everyone that this herb should be thriving in every garden. The finely chopped leaves impart a delectable flavor to many kinds of food: salad, grilled or roasted meat, soup, savory omelet, sauces, homemade cheese, and numerous others.

Dill   Dill takes about two and a half months from seed to harvest; so it will be well to sow it outdoors once the danger from frost is past, perhaps timing the planting so that it will ripen when those cucumbers are ready for pickles. The fresh dill leaves are picked when the flowers start to unfurl. Once the latter have matured, the ripe

Dill

seeds are harvested. If you're going to try your hand at homemade soap, details for which may be found in my *How to Live in the Woods on Pennies a Day,* try distilling oil from the dill leaves and mixing this with other essences for perfuming your output. Dill is also used extensively in home pickle-making, while the plant's younger tops and leaves will pleasantly aromatize fish sauces and even vinegar.

Lavender Lavender grows wild on dry, stony lands and when brought home seems to prefer a sunny spot in light, chalky soil. If you want to extend certain bushes, it is easy to perpetuate them from slips put in sandy soil. Lavender can also be grown from seed, begun indoors and later transplanted.

Lavender's stems and flowering branches are best cut on sunny afternoons, as close to the woody stalk as possible, but you should wait until the whole spike is in flower and the lowest bloom has started to darken. The volatile oil of aspic from lavender is used to dilute delicate colors for painting on porcelain, a pleasant and often profitable hobby by itself. Most of us have sometime hung the dried leaves and flowers in a clothes closet or laid them in a handkerchief drawer. They are also utilized, of course, in soaps and perfumes. The leaves are sometimes used in flavoring, while subtle sweets are made of the attractive flowers.

Sage Sage will grow in any good, well-drained garden. Varieties, generally narrow-leafed, can be started from seeds. Too, plants may be purchased from many stores and nurseries and later increased from cuttings and slips, preferably in the spring. The distinctively smelling leaves are harvested by stripping them from the bushes, then drying them in the shade to keep them from turning black. However, the young sage plants should not be cut too much the first year.

Someone trying to give up the provenly harmful tobacco habit may like to switch for a while in passing to sage leaves with their mildly astringent and tonic properties. As for the aromatic sage tea, this has long been a favorite household remedy for sore throats and colds. The oil distilled from the whole plant has a camphorous odor that is blended into soap, perfumes, and hair tonics. Dried sage leaves, used discreetly, as the herb is strong, distinctively flavor pork, cheese, sausage, and poultry stuffings.

Lavender

Garden Sage

Sweet Basil Sweet basil, easily raised from seed indoors or out, may be sown in your garden once the danger of frost is past. The seeds, which germinate readily, may be expected to produce plants from which a few leaves may be cut for the kitchen in about six weeks. This herb likes a sunny, well-drained exposure.

Limited numbers of pleasantly scented sweet basil leaves can be gathered as soon as the plants are large enough to stand it, and it is safe to cut them in quantities once the flowers begin to open. When you do lop back the leafy stems, the plants will be the better for rich compost's being stirred around the roots for stimulation. Then the more they are cut, the thicker they'll grow.

If you don't already have an indoor herb garden, pot a few of the plants when cold weather approaches and bring them into the house. Sweet basil, particularly effective with tomato dishes, will impart an agreeably different tang to soups and stews. Some also like to dust it over cheeses and atop fruit drinks.

Sweet Basil

Sweet Marjoram   Sweet marjoram, best started indoors in a cold frame or south window and the seedlings transplanted to the garden after perils from frost have passed, should have a sunny, dry, amply drained exposure. Incidentally, if you're raising a few sheep, you're well away, as the herb thrives best when fed with sheep manure. The leaves and flowering tops are cut just as the flowers appear, then the leaves stripped off the stems and dried in the shade. Sweet marjoram, used either fresh or dried, will do wonders for soups, garnishes, poultry dressings, and for giving a special taste to homemade sausages. For these reasons it was one of the most popular herbs in Colonial gardens.

Summer Savory   Summer savory is an annual, attractively spreading, sweet herb whose plants, sixteen to eighteen inches high, spice the air. The leaves, the part the cook uses, are small, slender, and soft. Green, they have the pleasantly mild overtones of pepper and camphor. This taste becomes sharper and more peppery once the leaves are dried. These dried leaves, steeped into tea, have long been an old-fashioned home remedy for colds and fever. In Colonial years the leaves were crushed and rubbed on bee stings, a swiftly acting remedy that still works.

Summer savory is easily grown from seeds which, outdoors, should be sown half an inch deep in the early spring in finely screened, mellow soil. The little plants withstand transplanting sturdily and can be so thinned to allow each one sufficient room in which to develop. When the delicately pinkish lavender flowers appear, green stalk tips and leaves can be gathered and dried in a shaded spot. Later pulverized as between your dry hands, they give delectable flavor to stews, gravies, sausages, veal and pork dressings, and poultry stuffings. The herb may also be mixed with parsley to add flavor to salads and to freshly cooked peas and beans.

Parsley   The ancient Greeks were among those esteeming parsley, one of the oldest as well as most useful of our garden herbs. Everyone has savored the delightful, tangy flavor that finely chopped parsley or dried and pulverized parsley flakes add to salads, stews, meats, and soups. In addition, the prickly green, fernlike attractiveness of deeply verdant parsley leaves boosts the eye appeal of many foods.

Parsley seeds are extremely slow to germinate, often requiring a

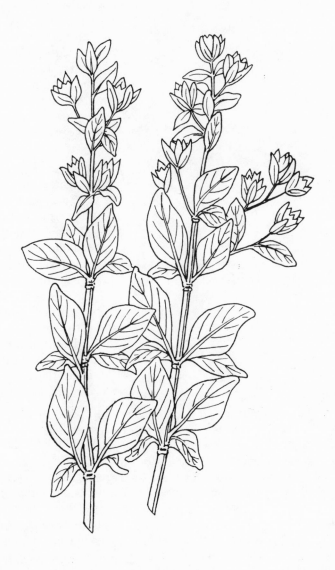

Sweet Marjoram

Parsley

month. The seed coats should first be softened, therefore, by soaking the tiny tidbits overnight in water that is slightly warm to start with. Sow them in early spring in fertile, mellow, finely screened soil, the rows being a foot apart and the individual plants up to the same distance from one another. Parsley is one of the many biennials and should be renewed from seeds every second year. Planted in flower pots and grown on window sills, it makes a dainty house plant that's both useful and ornamental.

Rosemary   Rosemary grows readily from seeds which should be started as early as possible indoors if the fragrant plants are to grow large enough for leaves to be cut from them early in the season. As for rosemary carried over the winter indoors, cuttings can be made during January or later. Once the leaves are taken, the soil about the

Rosemary

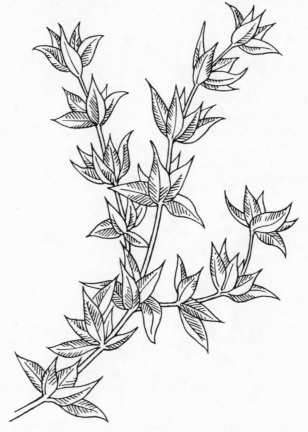

Thyme

plants should be carefully stirred and sheep manure or other organic plant food added. The fresh leaves can be used at any time. For drying, they're best picked once the herb flowers, then dried in the shade. The flowers, incidentally, are a stimulant.

Oil of rosemary, secured by distilling the leafy tips and the leaves themselves, can be used in homemade perfumes and soaps. For a sumptuous feast, try thick rare slices of red meat from a roast that has been heartily rubbed with dried rosemary leaves and salt before being consigned to the oven.

Thyme   Most of the thymes, except for those with variegated foliage, grow readily from seed which will do very well when sown outdoors in May. It is the broad-leaved English thyme that is used principally for seasoning. The plants should be cut when they are in full flower, then dried in the shade to preserve their color to the fullest possible extent. Both the blossoms and the leaves are used for flavoring. As for the oil of thyme that is distilled from the flowering tops, this is another scent for those kitchen-fabricated soap bars—maybe another business for you.

Garlic   Then there's garlic, one of the oldest and most universally known of the herbs that are dried. In fact, many just braid the green garlic tops together once the bulbs have been harvested and hang the long ropes out of the way in cellar or laundry. To plant, separate the garlic bulb into cloves and embed these half an inch deep with the roots, of course, downward. To grow these indoors, plant a half-dozen in a ten-inch pot. They'll take some weeks to come up in any event, but then each clove will start radiating green shoots which you can snip off and utilize as you would green onion tips or chives.

Anise   Anise is a hardy annual which thrives in even the colder states, has lacy leaves and white flowers, and does things for your cooking. Sow the seeds in very warm soil in May, thinning the results and keeping them weeded. Anise grows two feet tall; so plant in rows and keep the individual herbs a dozen to eighteen inches apart. The herb does best in soil that is not too rich. Anise seeds, it so happens, do not retain their fertility long, so use fresh seed not more than two years old.

Garlic Bulbs

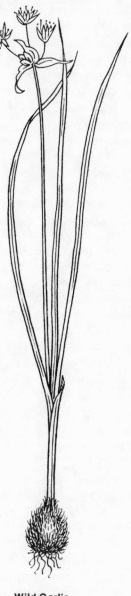

Wild Garlic

The leaves of anise are sometimes used for giving piquancy to salads, but it is the seeds for which the herb is best known. Save these by cutting off the seed heads before the seeds begin to fall. Spread the heads on cheesecloth, paper, or such to dry. Then rub out the twinkling little particles. Before you use the seeds in the kitchen, wash them thoroughly.

Borage Borage is a rough-stemmed, leafy annual, attractive with clusters of lovely blue flowers. The leaves are oval and exceedingly hairy. Borage is grown from large, rough, and ridged seeds with conelike bases. These retain their fertility well. The plants come into bloom quickly. In fact, many times the older plants self-sow and form a fresh bed which will bloom until frost nips the foliage.

In olden times borage was thought to keep away melancholy, not surprisingly, as it is a cheery, beautiful, and profuse blossomer. The flowers were formerly candied as a sweetmeat which was used to flavor cordials, something you may still care to try with your home-concocted beverages discussed in detail in Chapter 12. The tasty leaves are edible and may be cooked and served like spinach.

Burnet Garden burnet is a hardy, perennial herb with mats of long, compound leaves. The white or rose-hued flowers waver on tall stems. The plant germinates from seeds sown very early. The seedlings should be transplanted to stand some eight inches apart to allow for the spreading crowns. This herb is also propagated by root division.

The portion of the plant used is the young leaves, which thrive in the almost evergreen mats all winter. They are utilized in salads and even cocktails, lending all these a distinct flavor pleasantly resembling that of ripe cucumbers.

Catnip Catnip is a well-known perennial, so prolific that in some places it gets enough out of hand to become a garden pest. The way to grow it is from seed sown where the plants are to remain. These will thrive in poor soil and with less moisture than most of the mints.

Past generations used this herb extensively as a medicine for feverish colds and to induce sleep. It is still so employed to some extent, although today it is thought of primarily as an herb given to kitty to delight her and to keep her in good health.

Celery Celery is another biennial, under normal conditions

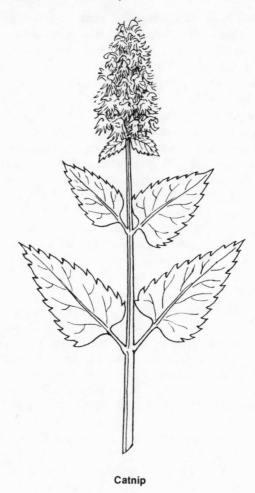

Catnip

producing seeds the second season. Inasmuch as it may be difficult to carry over the plants for seed production, it is usually advisable to buy the seed. Celery is an important vegetable crop even though it is somewhat hard to start. Good results are possible, though, if the seeds are sown in shallow flats or even cigar boxes. Fill the container with fine soft loam; then sprinkle the seeds over the surface and sift about one-eighth inch of sand or fine loam over them. Keep moist with careful watering, and in about ten days or two weeks the young plants will appear.

As soon as these are large enough, transplant them into other flats. Later set in your garden, about four to six inches apart, in rows three feet apart. When the seedlings are put in the ground without transplanting from the seedbed to a flat, there are usually not enough roots to withstand the shock. Celery needs heavy soil. It fails to develop well on upland sand, for instance.

The crisp stems and tender leaves are used for flavor in soups, stews, and salads. The seeds are also used in soups, especially when fresh celery is not available. Celery plants, stored in a good cellar

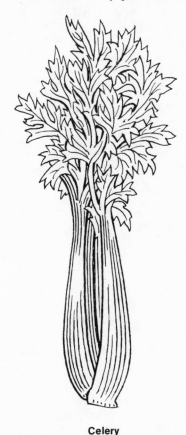

Celery

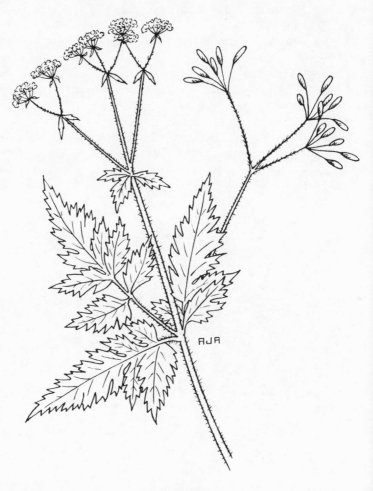

Sweet Cicely

with their roots in moist soil, will continue fresh and succulent for winter use.

Sweet Cicely   Sweet cicely is a European species, being a perennial herb with fernlike leaves and a thick root. The flowers are white. It seeds itself freely in practically any soil but thrives best in rich, loamy gardens in partial shade.

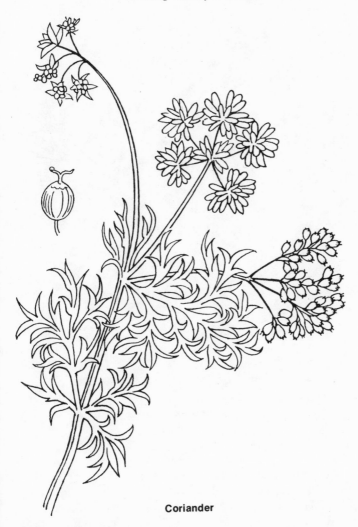

Coriander

The leaves, seeds, and roots are used both in cookery and medicine. The plant resembles our native, wild sweet cicely, which is officially called an *Osmorhiza*, Greek for scented root. You'll see the latter growing in rich, moist woods, flowering in late spring and summer. The sweet flavor of stem and root is much like that of anise.

Sweet Fennel

Coriander Coriander is an annual, distinguished by umbels of pale pink flowers set off by soft green foliage. It may be easily grown by sowing the seed in your herb garden in early spring. Thin the resulting plants to eighteen inches apart once they grow to be from one to two and one-half inches high. The excess will not transplant easily, by the way.

Coriander is grown chiefly for its seeds, which are used to flavor bread, poultry dressings, and the like. Strong-smelling and somewhat unpleasantly flavored when fresh, they become pleasing once dried. The seed heads are gathered when nearly ripe and spread on a sheet or tray to lose moisture. Care should be taken in gathering not to scatter the seeds, as they germinate easily enough to become a garden pest.

Sweet Fennel   Sweet fennel is a perennial with shining, tall stems and extremely feathery leaves. The yellow flowers are borne in umbels. There are two common varieties, both, although not too hardy, easily grown from seed and subsequently transplanted to rich soil. The seeds, leaves, and tender stems of the two are used in seasonings.

Rose Geranium   The rose geranium is commonly thought of as a house plant although it has its uses in the kitchen. It is a perennial in its native habitat, coming from the southern part of Africa. You no

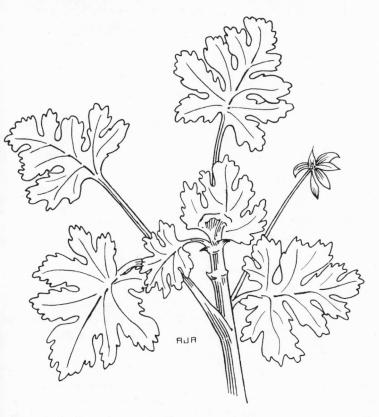

Rose Geranium

doubt know it as a shrubby plant with soft, hairy leaves, divided into three main divisions that are much indented. They give off a spicy, sweet odor not unlike that of roses. The flowers are small, pinkly lavender blooms in a loose umbel. This geranium is propagated almost entirely by cuttings.

The leaves are utilized in cooking to impart a rose flavor, one of the commonest uses being in flavoring apple jellies. They are also employed to flavor custards and puddings. Commercially, an oil is extracted from them which is used in blending perfumes. Give you any ideas?

Horehound Horehound is a shrubby perennial having white flowers in bristly whorls. It is very easily raised. As the seeds germinate slowly, they should be sown in poor soil very early. When about an inch high, transplant them a well-weeded six to eight inches apart. It is advisable to begin a fair-sized bed to allow for vigorous cutting when in bloom. Each fall cut the old stalks to the ground to keep the bed thick. However, to insure a constant crop, it will be well to start a new bed at least every other spring.

The flowers, leaves, and stems are dried slowly and then stored. Their primary use in olden times was in making a tea used in treatment of colds. Horehound is better known today when combined with sugar to make candy and cough drops.

The Mint Family Many of the mints are used for flavoring, the commonest of these being spearmint and peppermint. In general this genus does not produce seeds which are sure of germination, but propagation is easily enough accomplished by plant division or cutting. All that is necessary is to take a few stems with good roots and reset the latter in rich, moist soil.

All mints do well in clay, but they do not like lime. The bed may be cut freely. Mint seems to thrive when alternate portions are well sheared and is a most hardy perennial. For best results it must be sheared immediately after blooming, for the plants become exhausted if permitted to mature seed.

Spearmint, *Mentha spicata,* has dark green, toothed leaves, is strongly aromatic, and blossoms in pale purple spikes. It is a favorite for flavoring iced tea and other cool drinks. It is also utilized effectively in jellies, chewing gum, and in mint sauce to accompany that lamb from the flock you're maybe raising. The leaves and tips of

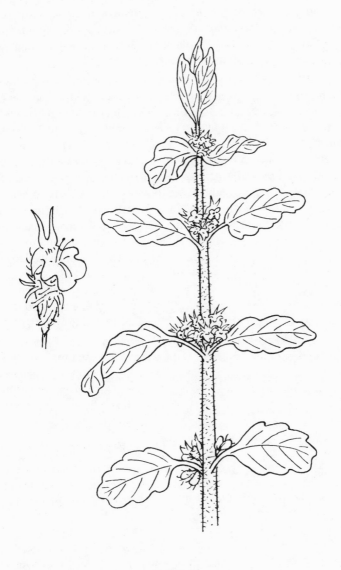

Horehound

the stem are used fresh and dry for these purposes.

Peppermint, *Mentha piperita,* resembles its above cousin but has narrower leaves and a reddish tinge to the stem. Although it is a popular flavor for candy and chewing gum, it is not cultivated as frequently as spearmint. The leaves and tender stems are the parts used for flavoring.

The mint, which gives such fragrance to the hands when you wash it for tea, has romantic connections. Mintha, it is told, was the daughter of the river god of Hades, Cocytus. As she stood on the banks of the river, Pluto passed by and fell in love with her. His queen, Prosperpina, being jealous, turned Mintha into a plant which we know as mint and which has ever grown near water. Baucis, of the ancient Greek legend, rubbed her dinner table with fresh green mint before she set the boards for the two gods, Zeus and his son Hermes. High connections these, but mints will still thrive by the smallest of brooks.

Watercress and Other Nasturtiums　　Although the nasturtium is not commonly thought of as an herb, it may well be included in our list of savory herb favorites. Both the freely growing common and dwarf varieties are used in cooking. These tender annuals, grown from seed sown in the garden and thinned, if you want, to stand six or eight inches apart for the dwarf and twelve inches apart for the tall, require a fairly rich soil and plenty of moisture.

The seeds, the flower petals, and the tender leaves of the nasturtium are all used in producing agreeably pungent food flavors. The flowers, tender stems, and the young leaves are utilized in sandwiches and salads, while the half-ripened seeds are added to mixed and mustard pickles. For tasty tidbits, relegate several handfuls of the ripe seeds to a vinegar-filled jar for several months, until they will almost melt in your mouth.

The popular watercress *(nasturtium officinale)* is a perennial with spreading root characteristics, white flowers that bloom throughout the summer, and oblong, glossy, dark green leaves. Besides thriving wild throughout much of the continent, watercress may be grown in shallow ponds and fresh streams, where it especially likes a location abounding in lime. While it is a surface water plant, it may also be raised in moist soil which has been adequately limed.

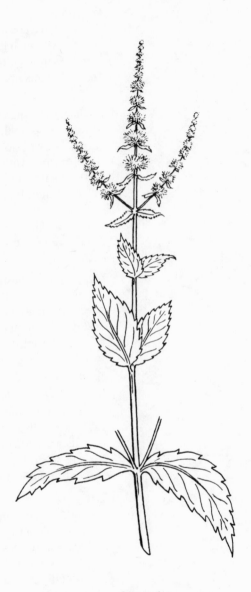

Spearmint

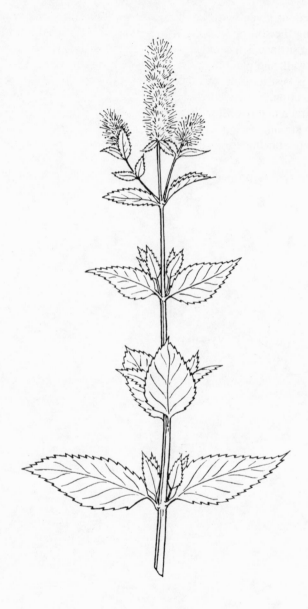

Peppermint

Directions given by those successful with watercress recommend screening the soil or working it over thoroughly, then adding lime until the surface is a decided white. Next, work this top in, moisten the soil well, and plant the cress about six inches apart in each direction. It is best to grow watercress in a special framework of boards for protection. For instance, it is sometimes seen abounding in a luxuriant green mat overflowing a shallow trough at the edge of a slow-running stream. Frequent renewal of the bed insures success. One bed can be starting, for instance, while a second is being used for cuttings.

Watercress is propagated either by seeds or by the tips of the

Watercress

stems, which root readily in water. Adding a little lime to this liquid helps to get good results. Watercress, it so happens, is not too hardy and will not stand severe freezing. In northern New England, for example, it is best to winter over enough to start a new bed by growing it in shallow boxes or in a greenhouse, keeping it moist and providing a well-limed soil.

Watercress's peppery, pungent flavor makes it popular as a garnish and salad plant. Watercress soup is also memorable. For one variety which we have found to be exceptional, heat 3 cups of fresh milk with 1½ teaspoons salt. In the meantime, run enough cold watercress through the meat grinder to fill a cup. Add this to the hot milk and simmer five minutes, keeping the pan covered as much as possible. Just before sitting down with your soup spoon, beat until smooth and add a cup of fresh milk or cream. Serve as soon as heated thoroughly, topped with sprinkled paprika and fresh sprigs of cress.

Winter Savory Winter savory is a woody, perennial shrub with dramatically purple flowers. It is grown from seed sown in the garden and later, growing sixteen to eighteen inches tall, thinned to a distance of from a dozen to eighteen inches. Like summer savory, it thrives best in poor soil, wintering most luxuriantly when the ground is neither too damp or too rich. The tender leaves and tips are the parts used in seasoning.

Southernwood Southernwood is an interesting perennial with sweetly scented, gray-green foliage and small, greenish yellow flowers in loose heads. It is propagated by cuttings or root divisions and spreads freely. The plant is grown more for its fragrance than its culinary uses in most sections, although it has also long been utilized along with nearly all the other members of the *Artemisia* family for its medicinal qualities.

Tarragon The popular tarragon is a perennial with dark, green, entire leaves, happening to be the only one of the *Artemisias* to have entire leaves. Closely related to wormwood, it is also marked with inconspicuous clusters of greenish flowers.

True tarragon does not develop fertile seed, the usual method of propagation being by root division in the early spring. Propagation by cutting of the stems may be successfully accomplished almost any time. The plants should be set twelve inches apart. A dry, poor soil is preferred, as in moist, heavy soils the herb is sensitive to

Winter Savory

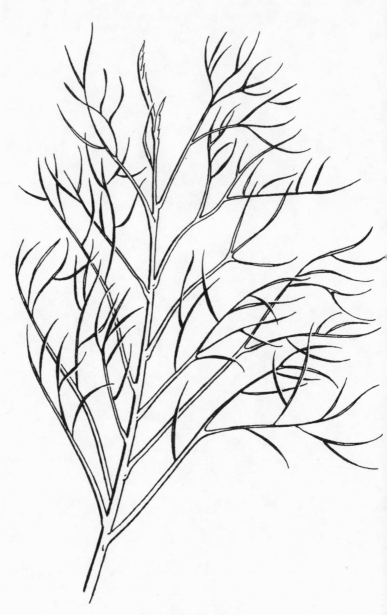

Southernwood

Tarragon

winterkill. It needs a scant covering of litter and leaves for cold-weather protection. It is well to relocate tarragon every three or four years to guard against disease.

Tarragon leaves are what are used. These may be gathered at any time once the plants have made a thrifty growth. Used both fresh and dried, these leaves have a delicate flavor resembling that of anise. They are used primarily for seasoning vinegar, pickles, salads, and table mustard, which, as detailed in my *Free for the Eating,* you can make and bottle yourself. Tarragon vinegar may already be a favorite of yours in dressing summer salads.

Lemon Verbena Your grandmother maybe spoke of lemon verbena. This plant is a perennial coming originally from Chile; so in much of the country it is not hardy and is usually taken in for the winter as a house plant. It is propagated by cuttings. If you are acquainted with this herb, you know that the leaves give off the pleasant odor of lemon peel. They grow in whorls, and are linearly lance-shaped and greenish yellow, darker and shiny above the dull beneath. They are rough to the touch. The flowers, growing on slender spikes, are small and bluish white.

As in the case of the rose geranium, the leaves are used extensively in making perfumes, but they are also utilized to flavor jellies. Too, they impart a lemonish flavor to both tea and cold fruit drinks.

Careful Soil Preparation

Careful preparation of the soil is essential for successful herb gardens. Inasmuch as many of the plants are perennials and will remain in one spot more than one year, it will be well to plow or spade the plot as deep as ten to fifteen inches and throughly work into the soil well-rotted manure and bone meal.

Fully five pounds of bone meal may be used on each 100 square feet, or ten pounds for a plot a handy ten feet wide and twenty feet long. The addition of five pounds of cottonseed meal will also prove a benefit. Rotted manure can be applied at any time in the form of a mulch or top-dressing around the plants, but a liberal amount of rotted manure worked into the soil during its prepara-

Lemon Verbena

tion will increase the organic content of the ground and improve its moisture-holding capacity.

The main points are to apply plenty of organic fertilizer and manure, to mix them thoroughly with the soil, and to pulverize this soil to the full depth that it is broken. If the ground is spaded, the lumps should be broken as each spadeful is turned. If the ground is plowed, it should be harrowed and then all remaining chunks broken by hand.

A large number of herbs can be started by sowing the seeds in the permanent garden locations, then thinning to the proper distances. This adds up to thin and careful sowing. A few tender varieties do best, as previously considered, when started in the house in flats or in a hotbed or cold frame, then transferred to the garden when weather conditions are favorable.

By the last of May or the first week of June in northern states, practically all seedlings should have had their final transplanting into the garden. If very cold nights follow, they may then need a slight covering.

The following herbs are easily grown from seed: sage, dill, parsley, chives, coriander, anise, horehound, caraway, thyme, fennel, basil, chervil, savory, catnip, burnet, and marjoram. All perennial herbs are best propagated by root division, layering, and cutting.

Indoor Herb Gardens

Want the fresh touch of sweet basil with your tomato dishes the year around, fresh green mint sprigs with your drinks, fresh thyme with that steaming fish chowder, fresh chives with that salad, and luxuriantly green parsley atop that omelette? Then reserve part of a southern windowsill for an indoor herb garden.

You can buy handy green plastic boxes, about two inches deep and a foot by two feet across, for such winter greens. Or build a similarly dimensioned tray and line it with waterproofing. A layer of gravel goes into the bottom of one of these, covered by an inch of sparkling sand. In the handiest corner, implant a very tiny cylinder or open-bottomed flower pot into which to pour your water when the time comes.

Then arrange your flower pots of herbs attractively in the tray, pressing each into the sand and giving it a slight steadying twist. The sand, swirling up into the holes of the pots, will form natural wicks, drawing the water slowly and steadily up into the pot's soil.

To kill harmful germs, as well as insect eggs or larvae, and to help control soil-borne plant diseases, it is a sound practice to disinfect all home-mixed house-plant soil before use. Perhaps the simplest effective method to pasteurize soil is to spread the potting medium in a kettle, add a cup of water for every gallon of solids, and bake for an hour at 180° to 240°. Turn the results out on a clean newspaper and let cool a full day.

If you have started your herbs outdoors, just transfer them to their indoor pots when they're a robust two inches high. If you're beginning the whole operation in the house, there's a little bit more to it, although a readily growing herb such as chives can be started directly in its final container, the thickly sown seeds pushing their grasslike spikes up through light alkaline soil within a very few weeks.

Herbs such as thyme and sweet basil will get better starts if you plant the seeds in seed pans or flat boxes, covering them at once with plastic or glass to keep the humidity high. Shade everything, as with an outspread newspaper, until the first green sprouts appear. Again, once the seedlings are some two inches tall, transfer them into their permanent small pots.

Tin cans with holes punched in their bottoms for drainage also make handy seed starters. Or you may like to capitalize on the effectiveness of the two-pot system. With this, start by covering the bottom of a large clay pot with pebbles or gravel, then a layer of dry moss. Set in the smaller, seeded pot and steady it by shoving more of the moss around its outer side. Water by keeping the moss damp.

Such windowsill herb gardens will thrive in the sunlight. The fact that it's generally cooler close to a window will be all to the good, as herbs will do best between the temperatures of 55° to 60°. If you can't manage this in your kitchen, although the nighttime drop of heat while you're sleeping will help, then a cooler sun porch may be the answer. If your home is warmed with thermostated electricity, you're really in for some delicious dinners. The fumes resulting from gas heat are not as good, so air out such atmospheres whenever possible.

By following these few handy hints, you can be enjoying the benefits and delights of fresh herbs when winds are hurling snow against the windowpanes like chilled shot and everything outside, except for the evergreens, is wintry and gray. Once the last frost has passed, just sink your pots of herbs in the garden. They'll be ready to come indoors again in the fall, probably either thinned out or potted in larger containers. And you'll be living and eating better the year around.

Winter Salad Greens by the Boxful

While we're on the subject of indoor gardens, let's give a moment to salad greens. All you need is a wooden box or two, filled with moist sand, and the necessary space, perhaps a sun porch, spare bedroom, garage, or the basement. The greens won't require much light.

Salad greens can be grown in sand from almost any edible root: carrots, beets, turnips, celery, parsley, Swiss chard, parsnips, and even wild chicory and dandelions. The main difficulty, in fact, will probably be getting the wooden boxes, as so often these days everything from dynamite to apples is being shipped in cardboard. But your grocer will usually be able to find something for you. At the extreme, build your own or buy several small galvanized baskets or small tubs from the hardware store.

Let's say you've found some of the very convenient wooden apple boxes. Prop up one end of each box with a couple of bricks set sidewise, and fill the lower part with sand. Atop this lay your first row of roots, tips downward. Cover with several scoops of sand. Then put another layer of sand in the box, higher than the first, and add one more row of roots, either different or the same. When you've reached the middle, lay the box level and continue the planting.

You'll find that such vegetables as parsnips, having long roots, will do best in the thickest sand. Shorter roots will fit in the center, while the very compact roots such as beets can occupy the shallower end. Cover everything with a final inch of sand. Then all you have to do is keep the sand moist and collect your greens as they appear. There'll be continuing healthy crops, rich in natural vitamins and enzymes.

Modernizing Prehistoric Herb-Drying Methods

The ancients understood the flavorful intricacies of herb-drying well, but today in our kitchens we can give the age-old art some

new twists. Even if you have only an outdoor herb plot, the crop
will be so bountiful that even the most liberal seasoner will be able
to use only a small part of it during the growing season. Excesses
should be snipped off when most tender and saved for the cold
months.

The conserving process may be as simple as hanging a sprig near
the ceiling to dry in the warm stirrings of air in the house. For
larger amounts of some of the green pungencies, though, a drying
rack will be well worth the few minutes it will take to make a small
frame, perhaps one foot by two feet, and set it on legs so that air
can circulate freely about it. Spread some highly porous material
such as cheesecloth, or for that elegant touch, silk, across the top of
the frame, and you're in business.

It will be best if you can keep your garden so clean that when
masses of herbs are brought indoors for drying, they need not be
washed and some of the essential oils thus lost. If they are dusty,
you can perhaps wipe off this film with a dry cloth. But if they
have become dirt-spattered by watering or rains, a cold-water rinse
will be in order, after which all excessive moisture should be
shaken from the stems and verdant leaves.

Arrange each harvest of herbs in a loose layer atop the drying
rack. Weigh down another clean cloth over the plants; then set the
whole business outside, preferably in a warm, breezy spot where
the air will circulate throughout the bounty. Shade is to be
preferred, as direct sunlight has a tendency to scorch the herbs and
blunt their essential flavors.

The process will take from one to two days, depending on air
circulation, temperature, and humidity. Check the rack frequently
once the herbs have lost most of their moisture. The greens will be
ready as soon as they crumble dryly between the fingers. If you
leave them exposed after that, they'll lose aroma and taste.

Pack them gently in sterilized jars and fasten on air-tight covers.
They're preferably stored where it's dry, cool, and dark. The
small containers left in the kitchen for daily use should not be too
close to the stove, and they should be out of direct sunlight that,
besides weakening their effects, would eventually bleach them from
taste-tempting greens to something resembling scraps of old
leather.

Drying Fruits

You can use the same general process and the identical rack for drying small amounts of fruits for winter use, although these do best in direct sunshine. Let's take tasty bell peppers for an example.

The fruit is first washed, then seeded and stemmed. Finally, each pepper should be cut into small strips. Soak these in brine, two tablespoons of salt to a gallon of cool water, for a couple of hours. Incidentally, half this amount of salt will be best for apple chips that are to be dried. Raisins, as we're considering in Chapter 12, require no bath at all.

Then rinse the peppers in fresh water, shaking off the excess moisture when this process is completed. Spread the tidbits evenly and sparingly on the rack before setting it outdoors in direct, midday sunlight. If the heat is near its summer peak, dehydration in most cases should take about six hours. Apples, on the other hand, will require more like two days. Whatever fruit you're drying, turn the bits occasionally so that they'll get the rays on all sides.

Dried fruits that are at all sticky should be stored in the usual airtight containers and kept in a cool place, perhaps the refrigerator or freezer if you've enough room in either. To get back to the peppers, these dried flakes can be handled like the other herbs, and their spicy aroma will fill the kitchen each time you open the jar.

Sachets for You and Your Friends

Garden perfumes such as those of lavender and the more strongly scented roses can be brought indoors, into closets and handkerchief drawers and even into boxes of stationery, by means of appealing little sachets. Such ornamental pouches can be sewn from silk or from one of today's bright miracle fabrics, a corner being left open for the stuffing in of the leaves or petals, then closed with needle and thread. Although a plain little sack will do, you may care to add lace and ribbons to a few, perhaps as gifts or even as a sideline occupation.

Lavender, which in the kitchen will also impart its fragrance interestingly to certain dishes, is a favorite for sachets, especially as its distinctive aroma becomes more noticeable with age. Dry the flowers and leaves as you would those of any other herb, trying to package them at their peak of effectiveness, as soon as they crumble dryly between the fingers. For variety, the petals of roses can be similarly dried and encased.

The climax of all these preceding processes will be better-tasting foods and better-smelling abodes—more spice to your life.

Ginseng and Goldenseal

Ginseng commands the loftiest prices paid for any herb or medicinal root. It is found sparingly in rich, moist soil in hardwood forests from Maine to Minnesota, southward to the mountains of northern Georgia and Arkansas. Too, ginseng has long been cultivated in small areas in the northern and central states and on the north Pacific coast, where $8,000 can and is being made from as little as half an acre and where a full acre planted to ginseng has brought as much as $22,000 at the present high prices, which see the root crop selling at around $25 a pound. Two thousand pounds harvested from one acre is considered by some authorities to be a good average yield.

Ginseng can withstand hot, dry weather better than most farm crops because it grows under partial shade and mulch. Goldenseal, occurring naturally in patches in high open woods and usually on hillsides or bluffs affording natural drainage, is grown much the same way as ginseng and may give you a companion second crop. Neither of these herbs will harm farm livestock.

Ginseng is an erect plant growing from eight to fifteen inches high and bearing three leaves at the summit, each leaf consisting of five thin, stalked leaflets. The three upper leaflets are larger than the two lower ones. From half a dozen to twenty greenish yellow flowers are produced in a small cluster during July and August, maturing later in the season to bright crimson berries.

Ginseng is valuable for its thick, fleshy, spindle-shaped root two to three inches or more in length and about one-half to one inch thick, often branched at the start. After the second year the root becomes definitely branched or forked. It is the branched root, particularly if it resembles the human form, which finds especial favor among the Chinese, who are its principal consumers. The Chinese

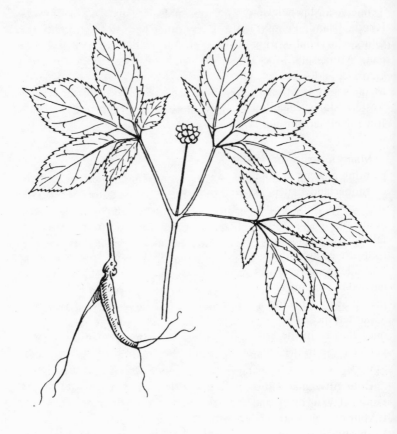

Ginseng

eat ginseng roots as a medicine to assure, they think, potency. The organic food markets in this country are beginning to sell small amounts of it, too, as a "medicine."

The root is dug in the autumn. If collected at any other season of the year, the root shrinks so much in drying that its appearance is injured and its astonishing market value diminished.

Although ginseng has been successfully grown in other parts of the continent, the best natural range for it is found in Maine, Kentucky,

Tennessee, Massachusetts, New Hampshire, Vermont, Connecticut, Rhode Island, Pennsylvania, Delaware, New York, New Jersey, Ohio, Maryland, Virginia, West Virginia, Illinois, Indiana, Michigan, Minnesota, Wisconsin, North Carolina, South Carolina, Georgia, and Alabama, as well as in eastern portions of Canada and as far south as Mississippi. Ginseng has also been raised in some western states, including Oregon, and in Arkansas, Missouri, and Iowa. Neither ginseng nor goldenseal will grow in Florida, by the way.

Many a landowner can easily spare part of his property to try planting ginseng or goldenseal—a wooded tract perhaps, or pasture or timberland that is not presently paying a penny. In the future, such crops could well put your child through college, build a new home, or provide retirement income. A look at the classified ads will tell where germinated seeds, planting roots, and seed-bearing-size roots are economically available.

Aside from weeding during the growing season, very little work is needed in growing either of these valuable crops once beds have been prepared by working the soil about six inches deep for seeds and about ten inches for larger roots. Freezing weather will hurt neither once they're in the ground. If you'd like to sow or sell the seeds, gather these in the fall when the picturesque pod has turned bright scarlet.

Both ginseng and goldenseal will grow in nearly any kind of soil, sandy, clay, or black loam being good and woods soil being the best. If your own ground is overly abundant in sand or clay, you can advantageously add top woods soil, rotten leaves, or rotten hardwood sawdust. Seeds may be planted a couple of inches deep or sown thickly in the bed, increasing the potential profitability of the valuable large, oddly shaped roots.

Beds can be conveniently made four to five feet wide and as long as you can manage. When planting roots, cover these so that the buds are set two inches deep. Immediately after planting, cover the soil with about an inch of mulch in the form of old rotted sawdust, leaves, straw, or the like. Leaving this mulch on the beds at all times, let the plants break through it in the spring.

Plants should have at least partial shade, and if trees for this are not handy, it will be worthwhile to build light lath shelters. If you have a tract of oak, hickory, poplar, dogwood, or a maple grove, grow your ginseng and goldenseal under these.

Unless you are pressed for cash, it will be best to let the roots mature for three or four years before that autumn day you harvest them. Then wash them, allow to dry for several days, and finally pack in boxes or barrels for shipment. The retailers of seeds and roots, who are potential buyers themselves, will furnish the names and addresses of cash markets including fur companies, drug firms, and exporters.

CHAPTER FIVE

Getting Healthy and Wealthy from Honey

KEEPING honey bees can be a profitable as well as a fascinating pastime, enjoyable more than one way. First, there's the freshly delicious honey the bees produce, far more sustaining and nutritious than commercial sweets. Then there's the bees' unparalleled services as pollinators of your crops. Finally, there is the fun of closely observing one of nature's most interesting insects.

After all, the honey bee, *Apis mellifera Linnaeus,* is man's most useful insect, producing in the United States alone some $50 million worth of honey and beeswax annually and at the same time pollinating more than $1 billion worth of invaluable agricultural crops.

There is no other branch of agriculture which, with little interference with other activities, can be made to yield so great a return on so small an investment of money as beekeeping. And in addition to the financial returns are to be reckoned the pleasure and fascination of beekeeping. This creates an absorbing interest in natural history and will not only bring you in contact with the honeymakers and all their enthralling habits but with the kingdom of plant life, a large portion of which is dependent on the pollinating industriousness of these insects.

In return for a minimum of expense and relatively little trouble, you can successfully keep bees almost anywhere in this country where the weather does not get too cold. The beginning beekeeper needs only a few dollars' investment in materials, a suitable location for the beehives, and the following elementary knowledge of the habits and loves of honey bees.

Using Honey Bees to Pollinate Crops

When clover was introduced to meat-raising Australia, it wouldn't pollinate until honey bees were brought in, too. In fact, maximum yields of many of the United States' fruit, vegetable, and seed crops often require more pollinators than are naturally present in an area at flowering time. For this reason, crop producers rent about 1 million colonies of honey bees each year to pollinate crops, another possible source of income for you. There's money, money everywhere in this land.

Although many other kinds of insects visit flowers in search of nectar, few are important as pollinators of crops. Generally they are too small, have too specialized food habits, or are too few in number. If it were not for honey bees, yields from many of our crops would be uneconomical. These honeymakers account for about 80 percent of pollination service to the nation's gardens.

The honey bee is an unusually industrious entity. It visits a wider variety of flower types than any other insect. In a single day, one may make a dozen or more trips from the hive, and it may tarry at several thousand flowers. But on each trip it ordinarily confines its premium-loading to one plant species, collecting one kind of nectar and distributing one kind of pollen. This characteristic, coupled with its large and hairy body, enables the industrious buzzer to accumulate and distribute an abundance of pollen, at the same time making it our most valuable agent for cross-pollinating crops.

Just to give you an idea, a few of the widespread crops that require, or at the very least benefit from, bee pollination are listed below. Not included are the range plants, medicinals, spices, and forest trees, many of which are also pollinated by the industrious insects.

There are numerous clovers, alfalfa, vetch; such fruits as apple, apricot, avocado, strawberries and many of the other delectable berries, cherry, some varieties of grape, melons, peaches, plums, and pumpkin; the nut crops such as almond, chestnut, and macadamia; vegetables like asparagus, cabbage, carrot, celery, cucumber, garlic and its onion and leek cousins, mustard, radish, squash, and turnip; and miscellaneous necessities such as cotton and flax.

The colony that you rent to pollinate crops—you're retaining all the honey, of course—should be housed in at least a two-story hive, contain a minimum of 30,000 bees, and have six to a dozen full frames of brood in all stages of development. Useful? You can even use them to distribute hand-collected pollen by placing this in a dispenser in the entrance of the beehive where departing bees come in contact with the special dust and carry it to the flower they visit.

Inexpensive Equipment

The basic equipment for a small operation should cost no more than about twenty-five dollars. It should include a hive to house your buzzing little workers, frames to support the honeycombs in which the bees will store their honey and raise their young, a so-called smoker to blow pacifying smoke into the hive when you want to work there, a hive tool with which to pry the frames apart to examine the hive or harvest the honey, a veil to protect your face and back from stings, gloves for guarding your hands, and a feeder with which to dispense sugar syrup until the insects start producing their own.

Life in Bee Communes

Honey bees, like people, are social individuals. With bees, this means that they live together in a colony and rely on one another for survival.

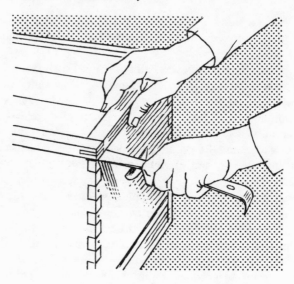

Hive Tool in Use

There it's mostly up to the females. The majority of bees in a colony are the sterile females that are known as workers. A few are drones, males, whose only function is to mate with the queen. Ordinarily there is one queen bee, the large fertile female who lays the eggs that maintain or increase the colony's population.

Worker bees number from 1,000 to about 60,000, depending on the egg-laying ability of the colony queen, the space available in the hive for expansion, and the food supply. These hustlers live only about six weeks. During that time they collect food and water for the entire colony, take care of all the housework, and guard the hive against intruders.

The workers also air-condition the hive, managing to maintain a constant temperature and humidity within despite the outside weather. Although work bees do not mate, they may lay eggs if the colony loses its queen. But these eggs will not sustain the commune's population as they develop only into drones.

The number of drones in a colony varies with the season. During the winter, for example, there may be none, as they are generally driven out of the hive in autumn once the worker bees can no

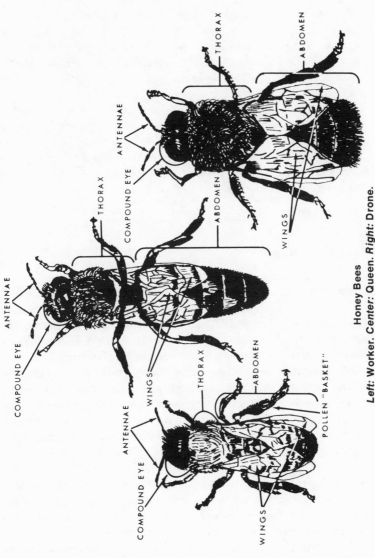

COMPOUND EYE

ANTENNAE

THORAX

COMPOUND EYE

ANTENNAE

WINGS

ABDOMEN

THORAX

ANTENNAE

COMPOUND EYE

WINGS

THORAX

ABDOMEN

WINGS

POLLEN "BASKET"

THORAX

ABDOMEN

WINGS

Honey Bees
Left: Worker. *Center:* Queen. *Right:* Drone.

longer collect food. By summer, however, there may be several hundred drones buzzing lovingly about.

The queen bee normally flies from the hive when she is about a week old and mates in the air with one or more drones. When she comes back to the hive, she commences laying eggs. During her lifetime she lays thousands of eggs, sometimes as many as 1,000 a day. She deposits each of these microscopic entities in a separate cell of the honeycomb.

Three days after an egg is laid, it changes to a larva. Then the worker bees, adding the role of nursemaids to their many other chores, feed and care for the larva until it changes into a pupa. At that time they seal the pupa into its honeycomb cell and leave it to finish developing. Three weeks from the day the fertile egg was laid, an adult bee emerges.

Breeds of Bees

The Italian strain of bees is the variety most common in this country. These bees are hardy, industrious, and relatively gentle.

The Caucasian strain is also widely kept. Bees of this breed are even more gentle than their Italian cousins, but the queens are dark colored and therefore difficult to locate in a cluster of bees. Why may it be important to be able to find your queen bee? You may choose to replace her after a year or two, especially if she does not lay enough eggs to keep the colony strong.

Caucasian bees also use an excessive amount of propolis in their hives. They collect this gummy substance from buds and injured tree parts, then use it as a cement in their homes. The problem is that frames which become heavily propolized may be difficult to remove.

Some especially bred hybrid bees, crosses between two or more strains, are available. A point in their favor is that they are generally more productive than standard strains. After a year or two, though, the offspring they produce may bear no resemblance to the original hybrid bee. If you keep hybrids, therefore, it will be sound practice to replace your queen each year, thus assuring a uniformly strong colony.

Obtaining the Bees

The best way to start keeping bees is to buy a bee colony already established in a well-constructed hive that has honeycombs built into removable frames.

If you already have a hive or are going to build one yourself, you can purchase a package of two or three pounds of bees with a queen, from another beekeeper or from a bee supplier, and put them in your hive. Be sure the bees you buy have a certificate of inspection to indicate they are free of bee diseases.

Another way to begin keeping bees is to capture a live swarm on your own and establish it in your hive. Bees are ordinarily gentle when swarming. Or you may transfer a whole colony, with its combs, to the hive from a cave or tree. On the other hand, for best results it is imperative to be relaxed around bees, so you may want to put off these two methods until you've worked some with the insects.

Wild bees and honey for free? Put a piece of honey-filled comb in a small, transparent plastic container. When you locate a bee on a flower, deftly coax it into the box and slap on the cover. That way you can watch until the bee is loaded down with plunder. Take off the lid then, and it'll happily arrow homeward.

That'll give you the direction to follow. This you can check when the bee returns with its fellows for more loot. Keep following the line, never advancing so far in any one move that the bees lose contact. Finally, with luck, you'll end up at a hollow tree or such. Then will come the part with smoke, ax, net, and gloves, all of which can add up to a sweet harvest.

The best time to establish a new honey bee colony is in springtime. Fruit trees and flowers are in bloom then and should supply the swarm with sufficient pollen and nectar. If you start with a new swarm or package instead of with an established colony, though, it will generally be a good idea to provide it with sugar syrup that is a mixture of half sugar and half water. This you can put in a feeder in the entrance of the beehive, where it will keep the bees from starving until they can make and store their own sweets.

Building a Beehive

Factory-built beehives and frames are best, their parts being of standard size and interchangeable. If you'd prefer to build your own beehive, therefore, it will pay to use a factory-made hive for your model. Then if you reproduce all parts exactly and keep all dimensions the same, the segments will fit well together and be interchangeable with corresponding parts in other hives.

The space between frames in your hive will be of especial importance. It should definitely be just about ¼ inch. If the space is less, the bees will find it too small to navigate and will energetically seal it off with propolis. If the area between the frames is more than ¼ inch, it will be too wide, and your bees will build honeycombs in it. Neither of these circumstances is desirable.

Herewith are the plans and dimensions for a ten-frame beehive, the most common size.

The Importance of Shade

This matter of shade for the bee colony, especially where the sun becomes torrid, is extremely important. Tests made in Arizona, for example, show that hives under solid shade produce as much as 50 percent more honey than a colony exposed to direct sunlight. Furthermore, the tests also reveal that unshaded colonies are more likely to be lost as a result of insecticide poisoning. The reason probably is that after a part of the working force has been killed by insecticide, the remaining bees in the unshaded hives cannot maintain the necessary brood-nest temperatures.

In the lower valleys of southern Arizona and adjoining California, where temperatures above 100° are frequent, numerous beekeepers have built permanently located artificial shades. These shades are usually about seven feet high and ten feet wide, the length depending on the number of colonies to be covered. A shade fifty feet long, for instance, is sufficient for fifty colonies, which should be arranged back to back in two rows, with a three- or four-foot walkway between. The shades run east and west.

Many materials have been tested to learn their effectiveness as shades of this sort. For effectiveness in reducing air temperatures beneath it, six inches of hay is the best roofing material. Aluminum, white on top and black on the bottom, is next, followed by

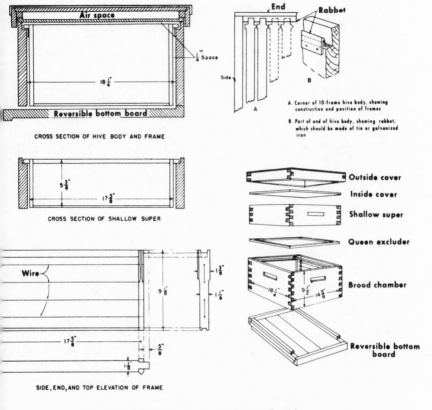

CROSS SECTION OF HIVE BODY AND FRAME

A. Corner of 10-frame hive body, showing construction and position of frames

B. Part of end of hive body, showing rabbet, which should be made of tin or galvanized iron

CROSS SECTION OF SHALLOW SUPER

Outside cover

Inside cover

Shallow super

Queen excluder

Brood chamber

Reversible bottom board

SIDE, END, AND TOP ELEVATION OF FRAME

Plans and Dimensions for a 10-frame Beehive

¼- to ½-inch plywood, new unpainted aluminum, ⅛-inch hardboard, snow fence laid in a double layer so that there are no openings, and Saran shade cloth of the type that produces 92 percent shade. Or you can construct a portable shade with wood or steel tubing and some fabric such as the aforementioned Saran shade cloth or a handy tarpaulin that may be lying around the place.

The hives should also be guarded from the heat radiating from the ground. This can be done by placing the hives on green grass or other vegetation. Keeping the hives covered with a substantial coat of white or other reflective paint also affords heat protection, reducing the amount of warmth these structures will absorb.

The Bees' Water Supply

When your hive is stocked with the working colony, put it where the bees will be unlikely to sting anyone. If you live in a warm area, situate the hive in the shade. If you live in country that has extended periods of freezing temperatures, expose it to the sun and protect if from prevailing winds, especially during the frosty months. Finally, make certain a constant supply of fresh, cool water lies nearby.

On a hot day a bee colony may use as much as a gallon of water. Some of this is obtained from nectar, but a colony unable to collect water directly, too, will die within a day or so. Beekeepers generally locate their hives as near a source of fresh water as feasible. If this is not done, the bees will have to carry water when they should be collecting nectar.

If a colony is more than a mile from water, it should either be moved closer or, for full efficiency, a source of cool fresh water made available within a few rods of the hives. Bees kept in a residential area may become a nuisance if they seek their water near the homes of neighbors. You can avoid possible trouble, therefore, by making water available near the colony.

If large numbers of the insects require water for an extended period, this should be furnished in barrels, in a tank, or directly from a pressure water system opening into some watering device, perhaps a trough filled with coarse gravel. Uniform water distribution can be obtained in the latter with a perforated tube in the bottom of the trough.

A cellulose sponge one or two inches thick can be floated in water in a trough or pan. The latter should be some two inches deeper than the thickness of the sponge. A float on the end of a water supply line will then make it easy to maintain the desirable water level.

Such watering units, whatever you may decide upon, should be thoroughly cleaned twice a month to reduce the possible spreading

Artificial Shade for Bee Colony

of bee diseases. A cover, such as a low shade, over the watering place will help to keep it clean.

Sources of Nectar

In addition to water, bees need three basic materials: pollen, nectar, and propolis. They make honey out of the nectar. They turn pollen into so-called beebread which is food for the young members of the colony. They use propolis to waterproof their hive and to seal cracks and crevices. Water is used to dilute their honey before eating, and they also utilize water in their hive's air-conditioning system.

Bees cannot make honey without nectar, the liquid sugary substance produced by flowers. Nectar is the raw material of honey and the insects' main source of nourishment.

Several hundred kinds of plants produce nectar. Only a few varieties are common enough, however, or give enough of the sweet to be considered major sources. The best origins of this invaluable ingredient, so vital for the production of surplus honey, vary from locality to locality. As a beekeeper, you'll be concerned with learning the plants in your area that are the richest sources of honey and, if it is warranted, perhaps grow some of them yourself.

Those plants which are major nectar sources in the United States include alfalfa, aster, buckwheat, catclaw, citrus fruits, clover, cotton, the spectacular and edible fireweed, goldenrod, holly, horsemint which can also pleasantly flavor your tea, locust, mesquite, palmetto, tuliptree, tupelo, sage, sourwood, star thistle, sweet clover, sumac, and the widely distributed willow, which can save your life if you're ever starving.

The flavor and color of the honey depend on the kinds of plants attended by the bees in their eternal search for nectar. Honey may be clear, amber, or even reddish. Try to locate your beehive where the buzzers can collect the kind of nectar that will make the honey you like best.

Sources of Pollen

When the worker bees gather nectar from flowers, tiny particles of

Drinking Water Container for Bees

pollen stick to their body and are carried back to the hive. The bees store this pollen as beebread in cells of the honeycomb, to be fed later to young bees that are developing into workers and drones.

Interestingly, the few young larvae selected by the workers to become new queens are fed a special food, royal jelly, made by the workers in their own bodies.

The average-size colony of honeymakers uses about 100 pounds of pollen each year. This is why you need to locate your hives near good pollen sources. Many wild flowers, weeds, trees, and shrubs produce pollen. Some especially rich sources include aster, corn, dandelion, the blossoms of fruit trees, goldenrod, grasses, maple, oak, poplar, and willow.

How Bees Work

The nectar that bees collect is ordinarily half to three-quarters water. After nectar is carried into the hive, the bees evaporate most of the water from it. While doing this, they change the nectar into honey. Then the bees seal the honey into cells of the honeycomb.

Beeswax begins as a liquid made by glands on the underside of the worker bee's abdomen. As it is produced, it hardens into tiny wax scales. Worker bees then utilize this wax to build honeycomb. If you don't want them to spend so much time performing this function, why not give them an assist?

Beekeepers often provide their charges with honeycomb foundation made of sheets of beeswax. Such a foundation fits into hive frames and becomes the base of the honeycomb. Besides enabling the honeymakers to speed up their comb construction, it provides a pattern for the building of a straight and easily removable honeycomb.

How to Move Bees

If you ever need to move your bee colony, remember that you must get the bees oriented to the new location. Otherwise, unless you move the hive at least several miles, the bees will continue to find their way back to the old site.

A trick of the trade? If you wish to move your bees only to another part of the yard, first take them several miles away and leave them there for about a week. When they are oriented to their new location, move them to the site you originally decided upon. Or shift the colony a few feet each day until it is where you want.

It is inadvisable to move bees during the period of honey production. The sweet already stored will add extra weight to the hive. The honeycomb may break loose. You may disturb your working bees and cause a slowdown in honey storage.

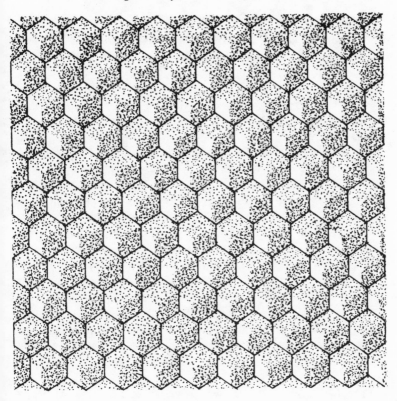

Honeycomb Foundation

Night is the best time to shift a colony. All the bees are then inside. If the weather is cold, you may completely close the hive entrance. Don't do this if the darkness is unseasonably warm and the colony strong, however. The bees might then suffocate if penned in for only an hour. Instead, cover the entrance and top of the hive with fine screen.

Staple, tie, or crate the hive so that parts cannot shift during the transfer.

Assuring Room and Food for Bees

As your bee colony grows, it will need more room. If the bees become too crowded and there isn't room for expansion of the brood-rearing area, they may fly away in large numbers, including the queen, to begin a new colony of their own. Naturally, you'll want to do everything possible to prevent such swarming, partly because the loss may leave the remaining colony too weak to store surplus honey.

To make more room for bees add extra boxes of combs, called supers, to the hive or onto the supers already in place.

Always leave plenty of honey for the bees. Remove only the amount you estimate to be more than they can use. Be sure there are at least fifty pounds of honey in the hive when winter begins. Otherwise, your bees might starve before springtime. Since one frame holds three to five pounds of honey, an average-size colony needs about ten to fifteen frames of honey to get through the cold months.

Extracting Honey from the Comb

Beekeepers generally measure honey production in pounds. The average yearly production of surplus honey runs about fifty pounds per colony, although a properly managed hive can produce several times that amount.

Probably the most efficient way to get honey out of the comb is to uncap the honey cells with a warm knife, then to spin the liquid honey out of the cells in a honey extractor. The honey is poured off, after which the emptied comb is returned to the hive to be refilled with honey by the energetic insects.

It may not pay to buy an extractor for the amount of honey yielded by only one or two hives. Instead, you may be able to borrow or rent such an extractor from a neighbor, dealer, or local beekeeper association. Be careful, though, that such borrowed equipment does not spread bee diseases.

The least expensive, and unfortunately least desirable, way to harvest liquid honey is to cut out the entire comb, squeeze the honey from it, and then strain this through a coarse cloth to remove wax particles. Although such a crushed comb cannot be used again by the bees, you can melt it and sell the beeswax thus salvaged.

Comb Honey

Some beekeepers produce comb honey by cutting out pieces of honeycomb, putting them in glass containers, and pouring liquid honey around them.

Another popular and practical method of producing comb honey is to place small wooden boxes in the top of the hive just before the honey flow begins. The bees themselves will then neatly fill the boxes with honey—about a pound in each box.

If you remove the boxes as soon as they are filled, you will have no problem with dripping or leaking honey, and no further handling or processing will be necessary.

Degranulating Honey

Honey tastes best when it is fresh, whether in the comb or in liquid form. But some honeys, even when fresh, granulate and become sugary. Too, most honeys will granulate sooner or later. The size of the granules, their appearance, and of course their flavor depend on the kinds of plants from which the bees collect their nectar.

Granulated honey is good food. In fact, many individuals prefer it to either liquid or comb honey. But if your honey granulates when you prefer it the other way, liquefy it by the following method.

Place jars of granulated honey in a container with enough water to reach the level of the sweet. Support the jars so they do not rest directly on the container's bottom, permitting water to circulate beneath them.

Heat gently until the granules disappear. The time required for this will vary, depending on the size of the jars of honey and the temperature to which you warm them. Be sure never to heat the water above 160°. Excessive heating will not only darken the honey, but it will also lower its quality.

Stir occasionally, both to distribute the warmth evenly through the honey and to determine when the granules have disappeared.

What To Do When Bees Sting

As a beginning beekeeper, you'll want to know what happens when a bee stings. A bee's stinger is barbed and has a poison sac attached to it. When the insect stings, the barb and sac usually tear out of the bee's body. Convulsive movements then push the stinger deeper into the flesh and pump venom into the wound.

If you are stung, remove the stinger immediately by scraping it off with a fingernail or knife. Do not try to pull it out because this will force more venom into your skin.

Stings are usually intensely painful when first inflicted. The pain is followed by reddening and swelling near the wound. Normally, the pain will subside after a few minutes, although the swelling may persist a day or more.

Generally, people develop a resistance or immunity to stings after they've been attacked a few times. A few individuals, on the other hand, become allergic to bee stings and develop a severe reaction to them. Such persons should consult the family doctor or an allergy specialist if they plan to work with bees.

How to Keep Bees from Stinging

Smoke pacifies bees. Always use a smoker when you are working with them. But use only enough smoke to keep the bees' minds away from stinging. This amount will vary, depending chiefly on the strain of bees and the weather. Bees, like people, are more irritable in cool, cloudy weather than they are when it's warm and sunny. Direct smoke into the hive entrance before you disturb the insects. When you remove the hive cover or an extra box of combs, apply smoke to the bees before exposing them.

It's also only reasonable to wear protective clothing: a veil over head and face, thin rubber gloves, and close-woven, light-colored overalls sealed at the ankles, wrists, and neck.

Bee Diseases and Pests

Several diseases attack honey bees. None of them is dangerous to humans.

Nevertheless, most states have laws to control bee diseases and to prevent their spread. In many jurisdictions it is illegal to offer for sale bee colonies and equipment that are not accompanied by a cer-

Smoker for Pacifying Bees

tificate indicating they are free of sickness. To play safe, before you buy or sell bees, notify the local or state bee inspector.

Your county agricultural agent is in a position to furnish specific information on local bee diseases. Or write for a copy of *AIB 313, Diagnosing Bee Diseases in the Apiary,* available for fifteen cents, not in stamps, from the Superintendent of Documents, U.S. Government Printing Office, Washington, D.C. 20402.

Keep your colonies strong. This is the best beekeeping practice. It is also your best protection against wax moth larvae, the serious insect pests that invade some unprotected honeycombs.

Getting the Help of Specialists

A good way to get information on keeping bees in your area is to talk with a local beekeeper. Most such individuals will be happy to show you how to open a hive and handle the bees, how to reduce the likelihood of being stung, and how to harvest the honey.

Your county agricultural agent should be able to supply pamphlets or direct you to other sources of information. Or it may be possible to take a course in beekeeping at your state agricultural college. You may also find it enjoyable as well as useful to join a beekeepers' organization, one or more of which are to be found in most states.

U.S. Department of Agriculture work on bee culture and insect pollination is directed by the Apiculture Research Branch of Entomology Research Division, Agricultural Research Service, Beltsville, Maryland 20705. Most bee research, however, is conducted in laboratories across the continent, usually in cooperation with state agricultural experiment stations and universities. In case you may sometime want some local advice, here is a list of the U.S. Department of Agriculture's bee-research labs:

Arizona: Honey Bee Pollination Investigations Laboratory, 2000 East Allen Road, Tucson 85721.

Louisiana: Bee Breeding Investigations Laboratory, Room 240, Agricultural Center, Louisiana State University, Baton Rouge 70803.

Maryland: Bee Disease Investigations Laboratory, Building A, Agricultural Research Center, Beltsville 20705.

Utah: Wild Bee Pollination Investigations Laboratory, Room 261, F. and B. S. Building, Utah State University, Logan 84321.

Wisconsin: Bee Management Investigations Laboratory, Room 436, Russell Laboratories, University of Wisconsin, Madison 53706.

Wyoming: Bee Disease Investigations Laboratory, University Station, P.O. Box 3168, Laramie 82071.

You'll get answers by addressing questions to these laboratories. Or perhaps you'll prefer to visit the research center nearest your home for some first-hand lore.

CHAPTER SIX

Raising and Selling
Rabbits and Earthworms

SOME ten million domestic rabbits are raised for meat each year in the United States. In addition, about 500,000 more rabbits are bred for medical and biological purposes. And it's all so easy. How would you like a piece of the action?

Rabbit raising is especially adapted to small homesteads and urban areas where other livestock projects are just not practical. Besides, rabbits make good pets, and their raising and breeding for show purposes is a popular hobby. Most domestic rabbits, though, are produced to provide such delicacies as jugged hare, rabbit stew, rabbit with sherry, and hasenpfeffer, to mention a few of the delectables detailed in my *Gourmet Cooking for Free*. Americans eat some 30 millions pounds of domestic rabbit annually. This meat comes in part from small backyard rabbitries.

Then there are the skins, which have a certain commercial value. Better grades are used in making fur garments and soft luscious trimmings, most of them being by-products of rabbit production. Too, you could utilize them in such money-making home projects as the manufacture of decorative little pin-on moccasins.

An increasing demand for rabbits for biological purposes offers marketing opportunities to breeders living reasonably near hospitals and laboratories.

Picking Your Breed

Once you've decided whether you want to raise rabbits for meat, fur, laboratory purposes, or for the spine-tingling competition of shows, pick the breed best adapted to this choice. Mature animals of the small breeds weigh three to four pounds, medium breeds nine to twelve pounds, and large breeds fourteen to sixteen pounds.

Rabbits best suited in size and conformation for meat and fur production are the medium and large breeds. If you have a good market for the skins, it may be desirable to pick one of the white varieties for meat production. White pelts ordinarily bring the highest prices.

If you are planning to raise the animals for laboratory purposes, check with nearby labs, hospitals, and city and county health offices to learn the type, size, and age most desired.

Rabbit fanciers can select from a large number of breeds for pet and show purposes. The American Rabbit Breeders Association lists standards for twenty-eight breeds and about seventy-seven varieties of these breeds. The standards cover type, size, color, and such.

The descriptions of some of the common breeds and varieties of domestic rabbits follow. The principal uses, approximate mature weights, and colors are listed for each breed and variety.

Angora.   Angora rabbits are raised primarily for wool production. The animals are sheared or plucked every ten or twelve weeks. Because of the competition from imported Angora wool and from other natural and synthetic fibers, the market price for the wool is generally low; so it is advisable to use Angoras as dual-purpose animals, handling them for both their meat and wool.

There are two varieties of Angora rabbits, the English and the French. They both come in black, white, blue, and fawn, with white being the preferred color. The mature English Angora weighs from six to seven pounds; the French Angora, over eight pounds.

American Chinchilla.   These are raised for both show and fur. The surface of the fur is gray over a deep blue-gray underfur. The

YOUR RABBITS CAN BE ALL THESE

Animals easily raised by anyone under any climatic conditions in all parts of the United States and Canada.

Animals, which for their meat, fur, wool, and laboratory use, enjoy a demand greater than the supply.

Animals that produce young thirty days after breeding, raising up to seven or nine younglings each litter, safely four to five times a year.

Animals that have proved an income producer for many. A real opportunity to engage in a hobby or business that brings pleasure and profit to thousands.

Animals that present a multitude of opportunities: delicious meat for home or for sale, fur and wool, scientific experiments, and even the sale of stock for breeding purposes.

Animals that must not be confused with ordinary pet rabbits. Standard-bred rabbits are larger, grow faster, produce meat quicker, have better fur, are more prolific, and, with health and vitality bred into them, are subject to few diseases.

Animals without peer as meat, fur, and wool producers. Multiply rapidly and reach marketing age quicker than any other meat animal; 2 to 2½ pounds of delectable portions at 8 weeks. Commercial animals that are already playing a big part in the meat, fur, and wool needs of the world.

bellies of these rabbits, which weigh from nine to twelve pounds, are a luxurious white.

California. Meat and show are the watchwords here. The rabbits weigh eight to ten and one-half pounds. Their bodies are white, with colored noses, feet, and wads of tail.

Champagne d'Argent. Besides standing out spectacularly at shows, these are also excellent meat animals. They weigh nine to a dozen pounds. The lush underfur is a slaty dark blue, lying beneath blue-white or silver surface fur, liberally sprinkled with long black guard hairs.

Checkered Giant. These rabbits, tipping the scales at eleven pounds or over, are excellent for both showing and eating. Their bodies are white, with black spots on the cheeks, sides, and hindquarters. There is a wide black spine strip. Black ears and noses, together with ebony circles around the eyes, really make them stand out.

Dutch. These are for shows and labs. Their black, blue, chocolate, tortoise, steel gray, or regular gray bodies weigh three and one-half to five and one-half pounds. They have white saddles over the shoulders, under the necks, and across the front legs and hind feet.

English Spot. These are triple threats, being fine for shows, frozen-food counters, and laboratories alike. Weighing nine to twelve pounds, they have white bodies with black, blue, chocolate, tortoise, lilac, gray, or steel gray spots. Additional head patches appear on nose, ears, cheeks, and as showy circles around the eyes. Side spots extend from the base of the ears to the middle of the hindquarters.

Flemish Giant. These meat and show monsters weigh thirteen pounds and over. Bodies are steel gray, light gray, sandy, blue, white, or fawn.

Himalayan. Weighing two and one-half to five pounds, these are destined for shows and labs. The color is the same as the California.

New Zealand. Meat and show. Nine to twelve pounds; body white, black, or even red.

Polish. These excel in both shows and laboratories. Weights average three and one-half pounds. Colors are white, black, or chocolate, contrasting with blue or ruby red eyes.

Rex. Show and fur are the key words here. Weights are seven pounds or over. The color of this variety can be representative of any breed.

Satins. These are raised for both shows and fur. They weigh eight to eleven pounds. The bodies, whose color scheme can be the same as the chinchilla rabbit or the Californian, are also black, blue, red, white, or copper.

Silver Martens. This is an imposing name for a mere rabbit, but these are beautiful chocolate, sable, blue, or ebony creatures with luxuriously silver-tipped guard hairs. They weigh six and one-half to nine and one-half pounds. These rabbits are raised primarily for their fur, but provide food as a byproduct.

Getting the Stock

The essential requirements for good foundation stock are health, vigor, longevity, ability to reproduce, and desirable type and conformation. If you are just getting started in rabbit production, select young animals for your basic stock. This will give you an opportunity to become acquainted with the animals and their habits before they reach production stage.

Begin on a small scale, one to two bucks and ten to twenty does, and expand operations as you gain experience and as market demands justify. National, state, and local rabbit breeders' organizations can suggest the names and addresses of nearby dealers who have stock for sale. Until you're more of a hand at the business or hobby, you can play safe by dealing only with reliable breeders who stand behind the stock they offer. For instance, brokers who handle live rabbits for market are seldom able to vouch for the conditions under which their animals were produced.

Housing and Equipment

The building and equipment needs for your rabbitry will depend on climatic conditions, any local building regulations, and the amount of money you can invest.

Where the climate is mild, hutches can be placed outdoors in the shade of trees or buildings. Or you may be a bit more elaborate and locate them under a lath superstructure. Good unadulterated sunlight will help maintain sanitary conditions, but the rabbits should be given their own choice between shade and sunshine at all times.

During hot weather make certain the hutches are adequately ventilated and that the little animals get the invigorating benefit of prevailing breezes.

In regions where strong winds and cold weather prevail, hutches can be protected by placing them in buildings that open to the south and east. During stormy weather these buildings can be closed, perhaps with the aid of curtains or panels. When weather is extremely cold, extra protection may be needed. Rabbits are sturdy creatures, however, and I've seen the wild ones hopping happily around in temperatures sixty degrees below zero.

Individual quarters should be provided for mature rabbits. Such hutches should be about two feet high and no more than two and one-half feet wide. You'll do well to make your hutches three feet long for small breeds, four feet for medium breeds, and six feet for large breeds, all these figures being inside measurements.

Hutch construction varies from all-wire hutches, quonset-shaped, for use inside buildings to partially enclosed hutches for use outdoors.

An inexpensive hutch suitable for small rabbitries is shown in the accompanying drawing. Note the hay manger between the compartments. Such a hutch is light and movable in addition to being easy to build. When the weather is balmy it can be set under trees or on the protected side of a building. When winter comes it can be moved into a well-ventilated building. Such a hutch can be thrown together with scrap lumber and wire mesh. There are also several types of metal and all-wire hutches on the market.

Several types of flooring can be used in building hutches. Wire mesh flooring is employed extensively in commercial rabbitries, where the convenience of self-cleaning hutches is desirable. Solid and slat flooring, or a combination of solid flooring at the front and slats or a strip of wire mesh at the back, are also practical.

If you decide on mesh flooring, be sure to examine the surface for sharp points, as the rabbit is a soft and fragile creature, hardy enough but not tough-skinned. Always put the smoother surface on top for this reason. Slat flooring? Use 1-inch hardwood slats and space them ⅝ or ¾ inch apart. To provide drainage, solid floors should slope slightly from the front to the rear of the hutch.

Nest Boxes A good nest box should provide seclusion for the doe when she gives birth to her litter, later affording protection to the youngsters themselves. It should be easy to clean and maintain, provide good drainage and ventilation, and be accessible to the young when they are large enough to journey from and to this sanctuary.

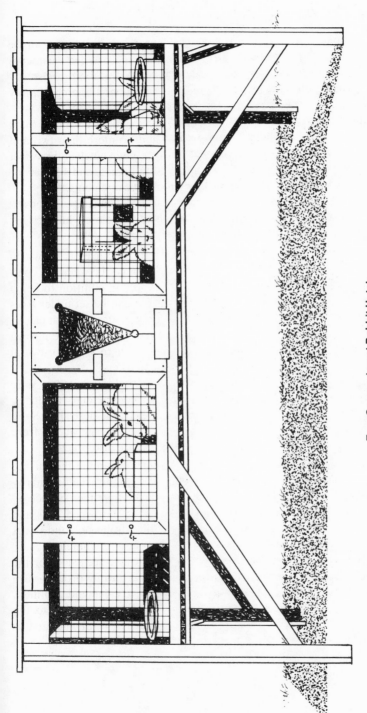

Two-Compartment Rabbit Hutch

Simple as well as inexpensive nest boxes can be made from the sturdy packing boxes available at your grocer's, apple boxes being ideal. Just cut an opening in one end of the box, or remove a portion of one end, so as to allow easy access for the doe and young. As an alternative, one end may be removed and replaced with movable slats. These you'll leave in place until the youngsters are large enough to leave and return to the nest.

Nail kegs from hardware stores also make fine nest boxes. Merely nail a board across the open end of the keg, covering about half of the opening. To keep the cylinder from rolling, extend this board a few inches beyond the edges. Drill several one-inch holes in the closed end of the keg for ventilation.

Your rabbits during cold weather may need more protection than the average nest box affords. A simple winter nest box is easily made, however, merely by lining the inside of a standard nest box with two or three layers of corrugated cardboard. After drilling two or three ventilation holes in the lid, fill the box with clean straw so that a doe can burrow a cavity for the nest.

Feeding Equipment Use feed crocks, troughs, hoppers, and hay mangers that are large enough to hold several feedings. Try to pick a type that will prevent waste and contamination of feed.

You will be able to buy crocks particularly designed for rabbit feeding. These crocks are heavy enough not to be easily tipped, and they have lips which prevent the rabbits from scratching out feed. Such crocks can be used for feeding pellets and whole grain.

When green feed or hay is included in the ration, hay mangers should be incorporated into the hutches. Here you can save space by having one central manger serving two hutches. Waste can be reduced by placing troughs under the mangers. These troughs can also be used to feed supplemental grains.

Hoppers save a worthwhile amount of time and labor when they are designed for self-feeding. Use them for feeding pregnant does, does with sucklings, and rabbits you are conditioning for market. Such hoppers can be made from cans, hardboard, wood, or other suitable material. An inexpensive self-feeder can be contrived from a five-gallon can with a little ingenuity.

Watering Equipment Rabbits need clean, fresh water at all

Handmade Hopper for Rabbit Food

times. During warm weather, for example, a doe and her litter will imbibe as much as a gallon a day.

Crocks or even discarded coffee cans are suitable watering devices for small rabbitries. In fact, coffee cans are particularly useful during cold weather because ice can be so easily broken and removed from them.

Automatic watering systems supply a steady supply of clean, fresh water. They are used extensively in commercial rabbitries to reduce labor, but their expense makes them impractical for use in small operations. This does not mean, however, that you can't figure out a small automatic system of your own; for instance, perhaps utilizing one of the automatic waterfall contrivances for gardens and changing the basic water supply more frequently than you would otherwise.

Feeding

Feed, although you can perhaps raise your own, is ordinarily one of the largest items of expense in the raising of rabbits. Too, the amount of personal work involved in the feeding depends on the type of diet you choose. Each herd presents an individual problem, and the thing to do is to suit the feeds to the type of production in which you are engaging.

Hays Just hay, often available merely for the cutting, will supply the bulk required for a balanced rabbit ration. Such high-quality feed will also provide much of the protein needed to balance the intake.

Legume hays—including alfalfa, clover, lespedeza, peanut, cowpea, and the bountiful vetch—are high in protein as well as being palatable. The grass hays—which include timothy, prairie, Johnson grass, Sudan grass, and carpet grass—are not only less tasty to the animals, but they also involve only about half as much protein. They are valuable for feeding, however, whenever legumes are not readily available. When grass hays are fed, include an additional protein supplement in the meals.

Fine-stemmed, leafy, well-cured hay can be fed whole. Chop any coarse hay, though, into about four-inch lengths to reduce waste and to have a more easily distributed food.

Grain Oats, wheat, barley, sorghum grain, buckwheat, rye, and soft varieties of corn can be fed whole or in milled form. With corn, feed the flinty hard varieties in the form of meal to prevent waste. All the grains are similar in food values, and one can be substituted for another without materially altering the nutritive value of the rations.

By-products from grain processing, including bran middlings, shorts, and red-dog flour, can advantageously be included in meal and pellet mixtures.

Supplements Sesame, peanut, linseed, and the invaluable soybean meals are rich in protein, being particularly desirable for balancing pelleted rations. It's a good idea not to mix these protein meals with whole grains, by the way, because then much of the meal will settle out and be wasted. If whole grains are fed, supply the protein in flake, cake, or pelleted form.

Rabbits, just like you and me, need salt. An easy way to supply it is merely by leaving small salt blocks or spools in the hutches for the rabbits to lick at will. If you prefer, though, it can also be furnished by adding ½ to 1 percent of salt to mixed feeds or pellets. If you happen to live in an area where the soil is naturally deficient in minerals, give the rabbits the same sort of mineralized salt that is being fed to other local farm animals.

Pellets Pellets take up little storage space and are easily fed. There are many brands on the market. In fact, in some regions they may be the only type of commercial rabbit nourishment available.

There are two general types of pellet rabbit food, all-grain pellets to be fed with hay and so-called complete pellets. These complete green pellets generally contain all the elements necessary for a balanced diet.

Pelleted rabbit food should be bite-size. That is, the pellets should be no larger than $3/16$ inch in diameter and $1/4$ inch long. If the tidbits are bigger, small rabbits will bite off part of a pellet and often waste the rest.

The ingredients and proportions used in making pellets vary, and it is basic good sense to follow the advice of the manufacturer when pellets are used in the ration.

Tidbits from Garden and Table Rapidly growing plants such as grasses, palatable weeds, cereal grains, and leafy garden vegetables that are free of insecticides, are customarily rich in vitamins, minerals, and proteins. These plants, therefore, make excellent feed for the breeding herd.

Carrots, beets, turnips, and other root crops are not only desirable rabbit food throughout the year, but they're also especially good in winter, when green grub is not ordinarily available.

Fresh green feeds and root crops should be considered as supplements to the regular diet. They can be used in the ration when they fit into the management program. However, they should be fed sparingly to rabbits unaccustomed to them. Never use feed that is spoiled or contaminated.

Dry bread and other table scraps, excepting meat and greasy or sour tidbits, are acceptable to most rabbits. They add valuable variety to the diet when used to supplement the regular ration.

Diet for Keeping Rabbits in Good Breeding Condition You'll naturally do your best to select rations that are suited to the needs of your long-eared friends. Dry does, herd bucks, and junior males and females need food that will keep them in good breeding condition. Pregnant does and those with litters require a high proportion of grain-protein concentrate in their rations.

Junior rabbits, mature dry does, and the ordinary run of herd bucks not in service but in good physical condition can be maintained on hay alone if fine-stemmed, leafy, legume hay is what is being fed. If coarse legume hay or grass hay is being used, supply each eight-pound animal with two ounces (⅓ cup) of all-grain pellets or grain-protein mixture several times a week. Using this ratio as a basis, you can easily adjust the amount of necessary concentrate to your particular animals.

The same amount of concentrate should be fed herd bucks that are in service. These lovers should also be given free access to choice hay.

Alfalfa pellets can be the sole food given to developing junior does and bucks from the time they are weaned to the moment when they are ready for breeding. Purchase pellets that contain 1 percent of salt and 99 percent of No. 2 leafy or better-grade alfalfa meal that itself is 15 percent protein. If such alfalfa pellets are not available, all-alfalfa turkey crumbles can be substituted with excellent results.

Feeding Pregnant and Nursing Does   To feed a doe properly, it is necessary to know definitely whether or not she has conceived. Palpating, described in a moment, two weeks after breeding is a quick and accurate way of determining pregnancy.

After the mating, keep the doe in breeding condition on good-quality hay. If she fails to conceive, as determined by palpation two weeks after breeding, mate her again and continue her on a maintenance ration until she is diagnosed as pregnant.

Once the doe is definitely known to be pregnant, give her all the concentrates she will eat in addition to good-quality hay. All-grain pellets or a grain-protein mixture can be fed with hay, or you can use a completely pelleted ration and no hay.

Change to the new ration gradually. Sudden changes in the rations fed during the gestation period may cause some does to go on hunger strikes.

After the blessed event, feed the doe in the same manner as during pregnancy. Keep her on the high-concentrate ration until the young are weaned. Provide additional food as the litter develops.

Breeding

The gestation period of rabbits, the time between mating and birth, is thirty-one or thirty-two days. Some litters may be born as early as the twenty-ninth day or as late as the thirty-fifth day, but 98 percent of the normal litters will be kindled between the thirtieth and thirty-third day.

Age to Breed The proper age of bucks and does for the first mating depends both on the breed and on individual development. Small varieties develop more rapidly and are sexually mature at a younger age than medium or large breeds. Too, some individual rabbits within a breed will mature more rapidly than others. Generally, the small breeds can be mated when the rabbits are four to five months old, the medium breeds at five to six months, and the large breeds at nine to twelve months.

Mate your does as soon as they reach maturity. If coupling is delayed too long, breeding difficulties may occur. Does that are kept in good physical condition should produce litters until they are two and one-half to three years old.

How Often to Breed If you're raising your rabbits to show, it may be advisable not to raise more than two or three litters per year. You'll want to arrange the matings so the offspring will be of proper age and development for show classification.

For meat and fur production, animals can be kept breeding throughout the year. Thereby, with a gestation period of about a month and a nursing period of eight weeks, a doe will be able to produce four litters a year. Does of heavy producing strains can be mated six weeks after kindling if they are in sound condition. If the litter is lost at birth, a doe can be rebred earlier than called for in the regular schedule.

Mating Procedure A doe shows signs of being ready for mating by nervousness and restlessness, by rubbing her chin on feeding and watering equipment, and by attempting to join other rabbits in nearby hutches. It is not necessary, however, to depend on external signs to determine when a doe is to be bred. Set up a definite schedule and follow it whether the doe shows signs of being ready for service or not.

You should always take the doe to the buck's hutch for service. This should occur almost immediately once you place the female within the male's domain. When the mating is complete, put the doe back in her own home. Make a record of the date of mating, together with the names or numbers of the two rabbits.

Try to maintain one buck for each ten breeding does. Vigorous, mature bucks can be used several times a day for a short period.

Determining Pregnancy An accurate method of determining pregnancy is important in managing the breeding herd. Test mating, i.e., the periodic placing of the doe in the buck's hutch, is not accurate. Some does will couple when pregnant, while others will refuse service when not pregnant. Trying to diagnose pregnancy by the development of the abdominal region and the gain in flesh is not dependable until late in the pregnancy.

Pregnancy can be quickly and accurately determined by palpating the doe twelve days to two weeks after mating. Hold the ears and the fold of skin over the shoulders in the right hand. Place the left hand between the hind legs, slightly in front of the pelvis. Place the thumb on the right side of the abdomen and the fingers on the left.

Exerting light pressure, move the fingers and thumb gently backward and forward. If the doe is pregnant, you should be able to distinguish the embryos as marble-shaped forms between the thumb and fingers. Be sure to handle the doe gently, using only light pressure on the abdominal cavity.

Does diagnosed as pregnant should be placed on a pregnancy ration. Nonpregnant does should be rebred and kept on a maintenance food routine until they are diagnosed as bearing.

Accurate determination of pregnancy by palpation takes practice. If you are inexperienced, repalpate a week later any does you've originally diagnosed as nonpregnant. Then if an error has been made in the first palpation, the doe can be placed on a pregnancy ration and provided with a nest at the proper kindling time. With practice, though, you may develop enough skill to diagnose pregnancy as early as the tenth or eleventh day.

Restraining a Doe for Palpating

Caring for Nursing Does and Their Young

Place a nest box in the hutch twenty-seven days after the doe is mated. A day or two before kindling, the prospective mother will begin pulling fur from her body to line the nest. She'll also usually consume less feed than ordinarily. Now is the time to give her small quantities of green rations. This will have a beneficial effect on her digestive system.

Most litters are born at night. Complications are rare when the doe is in good condition. After the births, the doe may be restless. Do not disturb her until she has quieted.

Does occasionally fail to pull fur to cover their litters, or they kindle their young on the hutch floor. When this happens, arrange the bedding material to make a comfortable nest and pull enough fur from the doe's body to cover the young. You can often save tiny rabbits by warming them, even if they appear to be lifeless. Keep some extra fur on hand for such cases.

Inspect the litter the day after birth. Remove any deformed, undersized, or dead young from the nest box. If you are careful and gentle, the doe will not usually object. On the other hand, if she is nervous and irritable, place some tempting food in the hutch to distract her attention.

The sense of motherhood in rabbits is strong, and you can transfer baby rabbits from a large litter to a foster mother with a small litter. For meat and fur production, seven to nine youngsters to a litter is desirable. Adjusting the number of young to the capacity of the doe will promote more uniform development and more satisfactory weaning. For best results, the young rabbits should not vary more than three or four days in age when they are shifted together.

The younglings should open their eyes ten or eleven days after birth. The eyes of baby rabbits occasionally become infected and fail to open normally. If the infection is treated promptly, the young one usually recovers without any permanent eye injury.

To treat such an infection, bathe the inflamed and incrusted eyelids with warm water. Once the tissue softens, separate the lids with a slight pressure. If pus is present, treat the eyes with an antibiotic eye ointment or with a fresh solution containing 10 percent of Argyrol.

Weaning the Younglings   Your rabbits will start emerging from the nest to eat feed when they are nineteen to twenty days old. If they come out of the nest sooner, they may not be getting enough milk or the nest may be too warm.

The doe customarily nurses her younglings at night or in the early morning and evening hours. If the litter becomes divided, the doe will either nurse the young in the nest or those on the hutch floor, not both. Furthermore, she will not pick up the strays and return them to the nest.

Leave the young rabbits with the doe until they are eight weeks old. By that time, the milk supply will have decreased and the youngsters will be accustomed to other feed. This means you're in business unless you've other plans. Fryer rabbits should be in marketing condition by the time they are weaned at eight weeks, and delicious they'll then be.

Delicious Fried Rabbit

This is my favorite way of cooking what, incidentally, is America's most hunted game. Divide the rabbit into serving pieces, disjointing whenever possible. Dip each portion in milk. Salt and pepper, and then roll lightly in flour.

Put ½ stick butter and 4 tablespoons cooking oil in a frypan over high heat and set in the pieces, any bony sides uppermost. Lower the temperature at once and cook, uncovered, until the portions are brown on one side. Then turn, just once, and brown the other side. The meat will be crisp and done in a total of slightly more than ½ hour. Spread it out on absorbent paper and keep warm while concocting the gravy.

For this, pour off all the fat except just enough to cover the bottom of the frypan. Stir in two tablespoons flour, ½ teaspoon salt, and ⅛ teaspoon of preferably freshly ground black pepper, smoothing it into a paste. Using the milk in which you dipped the meat, add enough additional milk to make a cupful. Pour this, then a cup of water, slowly into the pan, all the time stirring.

Simmer over low heat for twelve minutes, adding more milk and water if the gravy becomes too thick. Finally, sprinkle with paprika and parsley flakes. With everything served hot, the gravy has enough distinctiveness to transmute fried rabbit into an art form.

Roast Rabbit

Young rabbits have such a delicate flavor, too often overpowered by other ingredients, that—if you have a rotisserie—you may wish to roast a brace of them until just tender, seasoning them only by brushing them with melted butter every ten minutes. The result is rabbit pure and unspoiled: succulent, moist, simple, with a fragility of woodland flavor not otherwise obtainable.

If you have no rotating spit, roast the young rabbits in a low uncovered pan in a slow 325° oven until a sharp fork can be easily inserted and withdrawn, again brushing every ten minutes with melted butter.

Rabbit with Sherry

This, another of the recipes picked from my *Gourmet Cooking for Free,* is tasty for a change. Divide your rabbit into serving portions. Brown these in two tablespoons apiece of butter, shortening, and bacon drippings in a frypan over low heat. Then pour off all but enough grease to cover the bottom of the pan.

Chop a small bunch of watercress into fine bits. Mince a clove of garlic. Add to the meat in the frypan, along with a finely chopped, medium-sized tomato and a cup of sliced mushrooms. Sauté together for 5 minutes, seasoning to taste with salt and freshly ground black pepper. Then add ½ cup of dry sherry which may be from your own vineyard, cover, and simmer for about 20 minutes, or until the rabbit is tender. This is something to enjoy when just the two of you are alone with the crickets and the evening light.

The Role of Records

Mark each breeding rabbit for your record system. Tattooing is the best method because it is permanent and will not disfigure the ears. Simple tattooing instruments may be obtained inexpensively from livestock supply houses. Ear tags and clips are not satisfactory for marking because they tear out all too easily, at the same time marring the ear.

An adjustable box, such as the one shown in the accompanying drawing, is convenient for restraining rabbits for tattooing. Spring-type holders tacked to the lower side of a movable floor push the rabbit toward the top of the container. A movable cross partition holds the rabbit toward the front. Blocks of wood on each side keep the animal's head in the center of the box at the top, its ears extended through an amply large slot.

A convenient and simple record system is needed to keep track of breeding, kindling, and weaning operations. Information from such records can be used to cull unproductive animals and to select the most desirable breeding stock.

The essential features of a simple record system are illustrated in the reproductions of sample cards. Such record cards can be ob-

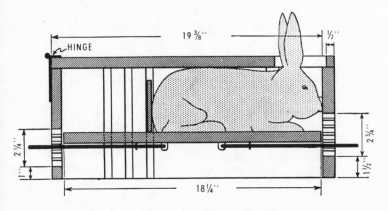

Box Used to Restrain Rabbits for Tattooing

tained from feed mills as well as from firms dealing in rabbitry supplies.

Hot Weather Care

A few changes in the general care and management of your rabbit herd may be needed during hot weather. Make sure, of course, that the animals have adequate shade and water. Good circulation of air through the rabbitry is essential, but strong drafts should be avoided.

Newly born litters and does in advanced pregnancy are the most susceptible to high temperatures. Heat suffering in the young causes extreme restlessness. In older animals, heat discomfort brings about rapid breathing, excessive moisture around the mouth, and occasional hemorrhaging from the nostrils.

Move any rabbits that show signs of heat suffering to a quiet, well-ventilated place. Moisten a feed sack with cold water and put it in the hutch for them to lie on. Placing water crocks or large bottles filled with ice in the hutches will also help keep the rabbits cool.

In well-ventilated rabbitries, wetting the tops of the hutches and the floors of the house itself reduces the temperature as much as 10° on a hot day. The tops of the hutches should be waterproof, as

HUTCH CARD

Animal No. __W 301__ Born __12/12/61__ Breed __New Zealand White__
Sire __W 394-__ Dam __W 604__ Litter No. __W 714__

DATE BRED	BUCK NO.	DATE KINDLED	NO. YOUNG BORN		NUMBER YOUNG RETAINED	LITTER NO.	DATE WEANED	NUMBER WEANED
			ALIVE	DEAD				
6/1/62	W418-	7/2	11	0	8	W19	8/27	8
8/24/62	W418-	9/24	9	0	8	W175	11/19	8
11/16/62	W418-	Passed 11/30						
11/30/62	W421-	12/30	9	1	8	W316	2/24/63	8
2/21/63	W421-	3/24	11	0	8	W465	5/19	7
Ⓐ								

PRODUCTION RECORD

LITTER NO.	WEANING			NOTES:
	NUMBER	AGE	WEIGHT	
W19	8	56	30.2	
W175	8	56	31.0	
Passed	11/30			
W316	8	56	32.0	
W465	7	56	28.0	
Ⓑ				

Record Cards for Breeding Rabbits

BUCK BREEDING RECORD

Buck No. _____

Breed _____   Sire _____

Date born _____   Dam _____

| Doe | Location | Date Bred | Result of breeding | | | Weaned | |
| | | | Kindled | | Passed | | |
			Alive	Dead	Date	Number	Weight

Record Cards for Breeding Rabbits *(cont.)*

rabbits must be kept dry. If the rabbitry has a concrete or soil floor that drains readily, overhead sprinkling equipment, if only a garden-hose attachment, can be used. You could even install an inexpensive thermostat to control the sprinkler automatically.

During hot weather it may be difficult to keep the young rabbits comfortably in their nest box. A cooling basket of wood-framed wire, hung in the hutch, will provide some relief from the time the young are born to the day they're large enough to get out of the nest by themselves.

During the hot part of the day, place the youngsters in the basket and hang it away from direct sunshine near the top of the hutch. Then in the evening return the litter to their nest box. If torrid temperatures continue throughout the night, put the younglings back in the cooling basket once they have nursed. Allow them to nurse again in the morning.

How to Prevent Sore Dewlaps

The dewlap, the fold of skin under the rabbit's chin, may become sore during warm weather. This is caused by frequent drinking from water crocks. When trouble occurs the fur in the dewlap becomes green and foul, and the skin on both the dewlap and the inside of the front legs becomes rough and irritated.

Remove the cause by placing a board or brick under the water crock, raising this high enough to keep the dewlap from becoming wet every time the rabbit has a few sips. If the skin does become irritated, clip off the fur and treat the area with zinc oxide ointment, applying this every other day until the irritation clears up.

Disease Control

Sanitation in the rabbitry is by far the best disease-control method. Remove manure, soiled bedding, and spoiled feed daily. Wash the feeding and watering equipment frequently in soapy water. Then rinse in clear water, drain well, and place in the sun to dry. If the latter step is impractical, rinse the utensils in a water-disinfectant solution; then rinse again in clear water.

Isolate any animals suspected of being diseased. Leave suspected animals in isolation for at least two weeks or until you can definitely determine whether they are dangerous to the health of the herd. Newly acquired rabbits and those returned from shows should be placed in quarantine for at least a couple of weeks. Bury or burn dead animals.

Effective treatments are not known for many rabbit ailments. It is usually simpler and safer to destroy a few sick animals than it is to treat them and risk spreading infection to healthy stock. This is especially true of rabbits with respiratory infections.

How to Lift a Rabbit

Rabbits are often injured by improper handling. Never, as is seen far too often, lift rabbits by the ears or legs. Instead, lift and

How to Carry a Small Rabbit

carry a small rabbit by grasping the loin region gently and firmly. Put the heel of the hand toward the tail. To carry a medium or large rabbit, grasp the fold of skin over the shoulders with the right hand and support the rabbit by placing the left hand under the rump. If the rabbit scratches or struggles, hold it snugly under the left arm.

The Proper Way to Cut Nails

Toenails of rabbits confined in hutches do not wear normally. The resulting long toenails often get caught in wire-mesh flooring, and the rabbit may injure himself trying to get loose. You can prevent this problem from arising by cutting the toenails periodically.

Hold the rabbit's foot up to the daylight and note the cone in

How to Carry a Medium or Large Rabbit

the toenail. Using side-cutting pliers, snip off the toenail below the tip of the cone. When done correctly, this operation will not cause hemorrhaging or injury to the sensitive part of the nail.

Marketing

Some producers sell live rabbits directly to brokers. In fact, such a concern as Behrens Farm, Inc., Box 148, Pearl River, New York 10965 will even supply you with up to $250 worth of breeding

stock without any cash changing hands except for an initial re-
fundable dollar to bind the bargain, taking their pay in the young
stock you produce.

On the other hand, numerous small producers do their own
slaughtering, packing, and marketing. Rabbits raised for meat and
fur are usually marketed at four to six months of age. Most medium and large breeds should develop a desired weight and finish by
the time they are weaned when two months old.

In some regions there may be a good market for roasters, which
are rabbits grown to maturity. Culls from the breeding herd can be
fattened for roasters, or it may prove profitable to develop young
rabbits to heavier weights.

Slaughtering

Slaughter in clean sanitary quarters, first checking with local
health authorities on any local regulations and restrictions. Rabbits
can be made instantly unconscious by dislocating the neck or by
stunning with a sharp blow at the base of the skull, the original
rabbit punch.

To dislocate the neck instantaneously and painlessly, hold the
animal by its hind legs with the left hand. Place the thumb of the
right hand on the neck just back of the ears and set the fingers
under the chin. Stretch the animal by pushing down on the neck
with the right hand. Press down with the thumb; then raise the
animal's head with a quick movement to dislocate the neck.
When done correctly, this method is painless and instantaneous.

Suspend the carcass by inserting a hook between the tendon and
bone of the right rear leg, just above the hock. Remove the head at
once to encourage thorough bleeding. Sever the tail, the front feet,
and the free rear leg at the hock joint.

Cut into the skin just below the hock of the suspended leg; then
slit open the skin on the inside of the leg to the base of the tail.
Continue the incision to the hock of the left leg. Separate the edges
of the skin from the carcass and pull the skin down over the
animal. It will come off like a glove. Leave as much fat on the
carcass as possible.

Once you've completed the skinning, make a slit along the me-

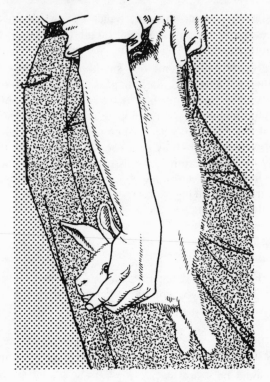

Dislocating Rabbit's Neck

dian line of the belly. Remove the entrails and gall bladder, but leave the delectable liver and kidneys in place. Unhook the suspended carcass and remove the right hind leg at the hock.

Wash the carcass in cold water, brushing the neck thoroughly in the water to remove the blood. Do not leave the carcass in water for more than fifteen minutes, as it will absorb water if soaked for a prolonged period. Chill in a refrigerated cooler.

Cutting and Packaging

Restaurants, clubs, hospitals, hotels, and other such establishments ordinarily purchase the whole carcass and leave it to their cooks to cut it into portions to meet particular requirements.

On the other hand, most housewives prefer the cut-up, packaged product. Use a knife to cut up the carcass. A cleaver leaves annoyingly splintered bones.

A paraffined box with a transparent plastic window makes a neat, sanitary, and attractive package for the chilled rabbit carcass. If the meat is to be frozen, wrap the box in a special sealable covering to prevent both freezer burns and loss in palatability.

A box 9 inches long, 4 inches wide, and 2½ inches deep is suitable for a fryer rabbit weighing from 1¾ to 2½ pounds. Arrange the cuts attractively, of course, perhaps with a few sprigs of parsley for color. Be sure to enclose the delicious heart, kidneys, and liver.

If you sell to the home trade or if you furnish butchers with rabbit that is to be enjoyed locally, you can make an inexpensive, sanitary, and appealing package by arranging the portions along with fresh parsley on a paper plate, then covering this with a piece of clear plastic.

Curing the Skins

Skins should be shaped while they are still warm. Draw them, flesh side out, over wire or board stretchers. You can buy the initial stretchers for a few cents, then if you want, whittle any others from shingles, shakes, or thin pieces of boards as the northern trappers do. Place the forepart of the skin over the narrow end of such a stretcher and make sure the legs are all on the same side. Press all wrinkles from the skin.

The day after skinning, examine your work. Make sure that the edges are dry and flat, the skin of the front feet is straightened out, and all patches of fat have been scraped off with your knife.

Although skins must be thoroughly dried before being tied together in handy bundles, do not hurry things along by drying the pelts in the sun or in artificial heat. Hang them so that air can circulate freely and let nature proceed. During warm weather, it may be a good idea to sprinkle the skins with naphtha flakes. Never use salt to cure rabbit skins.

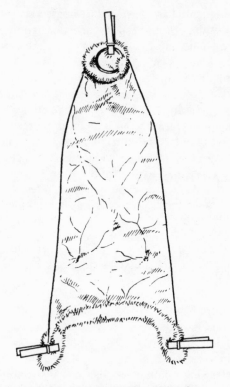

How to Place Rabbit Pelt on Stretcher

Baked Rabbit

Baked rabbit is excellent when you have some young rabbits and the time. It has enlivened more than one table, hand-hewn and otherwise. Divide the animals into serving pieces. Salt each and place, bony sides up, in a roasting pan. Sprinkle with paprika and cover generously with chips of butter.

Bake, covered to keep in the moisture, in a moderate 350° oven for 1½ hours, turning the pieces and shifting them from top to bottom as they brown. Then transfer to another pan and return to the oven to keep warm.

In the meantime, be simmering the livers and hearts in water so as to end up with ½ cup of stock for each rabbit. Again for each rabbit, add a tablespoon of sifted flour to the butter and juices in the roaster. Stir until smooth. Then add the stock and, mixing and heating, make gravy. Season to taste with salt and freshly ground black pepper and transfer to a gravy boat. Serve everything without delay.

When you eat rabbit like this, there seems to be a heavenly chorus singing in the foreground.

GROWING EARTHWORMS

In addition to your fun and profit with rabbits, you can raise earthworms under the hutches for extra income at no extra cost, no feed to purchase, and practically no work. Worms sell so readily to gardeners and especially the increasing organic enthusiasts— and to fishermen, researchers, photographers who want to bring birds closer to the lens, and to people who keep chameleons and other such pets or who have home aquariums, fish hatcheries, fruit orchards, poultry houses, roadside zoos, wildfowl farms, and to other rabbit raisers— that you can make more than $500 a month with this sideline, plus enjoying the most productive garden and best fishing in town.

If you are raising rabbits, you will automatically have some of the finest food available for earthworms; that is, rabbit wastes and the food that in spite of your best efforts will be scattered beneath the hutches. And men, women, boys and girls, the handicapped, and the retired can engage in this sideline with a very small initial outlay and with no previous experience. Too, it works right in with enjoying the best the earth has to offer, without ruining anything.

For example, a box or bin only three feet wide and fourteen feet long containing droppings and compost, situated under your rabbit pens, can hatch and produce 40,000 worms a week. By selling the worms at the wholesale price of $4 a thousand you'll be grossing $160 a week for $640 a month from worms alone.

Food for Earthworms

Inasmuch as earthworms live off the rabbit droppings and

wasted feed around and under the hutches, you don't have to buy any grub for your worms. In fact, the only initial expense you'll have to put out for is building the boxlike container to hold the compost and droppings. Even this can be constructed out of scrap or second-hand lumber, for worms are not fussy. Maybe you can even find what you need at the dump.

Start, then, by placing the boxes or bins under the rabbit hutches where they'll catch the droppings and waste fodder. Once these are about six inches deep, mix such waste materials as dead leaves, dead grass, and garbage to make a compost or, better, follow the compost directions in Chapter 3. Water the compost for a few days, during which period it will heat and then cool off. Once it has so matured, you're ready to add your breeding stock.

To each square foot of compost surface, plant 150 breeding earthworms. These are inexpensively obtainable from one of the dealers whose ads appear in the classified section of outdoor and gardening magazines. Even here, there's no hard labor involved. Just place the worms on the surface, and they'll soon happily burrow out of sight, staying near enough to the top, however, to consume the new waste matter and to eliminate offensive odors, manufacturing invaluable humus in the process.

All you'll have to add from then on is enough water to keep the beds wet but not soggy. So as not to pack the compost, this moisture is best sprinkled or applied in the form of mist. To keep the compost pulverized and porous, it should be forked every couple of weeks. That's all.

Even if you do not have a rabbit business or sideline, you can still enjoy earthworm profits. Build your box, using any old lumber and perhaps covering the cracks with flattened tin cans. Or scrounge around and find some old receptacles such as discarded garbage pails, bath tubs, deep freezers, and the like.

They need have no bottoms. If they do, make sure there is a drain hole. Six inches of gravel must go onto the bottom of all containers. If you lay wire, poles, or loose boards over this, you won't have the annoyance of disturbing it every time you fork the top filler.

For the latter you'll need compost, perhaps made of straw, manure, sawdust which has been soaked for a week before using, garden soil, and a scattering of garbage. All these, depending upon where you live, should cost little or nothing. Once the compost is well-matured, fill the containers, which, if you want, may be kept in a cellar or the back of a garage. Even if you still live in a city, you can raise earthworms.

To start with 5,000 breeders, you'll need a box eight feet long and four feet wide and deep, painted to keep it from rotting. No bottom is required, but there shouldn't be cracks in the sides. To raise worms outdoors in a cold climate, dig a pit some three feet deep and sink your box in this. Cover in winter with straw, leaves, or burlap bags. The beds should not be allowed to freeze.

When you don't have rabbits to do the job, your worms will need feed. Something such as chicken mash will suffice. Mix this liberally with water and sprinkle it loosely over the bed by hand so that it doesn't get too thick in any one spot. This precaution is particularly important if you are working indoors, as the mash will then sour and give off an unpleasant odor.

Caring for the Worm Bed

It will be a good idea to sprinkle the bed with water daily, keeping it moist but not sopping. If the worm quarters are outdoors, keep something such as some inexpensive roofing paper handy to cover the surface during downpours. Light rains are beneficial to worms.

The beds should be gently turned with a flat-bladed fork every couple of weeks. If one of your habitats is something as small as a garbage can, stirring the contents with a nail at the end of a stick will be sufficient. Change the bed entirely once a year.

The Breeding Cycle

All earthworms, being bisexual, are producers. After coming in contact with a fellow worm to be fertilized, each worm will lay an egg about once every ten days. The incubation period for these averages between fifteen and twenty days. Upon hatching, each egg produces from two or three to twenty young worms. Properly fed and watered, the youngsters themselves will become breeders in two or three months. Then after attaining breeding age, the individual worms will keep on growing for approximately five or six months before becoming fully mature. Money, money, money.

Marketing Tips

Besides giving you a garden that will be the cynosure of the neighborhood, earthworms can also more than pay their way. For example, put up signs, lay out small catchy newspaper ads, and arrange tie-ins if you can, as with a sporting goods store which can offer free worms weekly during the fishing season to anyone who buys his tackle there, all promoting the sale of your earthworms to local fishermen.

Anglers spend hundreds of thousands of dollars each year for bait, and it is not even necessary to live in the immediate fishing area to sell these top lures for this purpose. Innumerable individuals, sporting goods retailers, sportsmen's camps, roadside stands, and filling stations with bait-selling sidelines buy their wares by parcel post.

Millions of worms, in fact, are sold every year by mail. All you'll need is some waxed paper containers similar to those used for ice cream and cottage cheese. Just be sure to punch a few air holes in the top. Or buy containers especially designed for shipping earthworms by parcel post from Sealright Co., Inc., 2925 Fairfax Road, Kansas City, Kansas 66115. You'll want to put a padding of peat moss, soaked for a day and the water then squeezed out, in with the worms.

Large paper cups obtainable from the local grocery store can be used for local sales, or if you're going to make a special effort, perhaps filling orders from a number of nearby retailers, you might investigate the breather paper bags put out by R.C. Bait Bags, 224 Eleanor Street, Kalamazoo, Michigan 49006.

If you don't use it all yourself, the compost worked over by the worms and now particularly rich in readily absorbed calcium, phosphate, nitrogen, and magnesium will be invaluable to other gardeners. Then there's the continent-wide possibilities of disposing of your worms in quantity to nurserymen, orchardists, truck gardeners, florists, and to other enthusiasts like you who'd like to try their hand with the expanding earthworm industry.

Just get a name for your enterprise, begin advertising nationally in the outdoor and gardening publications who already have ads that can serve as models for your own terse, punchy layout, print a circular that you can mail inquirers instead of replying with time-consuming letters, and begin awaiting a welcome increase in your mail deliveries from those interested in breeding stock, soil building, and the best of all fish baits.

CHAPTER SEVEN

Running a Poultry Farm
Without a Hitch

HOW'S about pacing those hearty meals—for which the sort of healthy life we've been talking about will give you built-in appetites—with coq au vin, chicken cacciatora, omelette savoyarde, and eggs benedict, all from your own flock? Then get about fifty chicks. This number will allow for some losses from accident and disease, and it will supply enough eggs and some meat for a small family. A larger flock can become a source of a little extra income if there is a local demand for fresh eggs.

Several breeds of chickens are suitable for such small flocks. If eggs are your chief aim, then egg-production breeds such as White Leghorns will be the ones to consider. If you want your pens to supply both eggs and fried-chicken fodder, one of the general-purpose breeds will be better. Plymouth Rocks, New Hampshires, and Rhode Island Reds, as well as crosses of these breeds, are excellent for meat as well as egg production.

Chicks of good quality are usually available from nearby hatcheries. The way to start your own flock with the lowest initial cost is to buy day-old chicks. Such very young birds do require a

176

Chicken Breeds
Top left: Rhode Island Red. *Top right:* New Hampshire. *Bottom left:* Plymouth Rock. *Bottom right:* White Leghorn.

lot of care, however, and must be kept in a heated brooder house. For these reasons you may prefer to buy older chicks that are well started or even pullets almost ready to lay.

In any event, buy only from reputable hatcheries or breeders, making sure at the same time that the youngsters have been tested for and are free from pullorum and typhoid diseases. Most commercial hatcheries now have chicks separated by sex. This way you can choose mostly pullets for egg production or include cockerels that will be used for the table.

Feeding Chicks

Once you bring home newly hatched chicks, put them in the brooder house. Provide the younglings immediately with a starting mash in your chick feeders and plenty of water in the drinking fountains. Finely cracked corn, though, can be fed instead of the starting mash during the first two days after hatching.

Following these starting rations, except for some fine grit that can be mixed with the mash or fed separately, mash is ordinarily then used as the entire diet until the chicks are four to six weeks old. Allow one inch of space at the feeders and one-half inch at the drinking fountains for each bird. As the chicks grow, feeding and drinking room must of course be increased. In any event, keep mash and water available at all times.

When the birds are six to eight weeks old, replace the starting mash with an all-mash growing diet or with a combination of growing mash and grain. Begin by adding small amounts of grain and increase this gradually until the chicks are getting equal parts of mash and grain at about fifteen weeks of age. Grit, incidentally, must be included when the diet contains whole grain.

Grain is usually cheaper than mash. It contains less protein and fewer vitamins, but this is not a matter of concern. As the birds grow older, they have less need for proteins and vitamins. Grains fed to poultry include corn, oats, wheat, and barley. Most poultrymen now use commercially prepared feed whose quality is carefully controlled. It will be well to follow the manufacturer's directions precisely, therefore, when feeding these formulas.

If you'd like to mix your own feed from home-grown grains, get locally advantageous feed formulas and directions from your county Department of Agriculture agent or state extension board. Such formulas have been painstakingly tested, so follow directions carefully especially in the matter of mixing in minute proportions of vitamins and other additives to large batches of your home-blended feed. Be sure, too, that these additives are stirred into the whole sufficiently to distribute them evenly throughout.

If you've the space and if the weather is favorable, chicks can be put on range by the time they are six weeks old, insuring them exercise and sunshine.

For maximum egg production, laying mash fed either exclusively or with grain should make up the major part of the diet of laying hens. If grain is fed, add grit and oyster shell to supply the necessary calcium for normal eggshells. If mash alone is fed, check the manufactuer's directions to see whether limestone or oyster shell should be added. For the most part, mashes contain sufficient calcium.

Egg-production breeds such as White Leghorns generally start to lay at twenty to twenty-four weeks of age, general-purpose birds such as Rhode Island Reds at twenty-one to twenty-six weeks. About two weeks before pullets are expected to commence cackling over their first eggs, gradually replace growing mash with an all-mash laying diet or with laying mash and grain.

As might be expected, feed is the big expense in the egg business. Laying hens of light breeds, such as White Leghorns, eat an average of 85 to 90 pounds of feed a year. Plymouth Rocks and the other heavier all-purpose hens peck away at 95 to 115 pounds.

All this is happily offset by the average annual egg output of production-bred hens, from 200 to 240 eggs per fowl.

Chicken Houses and Equipment

Day-old chicks require a tightly built, draft-free brooder house that provides at least one and one-half square feet of floor space for every two fluffy youngsters. They will also need a brooder stove heated by coal, wood, oil, gas, or electricity. Electric brooders are satisfactory and are less of a fire hazard than other such arrangements. Some poultrymen use homemade brooders successfully.

On the other hand, as we've just considered, the care and expense necessary for day-old chicks may be avoided by purchasing older birds. Such more mature fowl can be raised in any building that keeps them dry and protected from cold, affords ample ventilation in hot weather, and permits easy tending of the flock. This building can be as inexpensively constructed as you can manage. In fact, you may be able to remodel an existing shed for the purpose. Allow three to four square feet of floor space per bird.

Chicken Roosts

If roosts are used, they should be located at the back of the house, well away from drafts. Roosts, which may be just single poles, should be two to three feet above the floor and about a foot apart.

Make a pit under the roosts to catch droppings, which will really do things for your organic garden, and to help keep the litter clean. Cover such pits with heavy wire netting to keep the chickens out of them. Removable dropping boards can also be utilized. In any event, clean the pits and boards often enough to prevent offensive odors.

Cover the floor with six to eight inches of absorbent litter in which the chickens can joyously scratch. Remove this litter when it becomes damp, as moist floor coverings harbor parasites and disease organisms. It's only reasonable always to clean and disinfect the flock's quarters, and to provide fresh litter, before housing new birds.

Chickens can be confined to houses, or a yard or range can be provided for them. Growing birds in particular do benefit from sunshine, exercise, and fresh air. Confinement of the flock generally cuts down on the expense, necessitating less money for land and equipment as well as less labor. Too, losses to predatory birds and animals are decreased.

Many poultrymen keep laying hens confined to the house at all times, with excellent results. If you want to lengthen the hen's day and thus stimulate egg production, turn on electric lights in the laying house falls and winters.

A house for laying hens should provide a conveniently located nest for every four or five hens. It will pay off in efficiency to build sectional nests along the wall in such a way that hens can enter from the rear and eggs can be removed via a simple door at the front.

Watch out for crowding. This can cause smothering of baby chicks, reduce egg production of the hens, and increase the possibility of disease. To help protect the fowl from the latter, always keep chicks separated from older birds.

Guarding the Health of the Flock

Get off to a good start by buying chickens from a reputable hatchery or breeder known to have a good disease-control program. Then if you keep them in a roomy, clean, well-ventilated house, many of the diseases and parasites common to young birds will be avoided.

Watch your flock for signs of disease and act promptly if any show up. Symptoms may include: coughing, sneezing, difficulty in breathing, watery eyes, droopiness, a sudden drop in feed consumption, and abnormal droppings.

When sickness is suspected, isolate the ill birds immediately from the rest of the flock. Get a reliable diagnosis and begin treatment at once. Kill very sick birds, unless they're particular pets, and burn or bury deeply the remains to help prevent the spreading of the disease.

Clean all feeders and waterers regularly. Remove droppings frequently. Keep clean litter on the floor. Thoroughly clean and disinfect the whole building at least once a year and especially after any sick birds have been held there.

Producing High-Quality Eggs

If you have fed and cared for your laying hens diligently, you should get high-quality eggs for yourself, the family, and perhaps even for the market.

Incidentally, cull the hens in your flock that are not producing and use them as southern fried chicken, savory chicken soup, and such. You can separate layers from nonlayers by looking for the egg-producing indicators; that is, changes in the appearance, size, or shape of the comb and wattles, pubic bones, and vent. A layer has a large, smooth comb and wattles. On the other hand, a nonlayer has dry, shriveled, undeveloped comb and wattles. Pubic bones on a layer are wide apart, those on a nonlayer close together. A yellow vent shows that a hen is not laying; while a pink, white, or bluish white vent indicates that the fowl is producing eggs.

Gather eggs from the nests twice daily, and clean and cool them. Eggs should be held at a temperature between 45° and 55° for best results. If you are going to market some of your output, try not to include undersized or thin-shelled eggs, inasmuch as size and shell quality affect price.

RAISING TURKEYS

Maybe you'd prefer turkey tetrazzini or even turkey divan? Well, turkeys can also be raised satisfactorily on one acre, even though they do need special care and equipment. For example, young turkeys must be kept warm and dry. But before they're half a year old, they'll be ready for eating.

Turkeys should not be allowed to run with chickens. For that matter, young turkeys should be kept apart from older ones. Turkeys should not be put in buildings that have housed chickens within the past three months. Land used for chickens or for other turkeys should not be utilized as range for a new flock until at least

Open-Front Laying House

three years have passed. Such precautions are necessary to keep turkeys from contracting blackhead and other serious diseases.

Marketing Ages

Turkeys, if you'd like to sell some, are usually marketed as mature roasters or broilers. Small-type mature roasting birds of both sexes are ready for the kitchen at twenty-two or twenty-four weeks of age, large-type at twenty-four to twenty-eight weeks. Large-type hens, however, often find their way into the stores at twenty weeks—a short span from egg to cash.

In fact, you can even better this. Small-type white turkeys make excellent broilers when marketed at about sixteen weeks. Large-type white females, marketed at a mere thirteen weeks, are excellent in this department.

To get started, you may well buy about 100-day-old turkey poults from breeding flocks tested for and found free from pullorum, typhoid, typhimurium, and sinusitis. Feed and water the birds at the earliest possible moment after getting them home.

Turkey Feed

For the first eight weeks, turkey poults need a starting mash containing 28 percent protein. After this, the growing birds should be fed a growing mash, loose or pelleted, containing 20 to 22 percent of protein, along with grain. It's all right to use either commercial feed or home-mixed feeds based on formulas recommended by state agriculture colleges or the U.S. Department of Agriculture.

Any common grain or combination of grains can be used effectively with the growing mash. If corn is fed, however, it should be cracked until the fowl are about sixteen days old. If confined turkeys are not fed supplementary green feed, give them a well-balanced growing mash. When direct sunlight and green feed are freely available, a less expensive mash without vitamin supplements may be used.

Housing

Poults require a well-built, artificially heated brooder house until they're eight weeks old. Allow one to one and one-half square feet as floor space per bird.

Use sand for litter the first two weeks. Then add wheat straw or splinter-free shavings. Litter is not needed if the birds are started on a floor with narrow slats three-fourths of an inch apart or on a floor covered with No. 2½ hardware cloth nailed to removable frames.

Older poults and adult turkeys are best kept in confinement in a well-ventilated building with a dry floor and tight roof. To exclude hungry small birds and predators, all openings should be screened with heavy wire. Litter the floor liberally with straw, hay, or splinterless shavings, all later excellent for the organic garden. Add to the litter as required for sanitation. Floor space required by poults to market age and beyond is about five square feet per bird if the turkeys are debeaked, seven to eight feet if they are not.

Range Rearing

Range rearing is practicable if you have facilities for moving both turkeys and equipment to clean ground every two to four weeks during the growing season. If the weather is mild, you can start poults on range when they are about two months old. If the weather is severe and range shelter is not available, wait until the birds are ten to twelve weeks old before you put them out on range.

The range may be a grass or legume pasture which should be well drained and fenced. Roosts and shade should be available. Some kind of portable range shelter on skids generally is needed. Wire walls on the shelter should be strong and tight enough to keep out predatory animals such as foxes, skunks, and even dogs. Care should be taken to latch the shelter door each night after the turkeys are inside.

RAISING DUCKS AND GEESE

One advantage in raising ducks or geese is that they ordinarily require less care and attention than the same number of chickens.

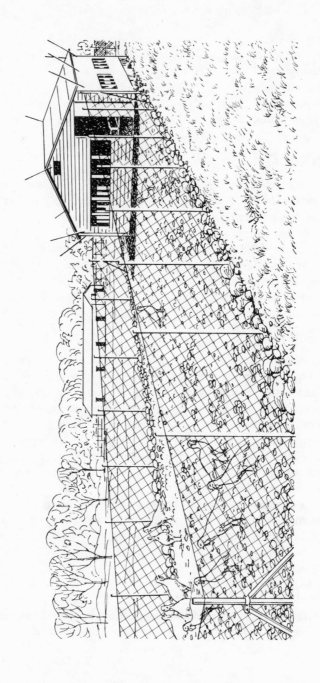

Permanent-Type Turkey Shelter

For example, young geese can be put on pasture when they are only a few weeks old. They will need little additional food as long as the grass is green.

Anyone planning to keep waterfowl should obtain additional free information on breeds, feeding, management, and care from his county agriculture agent.

RAISING SQUABS FOR THE TABLE

Squabs are young pigeons twenty-five to thirty days of age. Squabs for the family table can often be raised successfully on small farms not suited to chicken raising.

If you plan to market squabs, first investigate local market possibilities. Squabs ordinarily bring good prices, but the demand for them is more limited than that for chickens and eggs.

Pigeons can be raised in simple, inexpensive houses or in an unused part of a shed or barn. Adult birds feed their young on a substance called pigeon's milk, produced in the adult birds' crops. Each pair of breeders will produce around a dozen squabs in a year.

Breeds recommended for producing early maturing squabs of high market value are: King, Carneau, Giant Homer, and Mondaine. Squabs of these breeds should weigh fourteen to twenty-four ounces, a desirable weight and size for an individual serving. And what a serving!

Sometime when you're having another couple over for dinner, cut four squabs into pieces, rub well with butter, salt liberally, speck with a few flakes of freshly ground black pepper, and sauté briefly in six tablespoons butter in a pan. When the fowl have taken on a tempting tan, move to a casserole.

Add to the hot butter remaining in the pan ½ cup of chopped onion and ¼ cup of chopped celery. Cook, stirring, until the onion is soft but not brown. Then pour in a cup of boiling water in which a chicken bouillon cube has been dissolved, or use chicken or similar stock. Add a small can of pieces and stems of mushrooms, the juice included. Mix thoroughly, then turn everything over the birds. Cover and cook in a moderate 350° oven for about an hour or until the meat is tender.

Unless you have wild rice for this, try stirring and cooking two cups boiled rice in two tablespoons butter in a frypan over low heat for five minutes. Add two tablespoons chopped, preferably green, onion. Cook several minutes longer. Then add a beaten egg and stir vigorously until the white is set. Season with parsley flakes and salt. Serve everything hot. This will really set off the arriving night when the pale saffron glow overhead begins to fade into velvet darkness.

CHAPTER EIGHT

Setting Up
As a Sheep Farmer

DO you have grassland and good fences? Then a small flock of sheep may fit in with your way of living—with their two bountiful crops a year, lambs and wool, as well as sizzling shish kebabs for the table.

Sheep mean a whole lot less work than some kinds of livestock, and they get along well with low-cost housing and equipment. This means you can start with a few ewes and grow, if you want, into the sheep business. A small flock costs less, and you will be able to give it better care. There is generally less chance of disease and parasites.

If you do well and discover you like sheep, you can enlarge your flock merely by keeping the best ewe lambs. This way you can double the number of breeding ewes on your grass in just a few years, learning more about production and management as you are proceeding along this happy road.

What about cost? If you buy a breeding ewe for $25 and sell her in five years for $5, say, then your cost for five years is $20. The expenses for one year include the amortized $4 initial cost, interest of $1.25, the buying of about 75 pounds of concentrate and 500 pounds of mixed hay for $9, $.75 shearing costs, and a $3 breeding charge. This adds up to $18.

But you sell one lamb for $20 and one wool fleece for $5. The difference between these gross receipts and the total cost comes to $7, your return per ewe per year, not counting all that richly productive manure for the garden. This figure is based, too, on only one lamb per ewe per year. In many farm flocks four ewes will produce five lambs during a year, which would increase the hypothetical gross receipts to $30 and return $12 each ewe per year. Costs and returns will vary somewhat in different localities, of course.

Talk to the natives in your area who are raising sheep. How well are they doing? Where do they get their hay? What grains do they feed? Do they shear their own sheep and butcher their own lambs, further lowering overhead? Where do they sell their wool and lambs? When you get the answers to these queries, you can better decide if you want to take on sheep as a sideline.

Buying Your First Ewes

Autumn is ordinarily the best time to buy sheep. They cost less then.

Talk with your county Department of Agriculture agent and with sheepmen in your neighborhood who belong to local or regional associations. These individuals will know where to get good ewes and when sheep sales are held.

Look for future mothers that produce good wool and desirable lambs. A satisfactory, although not purebred, grade ewe of this type costs around $25 or more, depending on market conditions. Yearling or two-year-old ewes will be better buys for you than older stock. They have more productive years ahead of them.

If you purchase native stock, pick a breed that is doing well in your neighborhood. Get vigorous ewes that have produced well on pasturage and feed similar to what you'll be providing.

Ewes from western ranges, if you give them good care and breed them with strong mutton-type rams, often produce satisfactory lambs up to the time they are eight to ten years old. They usually sell for less than younger stock.

Your chances for success with sheep will be much rosier if you avoid buying: (1) ewes that are already bred, particularly as you then cannot be sure when they will lamb, (2) ewes that are lame, foot rot being a common and troublesome disease, (3) ewes with unsound udders, (4) ewes that have mastitis, and (5) ewes with worn or missing teeth, signs of old age.

Rams for Breeding

Even if only a few ewes are bounding over your acre, these should preferably be mated with a purebred ram. While you're at it, get the service of a ram with a record of producing good lambs. Depending on the locality, the breeding charge will generally average between $2 and $4 per ewe.

How about a ram of your own? When you are ready to acquire a purebred ram, expect to pay $65 or more for him. You can buy such a ram on your own, of course, or in partnership. Try to get one that is sound, fertile, and from a year and a half to three years of age. Such a male can be safely bred to fifty ewes in a period of forty to fifty days if he is strong, has good care, and is well fed.

Equipment and Housing

Fancy buildings and costly equipment are not necessary with sheep. Chances are, in fact, that you can use or convert a barn or shed already on the place.

If you are at all handy with tools, you can easily make pens, feeders, and troughs that may be needed. These do not cost much to build, particularly if you have usable poles or lumber at hand. For example, the illustrated five-sized hay rack is simple to construct, easily moved, and takes care of as many as ten sheep at a time. Each of the sides is about two feet long, with a center divider. Openings should be nine to twelve inches wide, the breadth depending on the size of your animals.

A rectangular hay rack, shown in the accompanying drawings, is

Five-sided Hay Rack

Rectangular Hay Rack

usually made eight to twelve feet long. Up to twenty sheep can be fed hay at one time with this simple contraption.

You should also provide some protection for the flock during frosty or dank weather. Then there's a dry, draft-free shelter for ewes and their young at lambing time. A shed or barn that opens to the south makes a fine sheep shelter. The animals enjoy a lot of sun, light, and air. Just a dirt floor will be entirely satisfactory.

Lambing Pens You should have one lambing pen for every five ewes in your flock. You can easily make such an enclosure,

Lambing Pen

as shown in the sketch, by placing a hinged panel across an inside corner. Each half of the panel should be three to four feet high and four to five feet long. Five-inch strap hinges can be used, top and bottom, to hold the panel halves together. Spaces between boards should be no more than three or four inches.

Making a Lamb Creep A lamb creep allows baby lambs to feed while keeping out the ewes. There are a number of ways to make a lamb creep as, for instance, per the accompanying illustration which utilizes a corner. The important point is that openings into the creep, where the youngsters' feed trough is placed, are some eight inches wide and about eighteen inches high. It will be important, of course, to place this creep near where the ewes feed and the lambs gather. Otherwise, the lambs won't get in the habit of straying into the creep to feed.

Fencing You'll do well to provide your sheep with the best fences you can afford. For one thing, without strong fences your losses from sheep-plaguing dogs can be heavy.

Lamb Creep

Unless you're lucky enough to have property already adequately fenced, the best kind of sheep fence can be expensive to build. This fence has a strand of tautly stretched barbed wire close to the ground. Above this is 36-inch woven-wire fencing with a four-inch mesh, and tight above this two more strands of barbed wire.

The cost of the materials required to enclose an acre with this sort of fence would be about $150. This sum would pay for the woven-wire fencing, the barbed lengths, and substantial steel posts but not for labor. A gate would be extra.

However, if you have a wood lot that will provide the posts, the cost of the fence will be markedly less. Cedar, black locust, and Osage orange make long-lasting posts. Other durable woods, considered at length in the chapter on home building, include tamarack, catalpa, red mulberry, black walnut, and the sassafras, whose bark makes such a memorable tea.

Useful Odds and Ends You'll need a vat or tub of some sort if it becomes desirable to dip your sheep to control mites, lice, ticks, and other skin parasites.

Other helpful items include: hand shears, foot-trimming tools, small pruning shears which will have other uses around the place, a sharp pocketknife for docking and castrating, drenching syringe for treating sheep for worms and other internal parasites, iodine for the navels of newborn lambs, pigment for the ram's chest to mark ewes that have been served, trough for treating foot rot, and a bottle of disinfectant.

This is not to say, of course, that you should attempt foot-trimming, castration, or even worming until you have had instruction in these practices. The Department of Agriculture, through its county agents, stands ready to give you free help in all these departments.

Pasturage

Pasture is the cheapest feed for sheep; so you'll do well to let them enjoy the fullest possible use of it. Sheep eat a wide variety of grasses though they prefer those that are short and fine.

Native bluegrass mixed with such grasses as clover, fescue, and orchardgrass provides excellent pasturage for sheep. A top dressing of one of the organic nitrogens on your bluegrass will insure early growth. The results? One acre of well-established bluegrass, adequately managed and fertilized, is enough to graze half a dozen ewes. If the pasture is unimproved, the same expanse may carry only two or three ewes.

Start your sheep grazing on bluegrass in the spring when new growth is three to six inches high. No other feed is necessary when this fodder is young and abundant. Do not rely on bluegrass for pasture all summer, though. When it begins to dry up, put your sheep on temporary pasture.

One way to grow pasture for mid-summer grazing, as well as hay for winter feeding, is by sowing a piece of land with Korean (annual) lespedeza. Sow this lespedeza in the springtime at the rate of ten pounds per acre.

As soon as it grows about ten inches high, cut it for hay. An acre can be counted upon yielding from one to one and one-half tons of the latter. Then when your bluegrass gives out in July and August, turn the sheep on the lespedeza. Let them graze contentedly there until the bluegrass returns in the fall. An acre of lespedeza will graze four or five ewes.

Sudan grass, rape, and kale can also be used for summer pasture. Fall-sown wheat, barley, or rye gives good grazing for about a month in spring or early summer. Combinations of grass and hay that are particularly suitable for sheep include ladino, clover and bromegrass, red clover and timothy, alfalfa and bromegrass, and bird's-foot trefoil.

Winter Feed

Good-quality legume hay, preferably alfalfa, is the most desirable winter feed for sheep. It contains the needed vitamins, minerals, and proteins. If you feed mixed or grass hay instead, include a protein supplement, linseed or soybean meal, daily with the hay to balance the ration.

Three to four pounds of alfalfa or other hay a day is sufficient for a ewe weighing 140 pounds or less. Begin to feed this hay as soon as ewes are taken off pasture in the fall. Continue with it until the ewes are back on pasture after lambing.

Hay is ordinarily fed for about five months on the average, but the length of time you stay with it will depend, of course, on the season and on the kind and amount of pasture available. You will need about 500 pounds of hay per ewe during the winter. This much alfalfa, if you don't raise it yourself, will cost about $10. Mixed hay will cost less, maybe $7 for the same amount.

Grain

Most of a sheep's living, in other words, comes from pasturage and hay. Grain is fed only at certain times during the year. Ewes generally need grain for about a hundred days. They should have grain thirty days before lambing. If the mothers nurse their offspring after lambing, it will be sound practice to continue grain daily until spring pastures become green.

One-half to three-quarters of a pound of grain daily per ewe is enough. Which grain? Feed the one that is most economical where you live. For example, ground shelled corn is a prime food for sheep, particularly if you want to put pounds on them. Ground oats and barley are also very satisfactory.

For a fresh or pregnant ewe already eating high-quality legume hay, a good day-by-day ration includes three to four pounds of the alfalfa, lespedeza, or clover hay, plus that one-half to three-quarters of a pound of corn, oats, or barley.

It will take about seventy-five pounds of grain, in addition to the hay, to winter one ewe. With the hay costing $10 and the grain about $1.60, the total cost of feeding one ewe this diet for 100 days is about $11.60.

A fresh or pregnant ewe who gets mixed or grass hay should be fed a daily winter ration of three to four pounds of this, plus one-half to three-quarters of a pound of concentrate. An efficient concentrate for a ewe not dining on legume hay is made by mixing twenty pounds of corn, a similar amount of oats, and six pounds of linseed or soybean meal.

This amount of concentrate would cost about $1.30 and would satisfy one ewe for about seventy days. The total cost of feeding a ewe mixed or grass hay and concentrate for 100 days would be about $9. In all these instances, if you raise all or part of your hay and grain, your feed costs will be pared considerably.

Growth Diet for Lambs

To get quick gains on lambs, start giving them a little ground grain in a creep when they are as young as five to ten days. Offer them, at the same time, a bit of leafy hay. Increase the grain and hay gradually as the lambs begin looking forward to it. By the time the young ones are sixty to seventy days old, they will be eating about one-half pound of grain daily.

Creep-feed lambs until they are weaned or marketed, at about four months of age or seventy to ninety pounds in weight. An excellent ration for creep-feeding a lamb is: seven pounds of shelled ground corn, three and one-half pounds of rolled or crushed or crimped oats, one pound of wheat bran, a pound of molasses, and three ounces apiece of salt and minerals. This amount of mixture, costing about $.40, will feed a lamb about a month.

Salt and Water Needs of Sheep

Incidentally, keep your sheep and lambs supplied with granular iodized salt the year around. If there is any shortage of certain minerals in your region, it will be sound insurance to use trace mineralized salt. Locate the salt box somewhere near the water supply, in a spot where it will be protected from wind and storm and in a shaded nook if possible.

Equal parts of either ground limestone or steamed bonemeal can be mixed with the salt. To help control internal parasites, phenothiazine may also be mixed with the salt. Your local Department of Agriculture agent or sheep supply store can give you the details on the amounts to add in specific areas.

See, too, that fresh, clean water is available to the flock at all times. Pregnant ewes and nursing ewes, in particular, require hefty amounts of water. A tip for winters? Sheep will drink more water in cold weather if the water is warmed.

The Mating Cycle

Autumn is the normal season of mating for sheep. Ewes generally are first bred when eighteen months old. They lamb when they are about two years of age.

Ewes come in heat in late August or early September. The periods in which ewes will breed last from one to three days and recur every fourteen to nineteen days. Ewes should be gaining weight when they are bred.

The length of time from breeding to lambing is from 140 to 150 days. Ewes bred in September, therefore, lamb in February. You can then market lambs born in winter before the summer season, when parasites get troublesome and your grass is poor.

If you buy a ram to service your ewes, get him well in advance of breeding time so he can get used to his new home. Give him a little grain to keep him happy and to get him in prime condition.

If the flock is small and has only one ram, you need a way of knowing when each ewe has been bred in order to be able to figure about when she will lamb. Pigment smeared on the ram's brisket every day or so will show which ewes he has mounted. Any commercial coloring—yellow, red, or ordinary lampblack—can be used. Mix the color with linseed, castor, or old crankcase oil.

After two weeks change the color of the pigment. If after a few days most of the ewes marked with the first hue are coming back into heat, a new ram should be put into service.

Lambing

Experienced sheepmen prepare well for lambing time. Extra care at this period both saves lambs and keeps their mothers in good condition.

As the natal day nears, observe the ewes carefully. At least two weeks to a month before lambing, clip wool and tags around the udder and hindquarters of the ewes with hand shears.

Separate every ewe about to lamb from the rest of the flock, taking particular care that she does not lamb outside in cold weather. In fact, just before or shortly after she gives birth, move her to a dry, well-bedded lambing pen. Set this enclosure up in the warmest part of the shed or barn. See there are no drafts.

A well-fed ewe seldom has trouble in lambing. However, if a ewe strains strongly and does not deliver within a half-hour, get help from someone who has had experience delivering lambs. If such an individual is not available, call a veterinarian. In any event, make certain beforehand that help will be readily available if you should need it.

Caring for the Lamb and Its Mother Shortly after the lamb is born, dip its navel into a 4 percent solution of iodine. This helps prevent navel infections. Make sure, of course, that the lamb is dried promptly and does not chill.

Be sure that the ewe has taken to her lamb and that the youngster begins nursing within a half-hour. Most lambs stand on their feet and nurse without help shortly after birth. If the lamb is cold, get it warm as soon as you can. If the lamb is wobbly, help it to nurse.

After the lamb has gained a little strength, it will usually get up

by itself. If it does not, repeat the feeding. It is especially important that the lambs get the ewes' first milk, colostrum.

After lambing, add grain gradually to the ewe's feed. By the
time her youngling is ten days or two weeks old, she should be enjoying a full ration of grain or concentrate along with hay.

Keep the ewe and lamb in the lambing pen for twelve to twenty-
four hours. This allows a mothering-up period and saves lambs
that might otherwise be disowned or trampled.

All lambs should have their tails removed, and male lambs
should be castrated by the time they are two weeks old. To find out
about these necessities, see your county agent.

Shearing

Sheep are usually sheared after lambing in the spring when the
wet, cold weather has passed. You can shear as early as mid-March
in most southern regions if you do it in a warm, dry shed. If your
property does not boast such a shelter, it will be better to wait for
mild weather. All fleece should be off before summer, however.

Hold all feed from your sheep for ten hours before shearing.
This shearing should be accomplished on a clean, dry floor or on a
heavy canvas spread over a bedded sheep pen. Make sure that the
wool is clean and dry before you cut it.

Shearing may not be too simple when you're beginning. In
some areas, county agents can direct you to a shearing school
where you will be able to learn the ins and outs of the procedure.
However, most owners of small flocks find it pays to get a custom
shearer. If this expert cannot come to your place, you can probably
take your animals to a neighboring sheep farm and have them
shorn while the shearer is there.

The usual charge for shearing sheep is about $.75 a head. Some
shearers dip sheep at a reasonable cost after shearing. A good
shearer takes all the wool from a sheep in one piece, with no second cuts and no injury to the animal.

Speaking of outside help, such can save you a lot of upsetting if
simple-enough routine when it comes to slaughtering and
butchering, although any Agriculture Department agent can make

you conversant with the procedure if you really have to count the dimes.

Once the fleece is off, spread it on a clean, dry floor with the skin side down. There remove all heavy tags, sweat locks, and short leg wool from the main fleece. Drop these clippings into a bag for separate sale.

Then roll the fleece from the rear toward the front so the shoulder wool is on the outside. Tie the fleece with paper twine. Do not use binder or coarse twine and certainly not wire. Insert the tied fleece into a regular wool bag, prepared for the purpose, or in a clean feed bag. Store it in a tidy, dry place until it is marketed.

The average fleece weight per sheep in the United States is roughly eight pounds. Some fleeces weigh as little as four pounds and some as much as twelve pounds, the weight depending on the breed.

Marketing the Wool

You and the other wool growers in your neighborhood may be able to sell your wool through one of the nearly 150 wool pools in this country. The Department of Agriculture can advise you if there is such a pool nearby.

In selling through a pool, you deliver the wool to a particular location on a certain day. The pool takes bids from buyers. As soon as a purchaser pays for your wool, the pool pays you, retaining a small marketing fee. By the way, many of the large wool pools offer other services such as supply departments that handle shearing equipment, wool bags, twine, and drugs. Wool pools inform their members of all activities.

In addition to the amount you receive privately for the fleece when you sell it, the U.S. Department of Agriculture provides an incentive to all persons in this country who raise sheep and sell wool. The incentive payment is the amount needed to bring the price per pound to $.65. This means that an eight-pound fleece, properly prepared for market, brings about $5.

To secure such an incentive payment, just bring your wool sale receipts to the local Agriculture Stabilization and Conservation office and make application. Such headquarters have been established in most counties in the United States. In due time, you will receive a check for the extra payment.

Keeping the Flock Healthy

Watch your sheep for signs of disease. Some of these can be helped by home treatment, but most should have the attention of a veterinarian. You can do a great deal to prevent illness by starting with and adding only healthy sheep from robust flocks, by housing the animals in clean, dry, well-ventilated quarters, and by feeding properly and providing clean water.

Sheep are attacked by many parasites. Prevention in this respect is better than cure. Your county agent will be able to give you the latest information on the local parasitic situation and on the disorders that parasites cause in sheep.

Ways to control parasites include: treating at least once a year for internal worms; keeping medicated salt available at all times; dipping for mites, mange, lice, and other parasites if necessary; weaning early; and changing grasslands whenever possible, as pasture rotation is important in parasite control.

Slaughtering

Practically, a lamb can be slaughtered for home use any time after it reaches 100 pounds live weight. Most ewe lambs, though, are kept for the flock.

A 100-pound lamb usually yields a 50-pound carcass and about 35 pounds of meat, worth $15 or more, for your table. Lambs reach 100 pounds in only 110 to 140 days. The point is, though, a lamb more than a year old does not put on enough weight to pay for its feed.

Extra feed can, of course, be made available to any healthy male lamb you decide to slaughter for home use. You can either see that he gets more concentrate while on pasture, or you can confine him and give him extra concentrate then.

The day before slaughter, pen the lamb so he can be caught easily. Give him plenty of water but withhold all feed for twenty-four hours before turning into table meat. This makes dressing easier. And, ah, the taste-tempting sputterings of those roasts.

CHAPTER NINE

Secrets of Successful Pig Farming—and Tips on Guinea Pigs Too

YOU can raise hogs on your place for less money per pound of pork than it takes to buy this tasty meat for your family. Not only will you be able to eat for less by rearing your own swine, but you may also be in a position to sell pigs to your neighbors or to a livestock dealer, helping the budget even more.

Hogs grow fast. Most eight-week pigs zoom from 35 pounds to 225 pounds in about 4 months. It will cost you around $11 to buy that pig which weighs between 30 and 40 pounds. And if you buy all the feed, it will cost you about $25 to feed the pig up to the 225 pounds that will yield some 150 pounds of chops, bacon, and other meat cuts plus 25 pounds of lard. If you can feed one or two pigs chiefly on surplus garden produce and table scraps, you'll be away ahead.

Obtaining Hog Stock

The best time to buy your starting pigs is in the spring or fall when they are being weaned. Be sure the pigs you purchase have been raised on clean ground and that they have been vaccinated for hog cholera. Incidentally, if you know little about hogs at the moment, the county agricultural agent can tell you where to obtain healthy stock and how to keep them hearty and robust.

Choose one or more pigs to fatten for butchering. Males selected for this purpose should be barrows; that is, pigs that have been castrated. A boar will produce meat with an undesirable flavor and odor.

The most rapid way to produce a litter is to buy a bred sow. You may buy a young gilt in her first pregnancy or an older sow that has raised one or more litters. A bred sow will cost you from about $45 to $65.

This cost is one that you can cut by raising and mating your own gilt. A well-developed gilt can be bred when she is eight months old and can afterwards produce a litter of pigs every six months. You can have a gilt bred for about $3; so it will surely not pay you to have a boar.

The selection of a breed—the old reliables Berkshire, Chester White, Duroc, Hampshire, Hereford, Spot, Tamworth, Yorkshire, and Poland China or one of the newer breeds such as American Landace and the inbreds that have been developed from crosses of two or more varieties—is a matter of personal preference. No one breed is perfect in every respect, so choose a breed of the type and color desired and one that seems to be best suited to the conditions under which your hogs are to be raised.

Individual excellence of animals is important and should be stressed in establishing and maintaining a herd, especially if the objective, partially at least, is to produce and sell breeding stock. Records on animals should be considered in selecting not only foundation pigs but also the replacements in the herd from year to year.

Production registry of breeding stock is sponsored by all the larger swine record associations. These organizations can supply information regarding herds that have animals that have qualified under the standards used. Then, too, you can obtain much useful information about the performance of the stock from the breeders.

Sow productivity, as measured by the size and weight of the litter at weaning, and acceptable growth rate of pigs are among the most important factors for you to consider when selecting breeding stock. Choose meat-type hogs that will produce carcasses of the most desirable quality and weight.

Market Weights

Meat-type hogs of nearly all the recognized breeds may attain market weights of 200 to 220 pounds from 5 months of age up. Mature boars in good condition generally weigh 600 to 900 pounds. Mature sows may weigh 500 to 750 pounds. Hogs of any breed may occasionally reach half a ton or more. You'll want to take into consideration, though, the fact that hogs heavier than some 250 pounds are made up of an excessive amount of lard, and the cuts are large and less suitable for the average consumer than those from lighter weight swine.

The aim of most hog raising is the production of pork for human consumption. Such a producer of swine, therefore, should have as his objective the efficient and economical production of hogs that dress out high-quality carcasses. Consumers demand lean meat of good quality. The amount of fat should not be excessive. The most desirable weights for market hogs are from 180 to 240 pounds.

Meat-Type Hogs

The intermediate-type hog, often referred to as the middle-of-the-road of the meat type, best meets present market demands. Intermediate-type hogs usually are superior to extremes in type that were formerly classified as small and large varieties.

The most desirable meat-type hog is one with a natural tendency to yield a maximum percentage of the highest-priced cuts—hams, loins, bacon, picnic shoulders, and shoulder butts—with enough finish to insure firmness. Light finish means less lard, a product generally retailing for less per pound than the live hog.

No one breed has a monopoly on meat-type hogs. These, in other words, can be produced from any of the breeds. In fact, breeders are now locating, identifying, and often certifying meat-type hogs to meet the increasing demand.

Many commercial producers today raise crossbred hogs for the market. If you want to carry on such a program in your own small herd, remember that half the inheritance of the litters will come from the boar, which, for this reason, should be sound and of a type that can produce the kind of offspring desired. To get the most from hybrid vigor, which is an objective in crossbreeding, mate hogs of completely different ancestry. Rotation of three or four breeds is helpful in maintaining hybrid vigor in a crossbreeding program. And who knows? Maybe you'll come up with your own new variety.

Shelter and Equipment

Get everything ready for your pigs before bringing them home. You'll need a hog house, a hog shade, a fence or tether, a feed trough, and a waterer.

The simplest of shelters will do for hogs if it has a dry floor, affords shade in hot weather, and keeps out drafts, snow, and rain. For instance, the hog house shown in the accompanying illustration

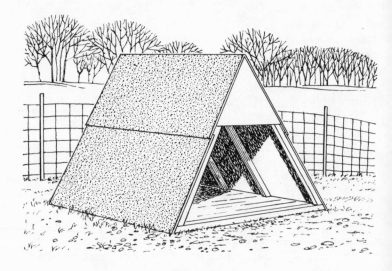

Hog House

Hog Shade

is easy to make. Besides a rear wall, it has a watertight roof that forms two sides. The front of the retreat is open, although if you want you can outfit it with a gate, door, or fabric flap. The house should be faced away from the wind.

Whatever shelter you use should be kept clean and well bedded with straw, leaves, pine needles, shavings, or sawdust. This should be changed frequently and never allowed to remain wet and dirty. Too, the house should be moved to clean ground at least twice a year. It will be a good idea to keep it at least 500 feet from any dwelling so that no one will be bothered by odors.

Shades Hogs can suffer greatly from heat and must have shade. Trees provide excellent shade, of course, but if they are not where you need them, you can put up a special hog shade with sheet metal or brush. For example, just set four posts in the ground, connect them at the top with a framework of poles or lumber, and cover this frame with sheet metal or brush.

Fencing Woven wire makes good hog fencing, but poles or lumber may be better for providing a small pen. A thirty-inch fence or pen with a single strand of barbed wire across the bottom,

Hog Tethered with a Cow Halter

two to three inches above the ground, is good. Each hog being fattened will need about twenty-five square feet of pen space.

Tethers You can also keep a hog from straying by chaining it to a post or some other object, perhaps a tree, that the animal can't budge. Another advantage of tethering, in addition to the money it saves, is that you can move your hogs from one location to another with comparative ease and thus control better grazing.

You'll need a shoulder harness to tether a hog. A dog harness, or even a cow halter, for instance, can be used. The hog shown is wearing one of the latter. It's easy enough, too, to make a harness with a piece of leather strap or cloth webbing, obtainable at surplus stores, long enough to pass around the animal's neck and body. Fit the harness over the neck, cross it under the chest, and wrap it around the body, attaching a chain to it where it crosses under the hog's chest.

Food and Water Troughs A good hog trough can be easily knocked together with scrap lumber. Make it long enough to let all the hogs eat at one time. The trough shown here, both effective and easy to build, will give you the idea.

Whatever feed trough you decide upon, keep it clean. If you feed slop, for instance, wash the trough every day so that left-over food won't sour. Once you clean a trough, dust it with slaked lime to keep it in top condition.

Hogs should have plenty of clean drinking water at all times. A 35-pound starting pig drinks about half a gallon per day, a finished 225-pound hog twice as much, and a brood sow who is suckling a litter about five gallons. A wooden trough makes a good waterer for one or two hogs. For more than that, a homemade barrel waterer will be better.

Feeding

Likeliest your biggest expense in raising pork on the hoof will be the cost of the feed. So one of the best ways to cut the cost of your meat is to reduce food fees. This you can do handily if you have surplus garden produce, pasture, or garden scraps.

Otherwise, when a hog is maintained on a straight concentrate ration it will need some 600 pounds of this to put on the 180 or so pounds difference between weaning and butchering weights. This comes down to about 5 pounds of concentrate a day. However, it is

Hog Trough

easier to measure feed than to weigh it. Mixed feeds commonly fed to hogs weigh some 1½ pounds per quart.

The concentrate ration should consist of grain and a protein-mineral supplement. Although corn is the standard grain for swine, wheat, barley, sorghums, or oats can also be advantageously used. When no green forage is available, yellow corn is superior to white corn.

Both soybean meal and commercially readied protein-mineral supplements will almost surely be easily obtainable where you live, although in some localities these might be replaced by meat scraps, peanut meal, tankage, or milk by-products. A good mineral mixture contains equal parts of steamed bonemeal, ground limestone or air-slaked lime, and ordinary salt. This should be kept in a self-feeder where the hogs can get at it at all times.

Hogs like root crops such as rutabagas and turnips. But even these root crops generally cost more to feed than pasture or hay. If hogs get good pasture, they will eat 10 to 15 percent less feed. You'll need one-sixth of an acre of good pasture for three growing pigs or for a sow and litter.

The following crops will provide this: alfalfa, ladino, red or white clover, alsike, bluegrass, timothy, bur clover, lespedeza, and Dallis grass. Rye, oats, wheat, cattail millet, rape, soybeans, crimson clover, and cowpeas will do for temporary pasture.

If you can arrange to obtain table scraps and selected garbage from several homes or a restaurant, you can reduce considerably the amount of feed you have to buy. Such garbage should be collected at least twice a week so that it does not become spoiled. Be sure it contains no paper, soap, glass, tin cans, washing compound, or dishwater.

Under a nationwide disease-control program, all the states now require the cooking of all garbage fed to hogs. Cook for half an hour at boiling temperature, 212°. This legal requirement is helping prevent hog cholera and other diseases.

Caring For the Sow and Her Litter

A sow will ordinarily deliver her litter in a brief 112 to 115 days after she is bred.

About three days before the exciting event, move the mother-to-be into a clean house or pen. Movable houses, if these are what you are using for farrowing, should be scrubbed with hot water and lye, one-half pound of the latter to ten gallons of fluid. After cleaning the shelter, move it to new ground. Add light bedding of short hay or straw, peanut hulls, or wood shavings.

Wash the sow with soap and water before you transfer her to the new surroundings. Be certain to bathe her teats, as such cleansing removes worm eggs that might infect the younglings and stunt their growth.

Normal, healthy sows and young gilts generally farrow without any signs of trouble. If possible, though, you should be on hand to give any assistance that may be needed. For instance, you may help by preventing the piglets from chilling, warming them after chilling, or starting breathing in youngsters that appear lifeless. You can often start a tiny pig breathing by slapping or rubbing its sides.

After delivery, paint the navel cords with fresh tincture of iodine. Clip the tips of the eight tusklike needle teeth of the piglets.

The sow needs no feed for twenty-four hours after farrowing, but she does require clean drinking water. Give her all of this that she wants, and if possible later feed the sow in a place separate from her offspring. This will prevent her from crippling or killing the piglets accidentally while her attention is on eating.

For information on vaccinations against disease, ask a veterinarian or your county agricultural agent. See that all male pigs not to be kept or sold for breeding are castrated when they are a month old.

If you'd like to raise two litters a year, wean pigs when they are about eight weeks old. Reduce the sow's feed for two or three days before weaning to reduce her milk flow. Then separate sow and piglets. The sow will come into heat and may be bred again three to six days after pigs are weaned.

You can let the youngsters run with the sow until she dries up if you raise only one litter each year.

RAISING GUINEA PIGS

Just why these natives of South America were ever called guinea pigs is a mystery. Actually, they're a member of the rabbit family and, incidentally, are just as delicious to eat. When the Spanish first went into the Andes in their search for gold, they found these little domesticated animals living in Indian homes where they were raised for food. In fact, there are still several species of wild guinea pigs in South America, where, considered a great delicacy, they are hunted as game.

Cavies, as they are also widely called in the United States, are entirely vegetarian in diet. thriving on just about the same grub as rabbits. They are hardy, tame, and healthy. They are also pleasantly clean in their habits and have no offensive odors. Moreover, they adapt themselves so easily to city or country conditions that, being practically free from diseases and epidemics, they are likely as easy to handle as any animal in the world.

Scientific Uses

Just a century ago guinea pigs were kept in Europe and this country almost exclusively as pets. Their utilization by Pasteur, Dock, and other scientists in experiments since that time has established their merit for use in the studying of disease symptoms in humans and animals.

Indeed, there is perhaps no animal so well adapted for scientific experiments as the cavy, a fact which keeps it in substantial demand. Because the reactions of guinea pigs to different tests are now well known, they are invaluable in genetic studies, in analyzing the effects of drugs, in standardizing vaccines and serums, and in determining the vitamin content of foods. These days, therefore, you can enjoy your pets while earning extra income by selling their offspring.

Guinea pigs are gentle, quiet little animals with short, stocky bodies, short ears and legs, and no tail. They eat vegetables exclusively, are easy to keep almost anywhere, and breed with engaging rapidity. Inasmuch as they do not bite or scratch, even the youngest children can enjoy playing with them. Because of medical uses, many pet stores have trouble in keeping them on hand for pets, and they bring higher prices for this purpose than for lab use.

Types and Colors

All domesticated guinea pigs are descended from stock originally found in Peru's cloud-scouring Andes Mountains. The principal types differ from one another in hair characteristics and in color. The cavy's coat may be smooth and short, rough and short, or silky and long. The short-haired English variety is the one most commonly raised and most widely known, and it is the one you should breed for commercial purposes.

The coat of the Abyssinian is short and rough, standing out in unique little rosettes. The picturesque Peruvian variety, the aristocrat of the lot but more trouble to keep inasmuch as its coat requires careful attention, is long-haired.

Most guinea pigs are attractively coated in solid colors including nugget gold, fawn, brown, black, white, and red. Some, though, have hair of mixed colors, alternating in bands of light and dark. Others are characterized by solid colors with harmonizing white spots. Commercial breeders have developed various hues and color combinations, and maybe in your breeding you'll be able to increase the number of these varieties. Today, guinea pigs with two and even three colors are not uncommon.

Buying and Selling

You may buy your starting guinea pigs from pet stores or laboratory supply houses. The price of them is so reasonable, though, that perhaps the safest procedure will be to purchase them from a responsible, widely known breeder who has a reputation to maintain. For a free list of dealers on the little animals, write the Institute of Laboratory Animal Resources, 2101 Constitution Avenue N.W., Washington, D.C. 20402.

Incidentally, if you intend to raise guinea pigs commercially, the Laboratory Welfare Act requires you to obtain a license, pay a small annual fee, and comply with the provisions of the law. Too, research facilities must register and acknowledge the Act's standards. For free additional information and a copy of the provisions, write to the Director, Animal Health Division, Agricultural Research Service, U.S. Department of Agriculture, Hyattsville, Maryland 20782.

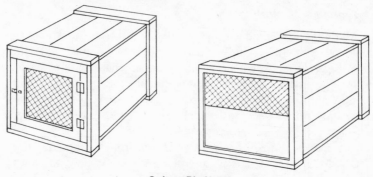

Guinea Pig Hutch
Left: Front view. *Right:* Rear view.

Breeding guinea pigs are ordinarily sold in pairs or in trios of one male and two females. Five females will not be too many. These animals are usually more expensive than the general laboratory types sold to hospitals, laboratories, and dealers.

Guinea pigs are sold for five main purposes: for food, for pets, for a hobby, for show stock, and for experimental purposes in laboratory and medical research. In fact, it will be a good idea initially to determine whether guinea pigs are needed in your area or if other laboratory animals are used. If there is a demand, then you can select the proper breeding animals and plan their housing and feeding.

Housing

A spare room can do until you get really started. So can a basement or a portion of your garage. However, guinea pigs may not be housed with any other species of animal. Except in mild climate, they are best housed indoors in temperatures maintained between 60° and 85°, even though if provided with ample bedding they can stand a lot of cold. They'll then find it easier to adapt to the average 70° of laboratories. Ventilation to minimize drafts can be supplied through windows and doors. Lighting should be adequate to permit routine inspection and cleaning.

In warm climates guinea pigs will thrive in outdoor pens, providing shade is available, especially if they are furnished with warm nest boxes. If you are raising cavies commercially, you must

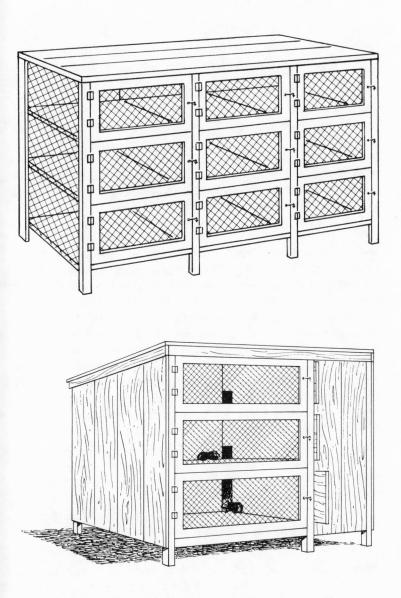

Guinea Pig Hutches
Top: Indoor hutch. *Bottom:* Outdoor hutch.

obtain the approval of the Director of the aforementioned Animal Health Division before housing them in the open.

Because guinea pigs customarily do not climb, jump, gnaw on wood, or burrow, the pens need not be elaborate. Most pens have screen wire or hardware cloth across the tops and sides. Ventilation is the important factor, a good reason for providing a small opening in the back top of the enclosure to aid air circulation in warm weather.

The average boy or adult will be able to build hutches similar to the several illustrated with discarded packing cases or fruit boxes and a bit of screening. As your colony enlarges, you'll likely find it handy to construct hutches that can be stacked.

A pen thirty by thirty-six inches, and twelve to fifteen inches high, is large enough for one male and five breeding females. A large pen, five by ten feet and one to one and one-half feet high, can accommodate thirty to forty guinea pigs. You'll probably find it more satisfactory, though, not to keep more than two dozen cavies in an enclosure.

Provide a shelf about four inches above the floor in a shaded corner of each enclosure. Guinea pigs like to sleep on such an extension, while females and their litters will seek shelter beneath it.

Cover your pen floors with wood shavings, straw, shredded paper, or similar material to absorb moisture. Sawdust, changed when it hardens and mats, is good. Peat moss, because it is so smooth and non-irritating, is fine although it does have a tendency to stain the coats of light-colored breeds. Wheat and oat chaff, with its qualities of absorption and of not matting, is excellent. Probably the best, longest lasting, and one of the most economical coverings is peanut shells, now stocked by many food dealers. Clean the pen floors at least once a week.

A Balanced Diet for Guinea Pigs

There are three general classes of guinea-pig grub; grain or pellets, greens, and hay. Dried bread is also good. Feed your cavies a balanced diet and supply them with fresh water daily. Suspend their food cups and water bottles above their bedding to prevent contamination by waste and dirt. Incidentally, you can substitute milk for water, particularly when there are thirsty mothers and youngsters.

Most breeders like to keep a sulphurized salt spool in each pen although this isn't absolutely necessary.

Ground oats, wheat bran, and soybean grit can supply the grain portion of the diet. Commercially prepared laboratory chows, made expressly for guinea pigs and available in pet and food stores, consist of a mixture of grains and minerals compressed into pellets. Too, a ready-made ration recommended for rabbits can be substituted for the commercial preparations designated for their cavy cousins.

Guinea pigs. like human beings, cannot produce their own vitamin C. Without it, they develop scurvy. Some food pellets supply all vitamin C requirements, but no matter what the source, this particular vitamin's potency lasts only a short time. The best all-around procedure when you can manage it, and a money-saver to boot, is to augment your pets' diet with fresh greens or hay.

Green alfalfa, lettuce, celery leaves, dandelions, beet and turnip greens, clover, parsley, and even lawn clippings will all supply this invaluable nutriment. When abundant, too, fresh greens satisfy the guinea pigs' need for water.

With hay, precautions should be taken to put in only as much as will be completely eaten in about half a day, especially as hay staying in the hutches too long mats, making the bedding wet and slimy. You should take care with greens, too, feeding only what will be cleaned up within a couple of hours. Incidentally, never give your cavies greens that are wet with frost.

To give you an idea of feed costs, each cavy should get not less than two ounces of nourishment daily. For the breeding pens of one boar and five sows, a reasonable standard is a handful apiece of lettuce leaves, hay, and grain, plus all the fresh water that can be consumed. Feeding in the morning and again at the end of the afternoon gives excellent results.

There is a difference of opinion about the efficacy of cabbage with cavies, and a reasonable compromise is to use it only in small quantities if at all. Some object to alfalfa as well, but other breeders find this gives completely satisfactory results if care is taken to balance it with other kinds of hay and never to use any that is musty or moldy. Potatoes, white turnips, and parsnips are frowned on by some breeders, while others find them harmless.

In any event, beware of overfeeding. It's better to keep your cavies a little hungry.

Growth Rate of Guinea Pigs

Guinea pigs, rugged and vigorous, can care for themselves almost from birth. In fact, they are born with hair and teeth and their eyes open. Within an hour after birth they are able to move about. After an interesting two or three days—and it's always a thrill to visit your pets in the morning and find the pen filled with young additions—they will be eating solid food.

However, it's a good idea to leave the young with their mother for about a month. Keep them in the same pen with their parents but never with other adults.

The younglings gain weight rapidly, weighing about a pound in four to six weeks. This may be all-important to your plans, as young cavies of this weight are preferred for many experiments. For the next year and a half their growth weight is slower. At maturity an adult male may weigh one and three-fourths to two and one-half pounds. At eighteen months of age, unbred females are generally some two ounces lighter. Cavies have lived past seven years of age.

Breeding Ages of Sows and Boars

Guinea pigs are prolific, and it is ordinarily easy to build up a sizable herd within a year or two. Sows become sexually mature thirty to forty-five days after birth and will breed at this young age. They come into heat every fourteen to seventeen days, this condition lasting about twenty-four hours.

The boars become sexually mature when only two months old. Remove those that are not to be used for breeding when they are forty to sixty days old, placing them in separate pens. For commercial purposes, it is good operating procedure to buy or swap males so as to have new boars about once every year. Stock not too closely related is apt to be stronger.

Number and Size of Litters

The gestation period of guinea pigs lasts sixty-five to seventy days, and a vigorous sow may give birth to four or five litters a year. The average litter contains three youngsters, while some are made up of five or more squirming little balls of hair.

The sow comes into heat immediately after giving birth and usually mates within ten to twelve hours. To assure regular mating, place the female in the same pen as the breeder boar at this time.

Breeding for Color

Would you like to establish a golden line of cavies? Then out of a mixed lot breed your most brightly golden male to the most vividly golden female. Afterwards, breed the choicest son to his mother and the most select daughter to her father. Keep on with this line breeding and eventually you should get solid golds.

Calculating the Profit

Money makers? Guinea pigs produce young until they are three years old and may continue to breed until the age of five. With each sow giving birth to a dozen or fifteen youngsters every year, each of them worth up to several dollars apiece, there is a big opportunity for profit.

Let's suppose you start your colony of cavies with five sows and one boar. The original guinea pigs should produce some fifty to sixty young ones a year, the young females of the first one or two litters also giving birth to youngsters of their own before the end of the first twelve months. All this should add up to about 120 cavies a year.

If the guinea pigs were disposed of at a price of as low as $1 each, these five sows would be bringing in about $120 annually. Think of what you could do with, say, 100 sows. However, if you start in a small way, very little risk will be taken. You will be getting your experience as you go along, at the same time amassing your own colony and adding extra stock to it as the operation grows.

Health Care

Guinea pigs essentially are remarkably healthy and rugged animals. They are basically so free from diseases that any difficulties along this line will probably be traceable to thoughtless care and feeding.

Start with sound, healthy stock especially chosen for breeding. See that their homes remain warm, dry, and well ventilated. Make sure that all food, expecially the greens, are fresh and sweet and that so much isn't put into the pens that all is not cleaned up. Keep the hutches clean and disinfected and change the bedding frequently. Give your pets reasonable care, in other words, and your efforts will be repaid many times over.

When laboratory guinea pigs develop a rough coat, lack appetite, or lose weight rapidly, a disease is likely the cause. Because many of the symptoms that affect the tribe are similar, even a trained individual may have difficulty in distinguishing one sickness from another. A veterinarian can recommend the best measures to control and eradicate illnesses among these usually stalwart little animals.

Sulfa drugs or antibiotics can be used in treating most infectious diseases of guinea pigs. These drugs should be used as approved by the Food and Drug Administration and only with professional advice so as not to injure the animals.

With some disorders, the best procedure is to dispose of the infected or exposed animals promptly and humanely. Burn the carcasses or bury them deeply. Burn all remaining refuse and disinfect the animals' pens, using one of the disinfectants that contain creosol. These are readily available at most drugstores.

You can do several things to guard against the outbreak of disease. Sanitize both pens and receptacles at least once every two weeks. Wash them with hot, soapy water at 180° and then apply a safe, effective disinfectant. Feed your guinea pigs a balanced diet, guarding against food contamination by mice and rats. Provide fresh drinking water in clean containers daily. Never transfer feed or water containers from one hutch to another. Protect your pets from cold, drafts, and excessive dampness. At temperatures lower than 60° they may get colds and other respiratory diseases such as pneumonia, and the young may be dead at birth or may perish shortly thereafter.

Although it's not likely, if disease ever does break out in your cavy colony, thoroughly sanitize the pens in which the diseased animals have been kept, waiting several weeks before securing fresh stock, and isolate new animals to prevent exposure to potential carriers and to reduce the possibility of introducing disease into a clean colony. All in all, guinea pigs are fundamentally sound and robust animals and you can have fun while making money.

CHAPTER TEN

Successful
Dairy Farming
with Cows and Goats

HOW'S about plenty of your own fresh milk, cream, and butter? Then there's wiener schnitzel, veal scallopini, and alla marsala in season, all from your own cow. What you need is a dairy cow.

A grade cow, well fed and conscientiously attended, produces enough milk to more than pay for her feed even if all food is purchased. She will give 3,000 to 6,000 quarts of milk a year, more than enough for a family of two adults and three children.

If you've ample hay and pasture in your hideaway, that will be all to the good. A comfortable and sanitary cow shelter must also be provided. No doubt, breeding service is offered somewhere in the community. Then, someone in the family must take it upon himself to be on hand every day to feed, water, and milk the new family pet. Even if you've a large family, such a cow will donate an abundance of milk and milk products. And what is more delicious than home-made cheese?

A milk cow will eat as much as twenty to twenty-five pounds of hay a day, three to four tons a year, if no pasture is available where

221

she can graze and luxuriate in the sun. In addition she will need one to two tons of a concentrate grain mix.

The cost of hay varies considerably over the country, but the usual price range is between $20 and $60 a ton. The price of concentrates depends on the protein content and may run from $30 to $80 a ton. Too, from 800 to 1,600 pounds of straw, corn stalks, or such are required for adequate bedding. The average cost of feeding and bedding a cow for a year, therefore, would be $100 to $300, this much only if your land will supply none of the necessities.

If part or all the food can be grown on your little nook, the expense of keeping a cow will be reduced proportionately. Generally, two acres of good land will provide most of the feed, mainly pasture, for six months of the year and cut feed costs in half.

Obtaining A Dairy Cow

It will be wise to select your cow from one of the five principal dairy breeds—Guernsey, Ayrshire, Holstein-Friesian, Brown Swiss, or the reliable Jersey.

Jerseys and Guernseys are often used for family cows because they are smaller and neither require as much food nor give such an over-abundance of milk as some of the larger breeds such as the Holstein-Friesian and Brown Swiss. Moreover, the milk of Jerseys and Guernseys is appreciably higher in butterfat than that of some of the other breeds.

Ayrshire Dairy Cow

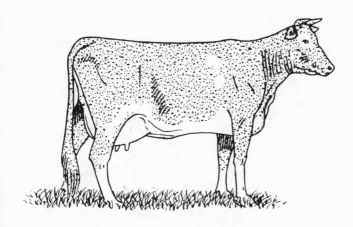

Dairy Cows
Top: Brown Swiss. *Bottom:* Guernsey.

Dairy Cows
Top: Holstein-Friesian. *Bottom:* Jersey.

A cow that is four or five years old and has had her second or third calf is generally a good choice. She will be young enough to have many productive years ahead of her and old enough to have shown her milk-giving ability.

Unless you can use or market a large amount of milk, there is no reason to pay the high price, both in initial cost and in subsequent upkeep, for a heavy milk producer. On the other hand, the cow you select for family use should be healthy and sound, easy to milk, gentle, and free of bad habits.

Examine the cow's udder. It should contain no lumps or hardened tissue, and it should have good-sized teats. A large udder does not necessarily mean high milk production. In fact, avoid large, meaty udders that do not shrink after milking.

See the cow milked by hand or, better still, milk her yourself a few times. Examine the milk for clots, flakes, strings, or blood. To do this, draw several streams of the first milk from each teat on a closely woven black cloth stretched over a cup, or do this into a strip cup designed for the express purpose of examining milk.

Do not buy a cow that kicks or one that wears a yoke, muzzle, or nose-piece. Such devices indicate that the cow has bad habits, such as breaking through fences or self-sucking.

Be sure, too, that the cow you buy is free from tuberculosis, brucellosis, and leptospirosis, especially as these diseases can be transmitted to man. Make sure that the animal has been tested for these diseases by a veterinarian within thirty days of the time you complete the sale.

Summer Feeding

Few things are more satisfying than seeing your own cow contentedly chewing its cud in a field near the kitchen window. If possible, use approximately two acres of land for pasture to provide summer grazing for the new family addition.

Permanent pastures of bluegrass or a mixture of grasses drop in production during the hot months of summer and may have to be supplemented to afford a uniform feed supply. In most of the states across the northern half of the country, alfalfa and ladino clover mixed with grasses such as orchardgrass and brome produce well

WILL IT PAY YOU?

The answer is that it will pay you to keep a cow if the cost of milk, cream, and butter your family needs totals more than 55 cents a day.

If you buy a cow for	$300
And sell her in 5 years for	100
Cost for 5 years is	$200

Cost for 1 year is	$ 40
Interest on $300 costs you	15
Breeding charge is	10
Cow eats 1 ton grain mix	55
And 2 tons hay	80
Uses ½ ton bedding straw	10
Which adds up to	$210
But you sell her calf for	10

So, keeping a cow 1 year costs	$200

. . . . or 55 cents a day

during the summer but have to be reseeded every three to five years.

Sudan grass and crosses of it with sorghum or soybeans make excellent summer pasture in the North. A half-acre of this temporary pasture can be planted next to the permanent pasture. This will not only provide temporary grazing for Bossy, but the excess can be cut and thrown into the permanent pasture for feed.

Be sure never to allow your cow to eat sudan during its early growth or during its regrowth after drought or frost. Sudan grass in the northern states may cause hydrocyanic acid poisoning. Do not graze sudan until it is at least eighteen inches high. Do not cut it for hay until it is a full two feet high. Tall, yellowish green sudan is relatively safe, but short dark green sudan is likely to be dangerous.

In the southern part of the country, coastal Bermuda grass, pearl millet, carpetgrass, Dallis grass, and lespedeza afford good summer pasture, although they do not come in early in the spring. In this region, part of the pasture should be planted in the late summer or early fall to crimson clover or to small grains such as oats, rye, barley, and wheat. This will provide some forage for winter and for late spring.

Your own organic vegetable garden, too, can furnish a little summer feed. Your pet will particularly relish pea vines, sweet cornstalks, sweet potato vines, and crunchy cabbage leaves.

Winter Feeding

The family cow's winter diet consists of hay and a mixture of concentrates. Alfalfa, soybean, alsike clover, or early-cut grass hay are all satisfactory. A Jersey or Guernsey cow will require at least ten pounds of hay a day, plus a pound of grain for every two to four pounds of milk produced.

A mixture of wheat bran and ground corn is a good concentrate to mix with hay. Some soybean oil meal or linseed oil meal may be added to rations of hay and grain for additional protein. Or you may buy a reliable ready-mixed feed made expressly for milk cows. About 30 percent of all concentrates fed to dairy cattle in the United States are commercially mixed. These feeds must comply with laws requiring a statement of minimum and maximum chemical composition and a list of ingredients on the tag.

The best-quality mixtures, it so happens, are generally low in fiber. A high-fiber feed contains some low-energy feeds such as oat hulls, corncobs, cottonseed hulls, or ground hay. Fiber content should not exceed 9 to 10 percent in a high-quality mixture. Fat content should not be less than 2.5 to 4 percent. When you purchase feeds, examine the tags and consider the reliability of the manufacturer.

The proportion of hay and concentrate may be adjusted. How this is done depends on the cost of feeds in your area and upon how much milk your cow is giving. Sixty-four pounds of concentrate furnish approximately as much nourishment as 100 pounds of hay.

Unless you want to take the trouble of adding loose salt to the cow's concentrate, mix at the rate of one pound for every 100 pounds of feed. Also provide a block of trace mineralized salt in a sheltered box for the cow, where she can lick away at it at her leisure.

Water the cow at least twice daily in winter and more often in summer. Best of all, of course, is a stream coursing lazily through your property.

Housing for the Cow

The family cow needs a sunny, comfortable shelter or stable. She may be left untied in a box stall about ten feet square, or she can be confined to a smaller space and held with a stanchion, chain, rope, or strap. A cow has more freedom but requires about three times as much bedding in a box stall than when she is restrained in a smaller space.

If a cow is confined with a stanchion, there should be a manger in front, extending beyond the stall, as well as a gutter behind the cow for the droppings that can be so invaluable in the organic garden. Allow four or five feet of space behind the gutter to make it easy for the cow to get into the stall and to facilitate the periodic removal of manure. If possible, have enough space beside or in front of the manger to permit feeding from the front. This way the forks of hay will not have to be carried wastefully and tantalizing from the rear.

If the cow is held by a stanchion, the sides of the stable should be constructed to prevent drafts in cold weather. This is not so important if she is kept lounging in a box stall. Except in very cold climates, in fact, the box stall can be open on the south if the other three sides are tight. Some sort of arrangement that permits the sun to shine into the box stall in winter adds to the cow's comfort. A stall that is entirely enclosed should be ventilated by a tilting window on the side opposite to the prevailing wintry winds.

Care of the Cow

Always handle a cow gently, slowly, and quietly. See that all fences are well constructed so that the animal does not develop a habit of breaking through, perhaps into the bean patch. A fence made of four barbed wires, tightly stretched and fastened to rugged posts, will keep most cows where they belong.

It's good practice to brush your cow daily. In any event, do not allow manure to cake on her flanks and thighs. Regular grooming is especially important if she is confined in a stall.

Cows are generally milked evenings and mornings. Before you milk, make sure that the udder and flanks are free of dirt that might drop into the milk pail. Wash any soiled parts thoroughly. Always wipe Bossy's udder and flanks with a clean, damp cloth before you milk, and be sure your hands are dry and clean. Use a small-top pail and milk with both hands, drawing the stream with as little discomfort to the cow as possible. Keep your fingernails short. Do not insert milk tubes or straws into the teats.

Consult your neighbors or local Department of Agriculture representative about any breeding service in your area. Artificial insemination will likely be available. Cows are generally bred to calve and freshen at about one-year intervals. It is a good idea for the cow to be dry for a month or six weeks before she calves again. In fact, this results in greater milk production. Cows can be made to grow dry by reducing their feed and gradually discontinuing milking.

Cows ordinarily do not have much difficulty at calving time, but the progress of labor should be checked frequently. If difficult labor is prolonged for several hours, a veterinarian should be summoned. In cold weather the cow needs a warm stall and plenty of bedding at calving time.

You may want to sell the calf, raise it for your own blanquette of veal and other table delectables, or keep a heifer calf for future extra milk. Newly born calves for the dairy breeds bring $10 to $30, the amount depending on their size and the current market. At two to three months, a fattened calf should bring considerably more. If your family does not need all the milk the fresh cow produces, the surplus can be fed to the calf.

Sanitary Milk Production

As soon as the milk is drawn, strain it through a clean cloth. Single-use strainer fabrics are best. If cloths are to be reused, wash and boil them after each employment.

The safest procedure then, although certainly not the tastiest, is to pasteurize all raw milk by heating it to 142° and holding it at that temperature for half an hour, or by warming it to 161° for fifteen seconds. Small electric home pasteurizers, which will make these exacting tasks a lot easier, cost about $40.

Once the milk is pasteurized, cool it as rapidly as possible to 50° or lower. Keep it in the refrigerator until you are ready to use it. Whole milk not needed for immediate use may be held for butter-making. Keep such milk in a deep container until the rich thick cream rises to the top. After about twenty-four hours, skim off this cream for churning. The remaining skim milk can be used on the table, in cooking, or for making your own delicious cottage cheese.

Rinse all milk utensils in cold water immediately after use. Then as soon as possible, wash them in hot water containing a dairy washing powder or detergent. Scrub with a brush. Finally, rinse the utensils with hot water, then scald them with boiling water.

Keep the sanitized utensils uncovered in a clean, airy place. Milk pail and other utensils should be seamless so there will be no crevices in which the milk can lodge.

Your Own Homemade Butter

High-quality butter can be intriguingly and satisfyingly made at home from sweet cream. Slightly sour cream can be used, too, but butter made from cream that has turned too much has a strong flavor and does not keep well, to boot. You'll likely wish to save the cream skimmings for three or four days before churning, though.

Churning uses mechanical means to pound, beat, or dash the cream until the minute globules of butterfat in the liquid stick together and form butter granules. You may have noticed the same thing happening to a lesser extent when you've hiked over a long distance, carrying a canteen of milk at your hip.

Probably the best kind of churn for making small quantities of butter is a one-gallon glass churn equipped with wooden paddles. Fill the churn only one-third to one-half full. Churning incorporates air into the cream and uses it to increase the volume. After you have churned for about half an hour, butter granules should form. If this seems too arduous, use an electric blender.

Butter granules form best when the cream is at a temperature of

54° to 58° in the summer and 58° to 64° in winter. Stop churning when the butter granules are about the size of corn kernels. At this time remove the bits of butter from the buttermilk, a delight in itself, and wash them with water that is about the temperature of the buttermilk or a little cooler.

Drain off the water, add salt if you want at the rate of one level tablespoon to each pound of butter, then work the butter with a paddle until the salt is evenly distributed and the remainder of the buttermilk extracted. There's a unique satisfaction to all this, difficult to appreciate until you've experienced it yourself.

DAIRY GOATS

There's another way around. The small family in particular may find it more convenient and economical to milk one or two goats than either to buy milk or to keep a dairy cow. Furthermore, goat milk can often be tolerated by infants and invalids who are allergic to other milk.

The rest of the story is that a good dairy goat produces at least two quarts of milk daily for eight to ten months of the year and can be fed for about one-sixth of the cost of feeding a cow.

A dairy goat costs $35 to $75, the amount depending largely on her breed and production record. Be sure, of course, that any goats you purchase are from a tuberculosis-free and brucellosis-free herd.

Food for Goats

Feed your milk-producing goat all the clover, alfalfa, or mixed hay she will eat, plus any root crops that are available from your garden such as carrots, turnips, beets, and parsnips. Good-quality silage can be substituted for root crops if you want.

If a goat giving milk is not on pasture, an excellent winter ration will be two pounds of good alfalfa or clover hay and one and one-half pounds of root crops or silage, plus a pound or two of concentrate. Mixtures of the latter should consist of oats, bran, and linseed oil or other protein supplement. Goats on pasture, maybe before your dining room windows, need slightly less grain or concentrate.

Pregnant does in fall or early winter should be fed all the roughage they will devour, along with a pound of root crops or silage and one-half to one pound of the same grain mixture fed to goats in milk.

However, any strongly flavored rations such as turnips and silage will be best fed after milking so that the milk will not be affected by off-flavors.

Keep rock salt before the goats at all times and occasionally, too, mix a small quantity of fine salt with the grain mixture. No other minerals are necessary if legume hay is used. If nonlegume hay is fed, though, calcium and phosphorus supplements will be needed. See that your goats have access to plenty of fresh water at all times.

Goat Care

Goats do not need any special kind of housing, but they should have a sanctuary where they'll be protected from rain, snow, and cold. They are natural climbers and, unless tethered, will climb on low buildings and anything else available.

Cleanliness is essential in handling and feeding dairy goats. Does kept in sanitary surroundings do not have objectionable odors. Bucks, the main offenders in this respect, need not be kept if satisfactory breeding service of some sort is available in your area.

How to Milk Goats

A milking stand built with a stanchion at one end and a seat for the milker at one side, as illustrated, is a real convenience when it comes to milking a goat. You can easily construct such a stand at little cost if you are at all handy with tools.

Young does often object at first to being milked, and a stanchion and stand help confine them. A bit of grain in the feedbox attached to the stanchion helps quiet them. Then after a young goat is milked a few times in such a stand, she becomes accustomed to the procedure and will generally leap on the stand and put her head in the stanchion without assistance.

Heavily producing does may need to be milked three times a day for a short time after freshening, but twice-a-day milking is generally enough for grade does.

Breeding Periods

Does come in heat regularly between September and January. Once this time has passed, they cannot usually be bred again until

Stand for Milking Goats.

late in August. They stay in heat one or two days. The period between heats is ordinarily about three weeks. Gestation averages 149
days, about five months. Does usually give birth to two kids. Occasionally, though, they may have three or even four offspring at one
kidding, all sources of additional revenue.

If you need the milk and your land produces only limited green
feed, you will probably want to sell the kids. The youngsters are not
hard to raise, however. They can be fed goat's or cow's milk in a
bottle, if you want, until they learn to drink from a pan, trough, or
pail.

A good goat will give rich, nourishing milk for eight to ten months
after freshening. One that produces milk for less than six months
should not be kept.

CHAPTER ELEVEN

Fish, Frogs, and Turtles for Profit, Food, and Fun

"THERE is certainly something in angling," noted Washington Irving, "that tends to produce a gentleness of spirit and a pure serenity of mind."

How would you like to do your angling in your own pond, besides letting others cast there for a price and still selling the excess trophies at a profit? Then perhaps fish farming is your thing.

"Ponds can be the biggest thing in Illinois fishing," says A. C. Lopincot, Chief Fishery Biologist for that state. "By themselves, they may not look like much. But counted in the tens of thousands, these little lakes add up to a lot of water and a lot of fishing. A few years ago in 1965 there were 62,627 ponds in Illinois (38,455 acres of water), and about 1,200 new ponds are being built each year. The majority of them are not managed for fishing. They would be—if their owners knew what they were missing."

Wise fishermen in every state covet good ponds, for they mean close-to-home action with scrappy trout, big bass, and strings of fat, fighting bluegills. At a time when good fishing is so highly prized and sportsmen want convenience and privacy, a good private pond is the answer to many a fisherman's prayer. Whether that angler is a freckled kid or a crusty old cutthroat specialist, the pond means magnificent sport. And as Stephen Leacock once noted, "Every man, deep down, is a fisherman."

But good fishing doesn't just happen. It's more than building a dam, waiting for rain, stocking some fish, and living happily ever after. Fish are a crop, and a pond must be managed and cultivated to provide good harvests. There are many fish you can raise, but let's concentrate on the universally popular trout.

Why trout? Well, try rubbing salt and freshly ground black pepper into your freshly caught catch. Then dip the steaks, fillets, or cleaned small trout for a moment into evaporated milk. Next, dust bread crumbs over them and fry them in a liberal amount of butter, just hot enough so that it is beginning to color.

Turn only once, as soon as the first side is brown. The total time depends on thickness. Test with a fork or toothpick. As soon as the trout is easily flaked, it is done. Remove at once to hot plates or a warm platter. Squeeze the juice of a lemon into the pan, add some chopped watercress, stir about a bit, and you'll almost instantly have a noble sauce to turn over the trout as you enjoy it sizzling from the fire.

Trout farming is the business of producing and selling high-quality trout or trout eggs. Many farmers and ranchers, for instance, are increasing their income by raising trout and providing related outdoor recreation services. For some, trout farming is a sideline. For others, it is the main source of income.

A trout-farming enterprise can consist of one or more of four kinds of commercial fish culture. These are:

1. Running a fishing pond for the public. Eight-inch and larger trout are stocked in a pond and fished by anglers for a fee. Some operators lease fishing privileges on an annual basis.

2. Raising small trout, fingerlings, to fish of market size. Fingerlings are grown in raceways until they are some eight to fourteen inches long. Raceways generally are narrow, rectangular structures 80 to 100 feet long with flowing water two to three feet deep. Production ponds of other shapes have also been successful.

One raceway usually spills into another in a series of two or more stairlike structures. The raceways can be excavated waterways, or they can be built of concrete or concrete blocks. Each must have water-control structures, preferably of concrete. Raceways and ponds fed by cold springs or cold-water wells may be suitable for trout farming at any elevation or in any latitude.

Trout in the raceways are raised on a prepared diet of dry pelleted feed. It takes about two pounds of food to produce a one-pound trout at water temperatures of 50° to 70°. If raised in water colder than 50°, trout take two or more years to reach market size. In water warmer than 70°, they grow slowly and are more subject to diseases.

3. Producing fingerling-size trout. Eyed eggs are held until hatched in special trays of running water. Several days after hatching the small fish, called "fry," are transferred to rearing ponds or raceways where they grow to fingerling size—one to six inches.

4. Producing eyed eggs. This requires rearing and holding adult trout in special ponds until the spawning season. The eggs are then stripped from the females and fertilized. These eggs are called eyed eggs once the eyes of the embryonic trout become visible, usually within two or three weeks after fertilization.

Income Sources of a Trout Farm

Income from your trout farm may come from one or more of the following sources:

1. Operating a fish-out pond. People come to your pond to angle. They pay for their catch by the inch or pound, whichever you say. You restock as needed to provide continued successful fishing. Then there's the area around the water, which can be used commercially for picnicking, birdwatching, camping, or even as a quiet and attractive trailer park.

2. Selling fry, fingerlings, or larger live fish for stocking trout farms, private ponds, or other waters.

3. Selling freshly dressed fish to local markets, hotels, and restaurants. In a large-scale operation, dressed fish are generally freeze-packed, but trout from smaller farms may be sold to larger

Trout Raceways

238 . . . *One Acre and Security*

operators for packaging, advertising, and marketing. Incidentally, the commercial processing of fish is closely regulated by local and federal laws, and the market often demands fish of a specific size.

4. Selling eyed eggs. Many farmers and private pond owners start the season's production with fertile eggs purchased from a commercial fish breeder. Today fish eggs can be air-shipped in special containers to almost any part of the continent.

Suitable Water

Most commercial trout farms use raceways that have a reliable, year-around flow of high-quality water from springs, wells, or streams.

Before starting anything, it is wise to study your water source diligently. The following standards must be met for a successful enterprise:

Temperature. Water between 50° and 60° is ideal for best growth and most satisfactory economic returns. Water between 46° and 55° is the most suitable for hatching trout eggs.

Oxygen. The water must have at least five parts per million of dissolved oxygen. Seven parts per million is the minimum where eggs are to be hatched.

Hardness. Hard water, 50 to 250 parts or more per million of dissolved solids, produces trout more economically than soft water. Management problems are fewer, too.

All in all, the number of trout you will be able to raise each year will be determined by the volume and quality of the water flowing through your raceways. Annual production from a well-managed trout fishery having high-quality water is about 10,000 pounds for each cubic foot of water per second. This means 450 gallons per minute of water flow in a temperature range of 50° to 65°. Therefore, a flow of good water at 5 cubic feet a second, which adds up to 2,250 gallons per minute, should bring you as much as 50,000 pounds of trout a year.

These estimates are based on government-accumulated data from established trout farms where raceways are designed for at least one complete exchange of water per hour. You could raise trout with less than one exchange per hour, but generally production would be lower and the possibility of disease greater.

Suitable Land

Select a site that has a slope of 1 to 3 percent if you want to keep raceway costs at a minimum. Make certain, too, that the soil at the site of an excavated runway or pond will hold water. If you plan to use concrete or concrete-block raceways, the land must also be safe for such construction.

Researching the Market

Marketing trout is highly competitive in some areas. At the outside, you might consider associating with other trout raisers in a cooperative marketing venture beneficial to all. The U.S. Department of Agriculture, either in Washington, D.C., or through its numerous local branches, stands ready to help you with your project. Too, here are some questions whose answers will help in reaching a decision.

Cities and towns are an important source of customers for public fishing ponds. Are you within reasonable driving distance of cities of 25,000 or more people? Or are you near heavily traveled tourist routes or major recreation areas? In this connection, is your land also adaptable to other kinds of outdoor recreation that would be profitable for you to develop?

Can you meet the competition from public fishing waters or other fish-out ponds in your region? As a matter of fact, what is the possibility of leasing your fish-out pond and any other recreational facilities to an organized group? Are there good roads to your pond? Is your pond in an attractive and natural setting?

Too, is there a local demand for live trout in stocking other fish-out ponds or private bodies of water? Is there a local or regional market for fry or fingerlings? Can you make an arrangement with the state fish and game department for the production of fish or roe? Is there a regional market for eyed eggs? Are there local markets, hotels and motels, or restaurants that might be enthusiastic at the opportunity of obtaining sleek, fresh trout from you?

Cost and Profit

To determine the cost of producing trout, first figure the cost of any permanent buildings and other facilities amortized for the estimated life of the structures at an appropriate interest rate.

Then add the annual expense of operating and maintaining your fishery. The total is the annual operating cost. If you want, you can divide it by the pounds of fish you raise to give you the cost per pound of producing trout.

Here is an example of estimated production costs figured by this method. Of course, you can hold down expenses to a considerable degree by doing most of the work yourself.

Let's assume that the estimated cost of constructing a small hatchery and storage shed, along with three earthen raceways, is $3,600.

With a flow of one cubic foot per second, 450 gallons per minute, of good water from a natural spring, the annual production capacity of this fishery would be about 30,000 ten-inch trout weighing 10,000 pounds.

The $3,600 initial cost, amortized over a twenty-year period at 6 percent, breaks down into an annual amortization cost of nearly $314. Add to this an estimated $3,150 cost of eyed eggs, fish food, labor, insurance, taxes, license, advertising, utilities, and other annual operations and maintenance items.

Amortized initial cost	$ 314.00
Annual operation and maintenance	3,150.00
Total estimated annual cost	$3,464.00

This figure divided by 10,000, the pounds of trout, gives a rough production cost of $.35 per pound of trout. Now profit is determined by subtracting operating costs from gross sales. Of course, all these figures are hypothetical.

Cost of Operating a Fish-out Pond

Production costs, 10,000 pounds at $.35 per pound	$3,500.00
Cost of fish-out pond operation	2,000.00
Total production and operation costs	$5,500.00

At a fee of $1.25 a pound, you can see that 4,400 pounds of fish must be caught to cover all costs. Poundage hooked in excess of this amount would be profit.

It is unlikely that all trout can be taken from the pond by a hook and line. Uncaught fish can be removed by other means, however, and sold to fishermen or local markets.

Saying you received $.45 per pound from a frozen-pack processor, you'd have to sell 7,777 pounds to recover your production costs of $3,500.

If you sold your excess fish instead to fresh-fish stores and restaurants, processing and marketing costs would raise the estimated production costs to, say, $.50 per pound. Then your cost for that same 10,000 pounds of trout would be $5,000. Say dressed trout are bringing $.80 per pound in your locality. Inasmuch as trout dress out about 80 percent of their live weight, then about 6,250 pounds of dressed fish would have to be marketed to cover costs. The rest would be profit.

All these estimates are based on trout production from a water flow of one cubic foot per second; that is, 450 gallons a minute. With a greater volume of water plus efficient management, it should be possible to produce trout at less expense and greater profit. Numerous small trout farms are profitably operated with flows of less than one cubic foot per second.

Then there's the matter of selling eyed eggs and fingerlings. Eyed trout eggs have been selling for $3 to $5 dollars per thousand, about twice the average cost of production. The retail value of fingerling trout has been ranging from $35 per thousand for two-inch fish to $250 and more for seven-inch fish. The margin of profit here depends on your efficiency in operating the hatchery and raceway.

Places to Get Help

It's a good idea to seek the advice of trout-farming organizations and to visit fish farmers and state or federal fish hatcheries in your area. Too, get in touch with the state or provincial fish and game department regarding any license requirements.

You can also apply to the cooperative U.S. Department of Agriculture for assistance in planning, constructing, and even financing your trout-farming enterprise and any proposed recreation developments.

Working through their Soil Conservation Service, the Department of Agriculture can help: (1) check the suitability of your water for fish production or recreation use, (2) design your hatchery, fishways, fish-out pond, and water-control system, (3) locate sites and prepare a layout for your outdoor recreation developments, and (4) develop an operation and management plan for your trout fishery.

For identifying market possibilities and providing yourself with information on fishery management, get in touch with the local representative of the Department of Agriculture's Federal Extension Service.

Then there are the finance and management plans for your recreation enterprise. Too, you may choose to arrange a loan to buy and develop land, construct buildings and facilities, and pay operating expenses for outdoor recreation enterprises including that public fishing pool. The local representative of the Department of Agriculture's Farmers Home Administration will help you in all these.

RAISING FROGS FOR THE GOURMET MARKET

The flavor and texture of frog legs are not unlike that of white chicken meat, although their taste is even more delicate. The smaller the frogs, the tenderer and sweeter they are. Strip the skin off like a glove. Practically all the meat worth eating, you'll then see, is on the hind legs. Like fish, frog legs are at their tastiest when fresh or when frozen fresh—a good reason for adding frog raising to your other activities, if only for home consumption.

For sautéing, they may first be rolled in lightly salted and peppered flour, cracker crumbs, or bread crumbs, perhaps after being initially dipped in cream. If you prefer a crusty coating, immerse them between rollings in egg beaten with a tablespoon of cold water.

Sauté in a liberal amount of butter or olive oil for about ten minutes or until the tender golden brown meat comes away from the bone.

You can often find a little watercress close by whose nippiness will help bring out the flavor. Tartar sauce and French-fried potatoes are the easiest accompaniments. Sautéed mushrooms also are excellent. Or you may prefer to sprinkle the sizzling delicacies with freshly chopped parsley and bring them out on hot toast along with lemon wedges. On any occasion they provide a worthy adjunct to even the most sumptuous of feasts without attempting to efface the deliciousness of the salad or soup.

Grilled Frog Legs

Frogs, believed to be the first animals to crawl out of water and live on land, still furnish some of the best food found in either domain. The odor of grilled frog legs will make any patio an even more pleasant spot. Dip the tidbits in cream if you'd like to try another of my *Gourmet Cooking for Free* recipes, then in fine cracker crumbs, and broil over open coals for ten minutes or until tender, turning occasionally and brushing with melted butter.

In the meantime, probably in the kitchen, sauté proportionately, depending on how large an amount of sauce you'll be needing, a small chopped onion in 1½ tablespoons of butter until limp but not brown. Then, stirring constantly, add a teaspoon of flour and cook two minutes more. Add a cup of sour cream and a tablespoon of fresh lemon juice. Stirring occasionally, simmer for ten minutes. Run through a fine sieve, salt and pepper to taste, dust with paprika, and pour over the still sputtering frog legs.

Breeders and Breeding Ponds

Besides being a year-around source of table delicacies, frog raising is fun, easy, and occasionally profitable. All you need are a few pairs of breeders, a properly arranged pond or two, and you're in business on a spare-time basis. Most conservatively, it will just be a hobby, with occasional banquets for yourself and your friends. Restaurants, high school and college laboratories, markets, pet stores, and of course individuals do buy frogs, though. The demand is nationwide, and the crops multiply quickly.

Even the giant bullfrog is clean and perfectly harmless, having neither teeth nor claws. Under favorable conditions, a pair of breeders can spawn up to 10,000 eggs and more a year, with 90 percent hatch. It is common for an encouraging proportion of such hatches to reach table size within a year or a year and a half. One way to tell males and females apart if you want to reserve as many as possible of the latter? The male has a greatly larger ear circle behind its eyes. Too, when fully grown the female is generally larger.

If there are already several small ponds on your property, you're all set. In building new ponds, the breeder pond should be separate from the tadpole pond and the growing waters. A 24-by-30-foot enclosure will take care of up to ten pairs of breeders, with about one-third water and the rest bank. You'll need a 40-by-100-foot pen, also one-third water and two-thirds bank, to accommodate fifty pairs of breeders.

Most of the so-called frog farms are simply natural marshy areas or ponds with food and environment suited to the needs of frogs. In such areas the frogs, left to themselves, will thrive and multiply. A pond or swampy area, for instance, may be stocked with adult frogs or with eggs.

In stocking with adults, better results can be obtained by introducing the frogs in late summer and fall to let them become accustomed to their new surroundings before the egg-laying season— April in the South and May and June farther north. In California, some species begin breeding in January and February. Smaller types might be hatched to serve as food for the larger edible varieties, but the cannibalistic habit which this suggests dictates a segregation of commercial species according to size to prevent their devouring one another.

Rice fields, incidentally, are suited to frog farming and, in fact, the raising of both frogs and muskrats can sometimes be combined to advantage. In any area designed for frog production, however, predaceous animals and fish such as snapping turtles, bass, pike, pickerel, cats, foxes, snails, and other enemies should be excluded. Encouragement, on the other hand, should be given minnows, crayfish, waterbugs, and of course smaller species of frogs. When adult, a big frog will snap at anything from an insect to a three-inch fish or a young turtle.

It's a fascinating business. The breeders ordinarily spawn in the spring or early summer. At that time the jellylike eggs are easily gathered and placed either in hatching tanks or in the tadpole pond. The hatching only takes from three days to a week.

Tadpole and Growing Ponds

For the tadpole pond, a 40-by-100 foot fenced space with a seven-foot bank will accommodate many thousands of tadpoles. The growing pond, if possible, should be as much as four times larger.

When the tadpoles go through their engrossing conversion to tiny bullfrogs, they should be transferred to a growing pond. This can be built in the form of a canal. All ponds should be approximately three to four feet in depth, depending upon how cold the winters become in your locality. The ponds should be deep enough so that they won't freeze all the way to the bottom, which, incidentally, should afford some six inches of mud for hibernating purposes.

Fencing for Frog Ponds

An ideal fence around your ponds, which should be dug on a slope from water level to whatever depth you decide upon for the center, can be made from new or used corrugated metal such as that used for roofing. The fence should be embedded from eighteen inches to two feet in the ground, and rise four feet or more above the surface. A second choice for fencing would be metal lying lengthwise along the ground, with eight inches embedded and sixteen inches exposed, above which poultry wire with a one-inch mesh should rise at least four feet.

To protect the frogs further, do not have any plants in the ponds that are sharp, bristly, or pointed. An excellent bank cover is clover, which both grows tall enough to afford shade and helps to keep out other weeds. As a bonus, clover is also edible.

Food for Frogs and Tadpoles

Stock your growing ponds with crayfish, which, besides being table delicacies in their own right, provide excellent frog food, in a short time affording a continuous supply of this. Minnows, worms, insects, and small frogs are also good foods for your future supplies of frog legs.

As for tadpoles, they thrive on natural pond growth. Tadpoles, which need very little feed, can be overfed more easily than they can be underfed. However, there are plant foods that can be placed in the ponds, including wild celery, arrowhead, water lilies, water lettuce, muskgrass, and the like. Algae, which forms naturally in ponds, is a very good tadpole food. So are cleanly washed potato peelings, carrots, lettuce, and such. Tadpoles need not be fed anything for four or five days after hatching. Then for the first few days thereafter, they will thrive on pieces of unsalted boiled potatoes and whole pieces of bread.

The baby frogs become robust and plump on insects, worms, flies, and their own larva. A handy tip? Place some wire baskets about either water or ground, on stakes reaching a foot above the surface. Meat scraps dropped into these will attract flies and insects. You might also spot a few electric lights just above the bank or water. These will draw many insects in the darkness for the hungry frogs to catch.

Frog Suppliers

You'll find the names and addresses of frog farms in classified ads in the outdoor magazines. One big supplier of both breeders and tadpoles is Leonard Slabaugh, Slabaugh Frog Farm, Route 3, Poplar Bluff, Missouri 63901. Jumbo bullfrogs are shipped by railway or air express in wooden crates, generally from April through September, along with full instructions.

RAISING TURTLES TO GUARD THE GARDEN

Want some extra help in your garden and for free? Turtles dine on cutworms, slugs, grubs, and insects, which they devour in quantity. What they eat in the way of outer lettuce leaf, some berries and beans, and the occasional fallen apple is negligible, particularly when you leave odds and ends of vegetables and perhaps a juicy melon rind in their paths.

Be sure to build a fence to keep the turtles where they'll be doing you all this good, as they are inveterate travelers except at the onset of cold weather, when you may see them digging into the compost pile to hibernate for the winter. When growing weather arrives again, though, out they'll waddle, ravenous to get back to their diet of bugs and grubs.

A fertile female will lay ten to a dozen soft-shelled eggs in late spring, excavating a shallow hole in some protected spot where the earth is soft and letting the dirt trickle back over the clutch to hide them when she's done. The youngsters, about the size of quarters depending on the breed, will soon take off in every direction through the apertures of any ordinary fence, unless you make special provisions for them. All in all, turtles are true allies of the organic gardener, besides being fun.

Quarters for Land Turtles

In addition to all their other attributes, turtles make interesting pets and usually become quite tame in captivity. They may be taught to take food from your fingers. If you'd like a cage for one, at least until it becomes used to the surroundings, this should be large enough for the turtle to move about in. A box or terrarium two feet long, a foot wide, and a foot and a half high will be satisfactory for a single turtle of average adult size.

A water pan large enough for the land turtle to get into, and sufficiently deep for it to submerge its bright-eyed head, is sufficient. Inasmuch as turtles spend most of their time on land, this should form a major part of the pen. Turtles are not good swimmers and would drown in an aquatic tank. They sometimes climb, so it will be well to have a screen atop the enclosure.

Quarters for Water Turtles

Water turtles, on the other hand, should be kept in an aquarium in which there is enough space for them to swim. Turtles such as Troost's and the Map particularly need large swimming quarters. Provide a rock or ramp on which they can rest, an area that should be entirely dry. A tank of the same dimensions as noted above will provide enough space for the painted, musk, and spotted turtle. Small specimens of all turtles can be kept in smaller quarters until their size indicates a change of cage is necessary.

Your pet will winter under the same conditions that are prevalent in summer, provided you do not allow the cage or water temperature to drop. It is not necessary for the reptile to hibernate under these conditions. Hibernation in close captivity is a delicate process and may result in the loss of your pet.

Best Temperature for Turtles

Heating should be constant at a warm 75° or 80°. When changing water, make sure that the temperature of the fresh water is the same as that of the water it is replacing. Keep the cage clean and the water fresh, always cleaning after each feeding, which should be three times a week. Keep your pet out of drafts, as turtles, too, are subject to cold. A symptom of this? Eyelids that are stuck together.

Turtle Diets

Aquatic turtles fed in water may have chopped fish and meat, whole small fish, and some lettuce. Land turtles provisioned on land do well on mixtures of chopped lettuce, carrots, apple, banana, celery, and meat. Soft-shelled and snapping turtles live on fish and meat. Both aquatic and land turtles will eat Blanding's turtle.

Incidentally, snapping turtles are capable of inflicting dangerous wounds, and they have bad dispositions to boot. Soft-shelled and musk turtles are also inclined to be vicious and to bite readily. These three turtles, therefore, are not recommended as pets for youngsters. But there are lots who are.

RAISING MEALWORMS FOR FISH AND PET FOOD

Worms, trout, frogs, and turtles go side by side. Besides, raising mealworms, *Tenebrio molitor,* is an interesting, easy, and economical means of keeping a supply of insect food for the fish and such you're keeping for pleasure or profit. The size of the mealworm colony may be dependent upon your daily needs. Once a successful culture has been started, program of enlargement is mainly a matter of space.

The mealworms you need to start with are generally obtainable from pet stores, bait dealers, or biological supply houses. If you're stuck for a supplier, write *All-Pets Magazine,* Fond du Lac, Wisconsin for names and addresses. In fact, you can even become a supplier yourself. Business chances abound all over.

Your eventual culture container may be of any length and width. The only requirement is that the inside depth should be at least four inches. For instance, the container may be made of tight wooden boxes, metal pans, unused or defective metal cans, or even large old-fashioned pickling or storage crocks. Whatever container is used, a preferably hinged, tightly fitting, escape-proof cover should be added.

Fill your culture container at least three inches deep with bran, easily obtainable at any feed store where poultry and stock foods are sold. Over the bran lay a single thickness of burlap large enough to cover the grain completely. Next, distribute your starting culture of mealworms on the burlap.

This culture may consist of any or all stages of the life cycle of the versatile insect: the adult beetle, the whitish cocoonlike stage which is the pupa, or the larva itself—brown to white, segmented, caterpillarlike, and no doubt a tasty creature with six legs at the front of the body. Inasmuch as adult beetles may have already laid their eggs, the initial stage of the prolific life cycle, it is safest to start with pupae or larvae.

On top of the culture, place another single thickness of burlap of the same dimensions as the first piece. You have now built up a four-layer arrangement consisting of bran on the bottom, a single thickness of burlap, the culture of mealworms, and finally another single thickness of burlap.

Care is easy. Mealworm cultures are fed by placing lettuce, thinly sliced Irish potatoes and carrots, and a few bits of boiled meat between the layers of burlap. Even then, the cultures are fed only when the beetles are adult or in the larval stage.

Care should be taken to make sure the colony is rationed sparingly. Too much food will rot and eventually destroy the culture. However, the vegetables, even after they are dried and shriveled, should never be taken out of the culture because this is where the adults lay their eggs. The top layer of burlap should be sprinkled very lightly with water, never soaked, twice a week.

Mealworms are best kept in a basement or other dark space with a reasonably constant temperature, preferably between 70° and 80°. The culture should never be allowed to ferment, sour, or mold. Sourness and mildew are caused most frequently by the application of too much water, keeping the culture where there is excessive humidity, or overfeeding. If you follow the few preceeding suggestions, you shouldn't have any trouble.

CHAPTER TWELVE

Groceries and Fine Wine from Grapes and Other Fruit

AMONG the deep-down satisfactions of living on the land are the pleasure of watching your own crops grow and the confident, self-reliant feeling that comes from providing not only the necessities, but also some of the amenities of life, for yourself and your family. Growing your own grapes and making your own wine from them can supply both of these satisfactions, especially since the climate throughout heavily inhabited North America is suitable for domestic grape culture.

Home winemaking is more an art than a matter of precise chemistry, although you'll have more margin for error if you measure and sift exactly. Yet natural yeasts and sugars vary, and there is always some difference in taste. Results, therefore, can be delightfully diverse. As with any art, if you get the basics right, it's difficult to go wrong.

With today's storage facilities you need not make your wines only at the harvest season. In fact, you needn't even use fresh products, especially if you are just getting started and don't want to wait until the dandelions have blossomed or the elderberries are

ripe. The wine supply houses that, increasing in number every
month, are scattered throughout the continent handle a number of
fruit concentrates that will turn out fine wines at only dimes more
in cost than those concocted from fresh wares and, provocatively
with half the work.

Winemaking as a whole is not only one of the most rewarding
hobbies, particularly if you have the gourmet's inquiring tastes,
but it's one of life's least expensive pursuits. Everyday kitchen
equipment—preferably glass or enamelware rather than bare aluminum or stainless steel—along with some jugs, will do the job. If
you like the results, that's the time to buy the extras that will add
to the assured results as well as the atmosphere of the whole under-
taking.

Perhaps you already have an accumulation of store jugs that
seemed too good to throw away. Too, most soda fountains will furnish gallon jugs for the quarter or so deposit, while the local supplier of spring or distilled water can sell you gleaming five-gallon
carboys for less than you'd expect to spend.

Free Winemaking Permits

"Any registered head of a family may produce, without payment
of tax, not more than 200 gallons of wine a year for family
use," Rex D. Davis, Acting Director of the U.S. Alcohol,
Tobacco, and Firearms Division, assured me. "This exemption extends to any person, regardless of sex or marital status, who is the
head of a family. For this purpose, a family consists of a group of
persons related to each other by blood, marriage, or adoption, who
are living together under one head."

Hard cider? "Cider or apple juice may be allowed to ferment by
itself and thereby become alcoholic. You don't need a permit to
do this; however, you can not help it in any way. The adding of
yeast, sugar, or any other material, or the treating of the cider by
adding preservatives or by pasteurizing, etc., changes the classification to apple wine, and you are restricted by law as to its production."

May you make beer, home brew, whisky, or just plain alcohol in
your home for your own personal use and not for sale? "No. The

Utensils and Jugs for Winemaking

law prohibits the production of other alcoholic beverages in or around the home or any other dwelling area and imposes severe penalties for such violations. These alcohol beverages may be made only by persons and on premises duly qualified under the law and on premises duly qualified under the law and regulations."

To apply for your winemaking permit, write:

Region	Assistant Regional Commissioner Alcohol and Tobacco Tax Internal Revenue Service
Central	6503 Federal Office Bldg. 550 Main Street Cincinnati, Ohio 45202
Mid-Atlantic	2 Penn Central Plaza Philadelphia, Pa. 19102
Midwest	35 East Wacker Drive Chicago, Ill. 60601
North-Atlantic	90 Church Street New York, N.Y. 10007
Southeast	Federal Office Bldg. 275 Peachtree Street N.E. Atlanta, Ga. 30303
Southwest	1114 Commerce Street Dallas, Tex. 75202
Western	Flood Bldg. 870 Market Street San Francisco, Calif. 94102

In Canada the making of wine by an individual is under provincial jurisdiction. The limit here is 100 gallons subject to authorization by the province's Liquor License Board. Interestingly, according to the Department of Customs and Excise, Excise Duty Division, any resident of Canada can make beer provided he first obtains a letter of consent from the Department to make beer at home. There is then no limit on the amount he can brew for his own consumption.

Growing Range and Climatic Requirements of Grapes

Wine, in the ordinary sense of the word, is a fermented beverage produced from grapes alone. Wine all started with wild grapes, and at least half the world's supply of these are native to this country, some two dozen or so species being widely distributed over the United States. One of the survival foods of the Lewis and Clark expedition and long an Indian mainstay throughout much of the continent, these include the large fox grape, the aromatic muscadine, the pleasant pigeon grape, and the notable scuppernong. They are the parents of more than a thousand domesticated varieties which now thrive in every state and in southern Canada, which, indeed, comprise one vast vineyard.

Favoring moist, fertile ground, the wild members of this beneficent family still twine toward sunlight along streambanks, beaches, fences, stone walls, and near the edges of woods. Birds find their dense foliage excellent sanctuary and even use the bark for some of their nests. Incidentally, fruit, leaves, and young shoots are all edible.

Everywhere these wild varieties grow in the woods and fields, the climate is suitable for domestic grape culture. Although temperatures approaching 20° below zero are as low as the unprotected grapes can withstand, such procedure as wrapping the vines or flattening and burying them enable domestic strains to survive where not even apples can bear the winter winds.

Two or three years after grapevines are planted they come into their own, bearing juicy crops. If they are given reasonably careful care, this cycle will go on during your whole lifetime and probably that of your children as well. The vines are particularly adaptable and will be at home on trelisses, the familiar grape arbors, stakes, fences, verandas, and even the sides of homes and garages.

Depending, of course, on the climate, if you select the proper varieties, you can enjoy the sweetly bursting tang of grapes from midsummer to early winter.

The hardy fruit will grow almost anywhere. Optimum summer weather is on the cool, rather dry side, with frequent breezes stirring the air, one reason why California is so successful with its vineyards. The most likely place for your home vineyard is on a sunny, southern slope near the sea, a lake, or other climate-influencing body of water. It is true that even in the most favorable areas the odd crop is spoiled by early fall and late spring frosts. Yet even in localities that have brief seasons you can select strains that blossom late and mature early.

Soil, after climate, is the next most important consideration for your vineyard. Gravelly and stony ground becomes radiant in sunlight, throwing up gentle bottom warmth which adds flavor and aroma to the grapes. On the other hand, moist ground does not produce good grapes, although such sturdy varieties as the Delaware, Niagara, and the universally favored Concord abound in soil too poor to sustain other species.

Cultivating Your Own Grapevines

Your grapevine may produce for half a century in one spot. For this reason, you'll probably want to make the soil as ready as possible before planting. Humus, for example, must be present. To assure this, compost or just plain horse manure should either be worked into the ground, or some such crop as rye or clover should be sown the year before and then turned under in autumn. Rake the ground in the spring, and you're in business.

Pruning, incidentally, starts the first fall after the leaves have fallen. Then most of the initial summer's growth is lopped off, leaving only the more robust canes, these cut back to two or three buds. Such pruning should not be carried out until just before winter. Once it has been completed, the ground is mounded around the grapevines for cold-weather protection. Then in early spring the canes are tied to wires or trelisses with string or raffia. The new shoots are similarly supported midway through the summer.

Grapes are less in need of care and fertilizer than any other

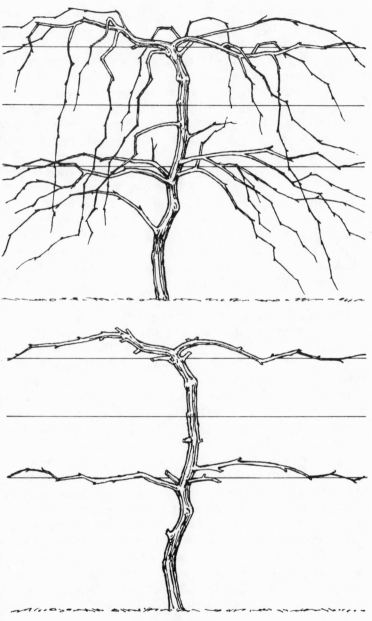

Pruning Vines
Top: Before. *Bottom:* After.

domestic fruit, although they'll thrive more strongly if kept reasonably free of weeds. Any hoeing should be shallow. Each grapevine, in fact, can be treated as an individual. If it is growing sturdily and producing good grapes, leave it to its own whims. This can go on for decade after decade.

Propagating Vines from Cuttings   Grapesvines are inexpensive. You can buy them at nurseries throughout the country. For real enjoyment, though, after you've got your start, try propagating your own vines, perhaps combining a proved commercial strain with locally resistant wild varieties.

Cuttings five to ten inches long may be secured from dormant vines during cold weather. In fact, the sooner such cuttings are obtained after the canes become dormant, the sturdier they'll be. Just slice them off at a slant with a sharp knife, severing them close to a bud on the lower end and leaving an inch of vine above the topmost bud. The commercial procedure is to tie these in bundles which are momentarily heeled into the ground with the butts up and covered with several inches of soil.

Then once your land can be worked in the springtime, press the cuttings firmly into place wherever you want, perhaps in rows, three inches apart, with the upper buds in the open air. Keep ground moist and fertile during the summer. Then by fall the little vines, pruned back to four or five buds, will be sufficiently mature to become part of your vineyard.

Propagation by Layering   The best way to propagate grapes in an established vineyard, though, is by layering. This is the ideal method of filling the empty spots that occur in even the best plantations of grapevines.

All you have to do is bend a branch into a hole or trench three or four inches deep, then cover this with moist, mellow, firmly compacted soil. As soon as the resulting shoots are three inches tall, completely fill in the depression. During the autumn after the original layering, the young vine should be cut from its parent.

Although a brand new vine may have trouble competing with its mature neighbors, the layered vine usually grows rapidly from the start and is producing its own fruit several years later.

Grafting   Then there's grafting, an easily learned skill that can do so much for both your production and pleasure. First,

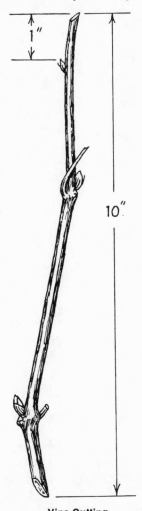

1"

10"

Vine Cutting

carefully dig a hole two inches deep around the vine to be grafted. Preferably using a fine saw, cut the vine off squarely with the ground.

Then, with the same thin saw or with a sharp knife, make a short vertical cut in the center of the remaining vine. Now you're ready for your graft.

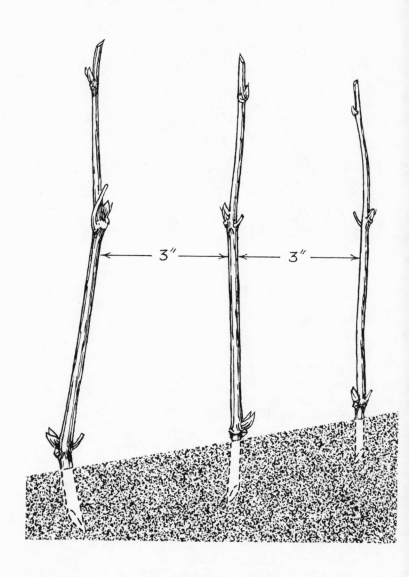

How to Plant Vine Cuttings

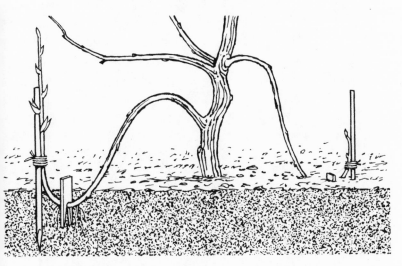

Layering

You'll want a strong, vigorous shoot with two buds. Make the end of this wedge-shaped so that it will fit into the cleft. Then, perhaps holding the opening apart with a knife, insert the new shoot. Tie the juncture securely with a wrapping of yarn.

That's all. Pile the soil in a mound around the graft. During the summer, cut off all shoots starting from the stock and all roots developing from the grafted newcomer. Who knows? You may be starting a new strain that will make you famous.

Your Own Grape Juice

There are two satisfactory ways of securing grape juice for use in the home, either from nearby wild vines or from your own vine-yard. For the first, wash, pick over, and stem your grapes. Have hot, sterilized quart jars or such waiting, arrayed on toweling away from drafts, and have water boiling. Tip two cupfuls of grapes into each jar. Add a cup of sugar to each, planning to sweeten the end results more later if necessary. Fill with boiling water. Seal immediately, allow to cool, label, and then store in a dark, cool place for about ten weeks before straining and using.

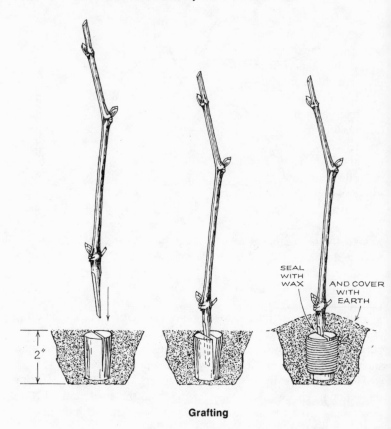

Grafting

For the second method, again wash, pick over, and stem your fruit. Mash the grapes in a kettle, not crushing the seeds. Cover with a minimum of water and bring to a simmer only. Heat that way for half an hour, with only an occasional bubble plopping to the surface. Season to taste with white sugar. Bring once more to a simmer, not a boil, for fiteen minutes. Pour into hot sterilized jars set on a towel, seal, cool as always away from drafts that might crack the glass, label, and store in a dark, cool, dry sanctuary.

Jelly That Won't Crystallize

Grape jelly including that from the wild varieties is luscious, but it takes some doing. The majority of the grapes should be on the underripe side. Wash, drain, and stem these. Relegate them to a kettle, mash them without crushing the seeds, and simmer until the fruit comes apart. Press through a sieve and then, not exerting any pressure, allow to drip through a jelly bag.

When the time comes to make the jelly, prepare only a quart of this juice at a time for perfect results. Here's another secret, too. Ordinary grape jelly has a tendency to crystallize upon standing. An easy way to prevent this? When preparing the juice, just cook a cup of diced tart apples with every four cups of grapes.

Allow four cups of sugar to every four cups of juice. Bring rapidly to a boil. Continue boiling until two drops form on the edge of a metal spoon, then flow together to make a sheet. The jelling point will be at 220° to 222° if you're using a thermometer. Skim off the foam. Then pour the sweetened juice into hot sterilized glasses, filling these to within half an inch of the top.

Either vacuum seal if you're using that kind of container or seal with paraffin, melting this in small bits over hot water and pouring a thin layer atop the jelly, carefully turning and tipping the glass so that the seal is perfect. Allow to cool. Then pour on a second thin layer of paraffin, cool, cover with a lid or with foil, and store where it's cool and dark.

Grape Leaves in Cooking

If like us you enjoy dining occasionally at Middle Eastern restaurants, you are already acquainted with the delicate acid savor that grape leaves lend to food. To use them for cooking, these should be gathered in the springtime when they have achieved their growth but are still tender.

A convenient way to keep a quantity for future use is to divide such freshly gathered leaves into piles of two dozen each. Fold each of these stacks once and tie it together with string. Bring a large pot of water to a boil and add salt until no more will dissolve—about ¾ cup of salt to every 3 quarts of water. Then dip each bundle into the boiling brine for 5 seconds.

Press the stacks tightly into sterilized jars, then tip in a bit of the saturated salt solution to condense and keep the leaves from becoming too brittle. Store in a dark, cool, dry place. These can be used—as long as they last—until the following spring, by which time you'll have a new crop of raw materials. Before employing any of them, incidentally, always wash the leaves well in cold, fresh water.

Stuffed grape leaves, far simpler to prepare than they may sound, are as exciting as they are exotic. Mix 1½ pounds ground lean beef, venison, lamb, or veal with ¾ cup of raw rice, two raw eggs, a small grated onion, ¼ cup minced celery, ⅛ teaspoon apiece of marjoram and thyme, plus salt and pepper to taste. Place about a tablespoon of this mixture on each grape leaf, well washed if they have been salted down, and wrap each neatly around it.

Sauté four diced slices of bacon in the bottom of a large kettle until they start to tan. Pour in three cups of canned tomatoes and bring to a simmer. Now carefully spoon the stuffed grape leaves into the hot mixture, top with another three cups of canned tomatoes, cover, and cook over moderate heat for an hour with only an occasional bubble ballooning to the top. Serve hot.

Such game birds as grouse take on added zest when cooked with grape leaves. Rub each cleaned and plucked small fowl inside and out with lemon juice, salt, and a sprinkling of powdered ginger and black pepper. Lard generously with thin strips of salt pork.

Place atop a nest of grape leaves in a shallow baking dish. Cover with additional leaves. Roast 30 to 40 minutes in a slow 300° oven until a sharp fork can be easily inserted and withdrawn. Remove the top leaves and the lardons. Then turn the heat up to a hot 500° just long enough to give the birds an appetizing bronze. Sprinkle with white bread crumbs, browned in an abundance of butter or margarine, and clear a way to the table.

Making Your Own Raisins

More than a quarter-billion tons of raisins are produced in the United States, mostly in sunny California, while Australia, Greece, Turkey, Iran, Spain, Cyprus, Argentina, and South Africa add their lots. You don't need to buy your raisins from any of them. Instead, why not have the worthwhile fun of making them yourself?

Thompson seedless grapes and the muscat of Alexandria are the two grapes mainly used for raisins, almost all the raisins produced in the United States coming from the former. Let yours ripen on the vines until they are as sweet as possible. Then cut off the clusters, handling them with care as this fruit bruises easily. Place the clusters in a water-filled container and wash them thoroughly, afterwards blotting them with a towel.

You can dry the grapes in these same clusters if you want, turning them about halfway through the process, stemming them later as when watching television. It's easier and more effective to remove them from the stems first, however. You'll now need plastic-coated or -lined trays or, if your crop is small, paper plates.

Spread one layer of the lusciously ripe grapes evenly on the container. For the finest results, cover such trays with wire screening, mosquito netting, or pieces of clean cheesecloth to protect the fruit from insects.

Set the trays of grapes, on blocks if necessary, in the direct sunlight to dry, away from dirt and dust and where air can circulate freely over and under each container. Once four sunny days have passed, test the grapes for dryness by squeezing them in your hand. If no moisture remains on your palm and fingers and if the grapes spring apart when the hand is opened, they are dry enough. They then should be pliable and leathery, like store raisins.

If the grapes are not dry, keep them in the sunlight and test them the same way the day following. Once they are ready, put them in glass jars. These may be stored in the pantry. If you don't use screens, though, the freezer is preferable as it'll keep any insect eggs from hatching.

If sunshine should fail you, you can always dry a small crop on radiators or in the oven. Gather and wash them as before but then dip the grapes into boiling water to crack the skins. Remove the fruit from the stems and spread one layer evenly on the tray. Place this in an oven, on a radiator, or even in an incubator if you happen to have one. Turn the grapes at least twice while they are dehydrating.

Let the grapes remain in the heat until they are pliable. Depending on temperature and humidity, this will require from two to six hours. The higher the temperature and the lower the humidity, the less time will be required. Store the raisins in glass containers as before. You're now really living off the country.

Winemaking From Start To Finish

Do you want to get going with that wine? All right, let's begin with a batch of lush ripe grapes, perhaps from your own starting vineyard. Ten pounds of grapes will give you approximately one gallon of table wine, a fruit-boxful from two to three gallons, and a bushel roughly five gallons. Let's put that in the form of a table of approximations for easy reference.

Grapes	Juice and Pulp	Water	Wine
10 pounds	1 gallon	5 cups	1 gallon
fruit box	2½ gallons	6 quarts	2 to 3 gallons
bushel	4½ gallons	3 gallons	5 gallons

Gently crush and mash the grapes in some container that's large enough for the job, and you're in business. In fact, vintners for centuries did no more than this. The trouble was that every so often, perhaps several years in a row, the crop was a failure. Science has changed all that. Now for a few dimes a lot, the home winemaker can be assured of a fine beverage and bouquet every time.

Incidentally, press your grapes only until the skins burst. Grinding the stems and seeds may give the end product an undesired bitterness. Temperature? This should be within ten degrees of 75°.

Yeast Wild yeasts were first depended upon for fermentation, but you can do much better today with a bit of store yeast. If a pound of this, to use round figures, is added to your juice and pulp, you'll be putting some 1,116,400,000,000 proved yeast cells to work. These yeast cells will outnumber the natural bacterial cells by about 150 to 1.

With so many more standardized cells than wild units, you'll have more of a controlled reaction. This is even more true because there are some 3,300 different known species of yeast to be found in nature wherever there is sugar of any kind. Those of the grape, it so happens, are to be discovered on the surface in its bloom.

These are some of the reasons we used to run into so many different flavors and consistencies in wine. With the help of store yeast, you can by all odds come up with a very satisfactory wine on your own the very first time and with every batch thereafter. Regular baker's yeast will do the job, although the special wine yeasts that are easily and inexpensively obtained from wine supply houses will provide a higher concentration of alcohol, up to 18 percent.

There'll be instructions with your wine yeasts, but with baker's yeast you'll find that a third of a package will do for a gallon of wine, while a whole package will get a five-gallon batch working. Proportions need not be exact, for these unicellular, microscopic plants start reproducing almost immediately by themselves.

With dry or cake yeast, thoroughly dissolve a tablespoon of sugar in a cup of lukewarm water. Be sure that the water is lukewarm only, not hot, as too much heat will destroy the yeast. Add the latter. Let stand ten minutes. Then stir well before adding to the pulp and juice, along with the first half of both the sugar indicated in the table below and the water indicated in the earlier mentioned table. More about this in a moment.

Active dry yeast may also be dusted directly over the surface of your mashed grapes and left to reproduce at will. Although this method requires a longer fermentation time, it is equally as effective. You still add the first half of both the sugar and the water, as we'll consider next.

Sugar   In speaking of wine, dry is the opposite of sweet. Again we have a table of approximations, useful for most other bases in addition to grapes.

Type	*Variety*	*Sugar in Final Gallon*
dry	usual table wine	2 pounds
medium dry	burgundy	2½ pounds
sweet	port	3 pounds
extra sweet	Kosher	3¼ pounds

You've already added half of the sugar and half of the water to your pulp and juice along with the yeast. The best way to do this is by simmering the mixture for several minutes, cooling the liquid to no more than body temperature, and then pouring it into a kettle as a syrup.

There's no need to struggle with big kettles in an effort to follow this suggestion exactly. Boil your sugar in a reasonable amount of the necessary water. Then boil the rest of the water in convenient proportions. Be sure never to add anything to the yeast-replete mixture that is appreciably warmer than your body temperature.

Straining The cake of pulp and seeds which floats to the top of the container—preferably an earthenware crock or wooden barrel twice the capacity of the fermenting nucleus, although you can get started with just a plastic wastebasket—should either be turned over or stirred into the whole in the early morning and again just before bedtime. Just letting the batch sit is a major cause of poor-quality wines.

After the batch has been fermenting for a week, you'll want to strain out the pulp and seeds. When this residue is heavy, as with grapes, make the first extraction with several layers of the cheap cotton gauze known as cheesecloth. Then strain.

Strain the juice again through some tightly woven cloth such as unbleached muslin. Make sure that this is new to start with and strong enough to endure all the scraping and squeezing, for if it tears you'll have the whole job to do over again.

Incidentally, it's wise to sterilize these cloths and all other parts of the paraphernalia between winemaking sessions, not only for cleanliness but because undesirable yeast spores otherwise left impregnating the materials may spoil what would have been an excellent batch. This is why you shouldn't use even good-quality polyethylene wastebaskets more than a few times, for the plastic is penetrable and may begin harboring unwanted bacteria.

The expressed juice of the grapes, or other fruit for that matter, before complete fermentation—that is, the new wine—is called "must" from the Latin meaning "young, fresh."

The Fermentation Process For the final fermentation, pour the remaining half of your sugar into the second half of the water, simmer for several minutes, cool to body temperature, and add to the must.

This new wine is now poured into sterilized jugs which are filled to within an inch of their tops. The temperature for this stage of fermentation may be a bit cooler if you want but not below 60°. As a matter of fact, ordinary house temperatures will do for the entire job and may save a lot of moving and shifting.

Gases will keep on being formed by the continuing fermentation, and there should be some device to let them escape while still keeping air out. Better than nothing is a wad of cotton batting stuffed into the neck of each jug, perhaps augmented with a patch of plastic knotted loosely enough to the outsides for the vapors to force their way through.

Better is a length of tubing inserted into the jug by a tight hole cut in the closing cork, then looped into a small container filled with water. The gases will thus be able to bubble free, while at the same time the water lock will prevent outside air from contaminating the must. Manufactured locks are so inexpensive, though, that you may later prefer to lay in a few.

Fermentation will be complete once the bubbling stops. To prevent popping corks, bursting bottles, and other such difficulties, it's a good idea to wait at least two weeks after all signs of fermentation have ceased before bottling your product. To do this, carefully siphon the undisturbed wine into clean containers, perhaps additional jugs.

If you can now wait at least a month, the wine should be beautifully clear and ready for carefully siphoning into the final bottles. Again, discard any sediment. If by any chance the wine refuses to clear, clarifying agents are obtainable at the store. If you've followed directions, though, you'll ordinarily have no such difficulties. Store preferably either in colored bottles or a dark place.

Wine should be allowed to mature in its final containers if you can possibly manage it. One month is good. Three months will be even better. Once you're in full production, such restraint should not be too difficult to manage.

You'll find that winemaking is an intriguing pastime, and to become really proficient at it you'll want to keep a record of past successes and the steps leading to them. Such records, which

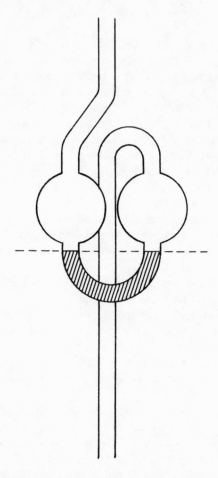

Device for Letting Gas Escape from Wine

should include dates and taste-and-quality differentiations among the basic raw materials, can be keyed to the mature wines by label numbers.

Colors? They don't mean much. You can secure a white wine from blue Concord grapes, for example, by straining out the skins, pulp, and seeds immediately after crushing, then fermenting the juice only. Pink wine? Put off straining a day or two.

Claret

A delectable second wine, such as a claret, can be fermented from the remaining skin, pulp, and seeds, especially if you do not attempt to squeeze these dry the first time around.

Go through the same procedures, adding yeast, sugar, and water as with the first batch. The total amount of added water should equal the volume of the initially extracted must. As before, pour in only half of it at first, saving the second half for the final stage. You'll likely enjoy the finished product more if its comparatively more subtle flavor is not harshened by too much sweetness.

Famous Dandelion Wine

Dandelion wine is notable. If you'd like to make four quarts of your own, pick a gallon of the flowers early on a dry morning, making sure that no parts of the bitterish stems are included. In fact, if you really want to be particular, pinch off the orange and yellow petals and use these alone.

In either event, drop the flowers into a scalded fermentation container and pour two quarts of boiling water over them. Leave for a week, stirring the mixture daily. Then strain out the blossoms and relegate them, like all such by-products, to your compost heap.

The pleasantly amber liquid that is left becomes your basic wine-concocting ingredient. To give it an enjoyable tartness, add the juice of two lemons and an orange when you put in the first half of the sugar. Now just follow the fundamental procedures, taking into consideration the two quarts of water already present.

If you don't want to go to even that much trouble, here's a formula that I've seen successfully used in the country. Get your gallon of dandelion blossoms as before. Press these into a two-gallon crock. Pour a gallon of boiling water over them and leave for at least three days, preferably a week. Then strain through a tightly woven cloth, squeezing all the liquid from the flowers.

Add the juice and thinly sliced rind and pulp from three oranges and three lemons. Stir in three pounds of sugar. Add one ounce of yeast. Cover the crock with a cloth and let it stand, out of the way, for three weeks while the mixture ferments. As soon as the bubbling has stopped, strain, bottle, and cork or cap tightly. There are vitamins in this.

Wines From Other Fruits and Vegetables

You can make wine, too, from raspberries, strawberries, black-berries, blueberries, wild cherries, gooseberries, mulberries, bil-berries, currants, rose hips, and any of the wild rhubarb and other ripe fruits that are free for the gathering. For a delicious gallon of elderberry wine, for example, mash four pounds of ripe elder-berries, then follow the basic wine-making procedures. Did you know that Portugal forbids the growing of elderberries in its wine country lest winemakers be tempted to mix elderberries, which lend an intense red color, with their paler ports?

The output of your own small garden will produce other winemaking ingredients, from peapods and parsley to parsnips, carrots, turnips, and beets. The carrots and parsnips are peeled, for instance, then boiled until soft enough to pulp and strain. Beets, which otherwise have an earthy flavor, are best made into sweet wine. Parsley must have something such as lemon and orange juice added to it to support good yeast growth. You can make wine from potatoes, too, and even from cereals that are bolstered with either dried fruit such as raisins or fruit juices.

Wines From Frozen Grape Juice

If you have frozen part of your home-grown grape juice, you can still have wine. Or just go down to the store and pick up seven 12-ounce cans of frozen grape juice. With this you'll also need seven pounds of sugar, a ½-ounce package of yeast, and five gallons of warm water.

Drop the dark blocks of frozen grape juice into the water, stir-ring until all is in solution. Add the sugar, gauging the amount by how dry you want the finished product to be. Dissolve the yeast in a cup of warm water, no hotter than body temperature, and pour that into the juice.

Once you've stirred everything well enough to assure that nothing is left undissolved, pour your mixture into glass containers and put on the previously described air locks. Fermentation should take five or six weeks if the new wine is handily kept at house temperature. Once the bubbles have stopped lifting through the richly dark liquid, siphon the batch into sterilized glass bottles.

The wine may take on a cloudiness after standing for several days. If so, for a five-gallon batch just dissolve a single ¼-ounce package of gelatine in one cup of hot water. Distribute this among your bottles. Then as soon as the cloudiness vanishes, you have wine ready for enjoying.

Blackberry Cordial

Blackberry cordial, which besides being delectable has long been a favorite home remedy for diarrhea, is easy to make when blackberries are plentiful. You'll need eight quarts of them for this particular recipe, although the formula is one that can be easily halved or quartered. In any event, pick over the blackberries if necessary, place in a kettle with two quarts of cold water, boil until mushy, and then strain.

For every quart of the resulting juice, stir in two cups of sugar. Then tie one tablespoon apiece of clove, nutmeg, cinnamon, and allspice in a bit of cotton cloth. Drop into the juice and simmer for twenty minutes; then remove the spices and discard. After the beverage has cooled, add one pint of brandy or whisky to every quart of syrup. Pour into sterilized bottles and cork securely. This will mellow with age.

Cherry Bounce From Rum Cherries

Rum cherries picked up their cognomen by being used by old-time New Englanders to mellow rum and other brandies, as well as whiskies. The procedure was to sweeten the strained and sweetened juice of crushed rum cherries with an equal volume of sugar, then add it to the raw liquors. The process was favored because, in ad-

274 . . . *One Acre and Security*

dition to its soothing effect, it also thriftily stretched the available supplies of the ardent spirits.

Cherry bounce still works out well with rum cherries, the proportions being one quart fruit and half a pound of sugar to a pint of whisky. Clean and stem the fruit. Start by covering the bottom of a wide-mouthed jar with a thick layer of the wild cherries. Top these with a single layer of sugar cubes. Some connoisseurs then dust on small amounts of clove, nutmeg, cinnamon, and allspice. Continue this process as long as the fruit and sugar last. Then pour in the whisky. Seal, put away in a dark place, and go about other matters for at least two months.

Brandied Rum Cherries

Brandied rum cherries, also popular during the early trading days of New England, can be made by boiling two cups of sugar in a quart of water until a clear syrup is formed. Pour this over two quarts of cleaned rum cherries and let stand overnight. The next day drain the syrup into a glass or enamel pot, bring it slowly to a bubble, carefully add the cherries, and simmer for ten minutes.

Then scoop out the cherries with a slotted spoon and pack them in sterilized hot glass jars. Cover them temporarily while boiling the syrup until it is thick. Stir in a pint of rum or other brandy, pour immediately over the cherries, seal, and put away to age.

Homemade Champagne

You can even concoct your own private champagne. This process is trickier than that of making simple wine, however, and because of the pressures that will be generated it is always advisable to use new or used champagne bottles, never ordinary wine containers. In fact, exert every caution throughout, particularly during the final step of disgorging. The proud, bubbly results will be well worth it.

Commence by making your grape wine in the usual manner, but keep close tabs on the must with a saccharometer, available inexpensively at any liquor supply house. Always use strained juice for each reading, incidentally, as otherwise sediment will clog up the works. When the new wine shows a reading of 2 percent or 2⅕ percent sugar, indicating that approximately 1 percent of alcohol remains to be fermented, you're in business.

Now it is time to bottle the juice. Only be sure that you use champagne bottles, perhaps retrieved from a nearby club. Close these with regular corks or, better, with the reusable plastic stoppers that can be inserted by hand and will remain inert, doing away with the necessity of storing the wine on its side. In any event, wire down the stoppers with strong wire hoods.

Storage time comes next. Stand each bottle on its cap so that the sediment, precipitating as the wine continues to ferment, will tend to settle in the neck, where it can later be more satisfactorily removed. To encourage the action, give each bottle a robust twist at least once daily, perhaps just before you retire for the night.

The day when you see the end of the bubbles that have been coursing through the liquid, the fermentation will be complete. Note the date in your records. Then let the wine stand for several weeks more until it is, ideally, entirely clear. Now the action starts, in the form of disgorging. It will be well to do this some place where a mess will not matter too much. Protective clothing and shatterproof eyeglasses if you can manage them may well be worn in case of possible trouble.

You'll need about twenty pounds of dry ice, broken into chips that will fill six inches deep a box large enough to hold a half-dozen bottles at a time. Handling each bottle extremely cautiously so as not to disturb the sediment, bury the necks of the still upside-down bottles in the ice right up to where each bottle widens to its fullest diameter. Leave them until a cylinder of ice forms in each neck. Now turn each bottle upright, loosen the wire guard, draw the cork, remove the sediment, and insert a clean cap. This should, too, be immediately wired into place.

If the pressure expels the ice from the container, a bit of the wine may be lost. Then just set one bottle aside for refilling the others. On the other hand, if the pressure is not released, give it an assist with a carefully wielded ice pick. All this insures the venting of enough pressure so that an undue proportion of cork-popping power won't remain to spoil the effect when you finally thumb the cap off at the chastely spread dining table.

Except for a wait of at least two or three weeks before imbibing, that's all. During this hiatus, store your champagne—on its side unless you used plastic caps—in some dark, reasonably cool sanctuary. Your health!

CHAPTER THIRTEEN

Hitting the Trail from Your Acre

SMALL uncrowded spots are what you need to find yourself. Even after you've established yourself on a secluded acre, it is always relaxing to explore a little farther into the surrounding country, and there'll be better fishing and better foraging even more distant from civilization's rat race.

"Hiking a ridge, a meadow, a river, is as healthy a form of exercise as one can get," says Supreme Court Justice William O. Douglas. "Ten to twenty miles on a trail puts one to bed with his cares unraveled. Hiking—and climbing, too—are man's most natural exercises. They introduce him again to the wonders of nature and teach him the beauty of the woods and fields in winter as well as in spring. They also teach him how to take care of himself and his neighbors in times of adversity.

"We need exercise as individuals. We need to keep physically fit and alert as people. ...History is the sound of heavy boots going upstairs and the rustle of satin slippers coming down. Nations that are soft and slack—people who get all their exercise and athletics vicariously—will not survive when the competition is severe and adversity is at hand. It is imperative that America stay fit. For today we face as great a danger, as fearsome a risk, as any people in history."

Hiking with today's modern equipment and improved methods, formerly known only to a few, lets you combine the satisfaction of walking and camping with fishing and hunting in unspoiled wilderness, all this at costs you could not even approximate any other way. In fact, living to a certain extent off the country as is possible in the true wildernesses of this continent, you'll often actually spend less than you would living at home.

Done right, there is nothing hard about vacationing with a packsack. You wander free and unfettered, with just enough exercise in the pure air to make life thoroughly enjoyable. Such trips are for anyone healthy and fairly vigorous. They can be enjoyed equally by parents, teen-agers of both sexes, elderly people in good health, and certainly by children. In fact, one of the important sidelines of the packsack companies is the arrangements like Himalayan Industries' Hike-A-Poose, which Richard Mack has designed so that the youngster riding an adult's back, somewhat like a papoose of yore, can face either forwards or, especially in bush country, backwards.

Hiking Trails

These days only two things are essential for backpacking vacations: drinking water, which you can purify if you must, and country where you can walk and camp without trespassing. Hikers in the United States, in addition to Canada, are therefore especially fortunate.

Within the 154 national forests in thirty-nine states and Puerto Rico are 182,000,000 such acres and well over 100,000 miles of trails, all open to backpacking. National parks are crisscrossed with thousands of miles of well-maintained trails. Innumerable public campgrounds are enmeshed by well-marked webs of hiking paths which lead to every type of attraction. Considerable undeveloped countryside everywhere, within reach of even the largest cities, calls for exploration on foot.

If you live near crowded New York City, for example, there are the Catskill Mountains only three hours away by car. North of

Boston, beyond the inviting backways of Essex and Gloucester, are the White Mountains with the Little Imp and other unforgettable trails. Just east of Philadelphia are the South Jersey pine barrens. From the very Capitol of our country, the cloud-scored Blue Ridge so beloved by the late Colonel Townsend Whelen is only two hours distant.

The Long Trail   Then there are the great trails of which Vermont's Long Trail, extending from Canada to Massachusetts along or near the crest of the state's historic Green Mountains, is a worthy cousin. Some ninety side trails, together with frequent crossings of country roads, provide such frequent access to supplies that it's practical to trek this wilderness footpath with ultralight equipment. The length of the Long Trail is a fraction over 255 miles, with more than ninety side trails adding another 200 odd miles. There's a shelter for about every four miles of trail. For detailed information, write the Green Mountain Club Inc., Box 94, Rutland, Vermont 05701.

The Appalachian Trail   Then there is the 1,995-mile footpath known as the Appalachian Trail, with its chain of free lean-tos and fireplaces, which twists from Mount Katahdin in Maine to Springer Mountain in Georgia. This is a free, serene, slightly incredible footpath that crosses the sparkling lake and mountain country of Maine, goes through the Green and White mountains and the Berkshire Hills, and finally leads through the restful wild areas along the crests of the Catskill and Allegheny Mountains, Blue Ridge, and the Great Smokies to its southern terminus. This trail is a volunteer recreational project, supervised and maintained by the Appalachian Trail Conference, 1916 Sunderland Place, N.W., Washington, D.C. 20036.

The Pacific Crest Trail   On the other side of the continent, the rugged 2,156-mile Pacific Crest Trail extends from Canada to Mexico in a country-wide slash from near Mount Baker in Washington to Campo in San Diego County, California. As is its eastern mate, it is supplemented by hundreds of miles of secondary trails that invite side excursions. Much of the rugged course, zigzagging to altitudes one and two miles above sea level, is suitable for well-shod pack animals as well as for hikers. Because of snow in the high country, portions are not always penetrable until at least mid-July

The Sierra Club (1050 Mills Tower, 220 Bush Street, San Francisco, California 94104) is an organization that has done much in bringing the Pacific Crest Trail to the attention of the public and in fostering a great deal of what it stands for. Founded in 1892, with naturalist John Muir the first president, the Sierra Club with its present thousands of members each year organizes knapsack trips here and elsewhere into the high hills, "offering the freedom and challenge of wilderness exploration with everything you need on your back." For details, write the Outing Department at the above address.

However, the Sierra Club is not the source of information for the Pacific Crest Trail, having no jurisdiction there nor administering the route in any way. Instead, write the Regional Forester at Region Six, 319 S.W. Pine Street, Portland, Oregon 97208 or at 630 Sansome Street, San Francisco, California 94111.

More National Scenic Trails

In pace with the unprecedented surge of interest in countrywide backpacking, a pleasure which during the past few years has grown faster than any other major outdoor recreation activity, Congress has designated fourteen other routes for study and possible inclusion in the National Trails System. These are:

(1) Continental Divide Trail, a 3,100-mile path extending from near the Mexican border in southwestern New Mexico northward, generally along the Continental Divide, to the Canadian border in Glacier National Park.

(2) Potomac Heritage trail, an 825-mile route extending generally from the mouth of the Potomac River to its sources in West Virginia, including the ancient 70-mile Chesapeake and Ohio Canal towpath.

(3) Old Cattle Trails of the Southwest from the vicinity of San Antonio, Texas approximately 800 miles through Oklahoma via Baxter Springs and Chetopa, Kansas, to Fort Scott, Kansas,

including the Chisholm Trail, from the vicinity of San Antonio or Cuero, Texas, approximately 800 miles north through Oklahoma to Abilene, Kansas.

(4) Lewis and Clark Trail from Wood River, Illinois, to Oregon's Pacific Ocean, following the routes of the Lewis and Clark expedition.

(5) Natchez Trace, from Nashville, Tennessee, approximately 600 miles to Natchez, Mississippi.

(6) North Country Trail, from the Appalachian Trail in Vermont approximately 3,200 miles through the states of New York, Pennsylvania, Ohio, Michigan, Wisconsin, and Minnesota to the Lewis and Clark Trail in North Dakota.

(7) Kittanning Trail from Shirleysburg in Huntingdon County, Pennsylvania, to Kittanning, Armstrong County, Pennsylvania.

(8) Oregon Trail, from Independence, Missouri approximately 2,000 miles to near historic Fort Vancouver, Washington.

(9) Santa Fe Trail, from Independence, Missouri approximately 800 sun-beaten miles to Santa Fe, New Mexico.

(10) Long Trail, extending a bit more than 255 miles from the Massachusetts border northward through green Vermont to the Canadian border.

(11) Mormon Trail, extending from Nauvoo, Illinois, to Salt Lake City, Utah, through the states of Iowa, Nebraska, and Wyoming.

(12) Gold rush trails in Alaska, including the path over stirring Chilkoot Pass.

(13) Mormon Battalion Trail, reaching 2,000 miles from Mount Pisgah, Iowa through Kansas, Colorado, New Mexico, and Arizona to Los Angeles, California.

(14) El Camino Real from St. Augustine to Fort Caroline National Memorial, Florida, approximately 30 scenic miles along the southern boundary of the St. Johns River.

The U.S. Bureau of Outdoor Recreation in cooperation with the Forest Service and other federal as well as state and local agencies is already working on this vast plan, studies of which are expected to be completed by 1976, the nation's 200th anniversary. Up-to-the-minute information on current developments along any of these luring bypaths may be secured by writing the Bureau of Outdoor Recreation, Department of the Interior, Washington, D.C. 20240.

As J. E. Jensen, Associate Director of the National Park Service, so aptly tells me:

"We realize that in order for man to increase his awareness of the natural environment he must have contact with it. And through such experiences as hiking in the back country he can find solitude, inspiration, and aesthetic enjoyment, all contributing to his awareness. Therefore, in order to preserve this unique experience for all generations, present and future, we must maintain those natural phenomena inherent in a given area. Although we cannot shut down these places, we all can restrict our use in those areas now available and strive to obtain additional ones in order to shift the load.

"One such plan is to acquire parks and recreational lands near our urban centers. And we are presently doing this. This move would not only allow more people a chance to obtain a park experience but would also reduce travel requirements and lessen the impact on previously established areas."

Weight of the Backpack

To travel any of these routes, and explore the regions adjacent to them, an easily carried outfit containing equipment and food for each individual is indispensable. For backpacking, everything should be cut down in weight and bulk to absolute essentials. Food should be largely dehydrated.

Briefly, the total weight of the backpack for pleasant mountain travel should not exceed about thirty-five pounds for young, vigorous men. This maximum should be pared down to some fifteen to twenty-five pounds for juniors and women. As for proportions, the equipment proper in the largest pack should not weigh over fifteen pounds, thus allowing a food load of at least twenty pounds. In this day of lightweight grub, you can take off for months at a time. And even this interval can be stretched when rations are supplemented with wild edibles, like fish and berries, as you go along.

And so at the end of the paved road, you shoulder your pack and head into the country. You leave a lot of hustle and bustle, and expense, behind. There's no other kind of vacation that can compare to these backpacking trips, none that can take you so close to peace and utter freedom.

The Pick of the Packs

Only two packs are really satisfactory for this sort of vacation. One is the alpine type of frame rucksack, generally with a single large and several smaller fabric containers built around a strong, light, metal frame to which shoulder straps are fastened. The other is the packboard, essentially a rectangular frame over which fabric is so tightly doubled and laced that a bundle lashed to it never touches the hiker's back. Both are obtainable in various sizes.

The best packs in the world for this type of recreation are variations of the packboard made in the United States and obtainable by mail and from stores throughout the country. Light, strong, and durable, such packboards are usually made of tough aluminum tubing, although such metals as magnesium and stainless steel are also used. Webbing, usually nylon, keeps all hard surfaces away from the back.

Carrying bags that can be secured from the same sources fit on the frames. The result is utility plus convenience and comfort. Anyone planning to cover very many miles of recreational backpacking would do well to make such a pack the basic part of his outfit. The wrong pack has ruined more vacations than any other single item.

Selecting A Sleeping Bag

The sleeping bag, next to the pack itself, is the most important piece of equipment to be selected for a backpacking vacation, especially as it is the most expensive item. You can bull along the trail with a poor pack. But the sleeping bag, in which you're going to be spending on the average a third of every day, has to be adequate if you're going to be refreshed enough to keep enjoying the trip under full steam.

In really cold weather a poor bag can actually be dangerous. If you are going to be hiking in mild weather, you have a wider

284 . . . *One Acre and Security*

choice. A roomier bag can be picked. Styling, such as provisions to keep the top around your head in frosty going, can be overlooked. The way the filler is held in place, even the filler itself, will be less important. Ideally, though, any bag you buy should be the most functional obtainable, as anything less will mean additional bulk and weight to carry.

In the mild weather enjoyed along many trails in the summer vacation season, mistaken choices will be felt most in the pocketbook and on the shoulders. There is considerably less latitude in really cold weather. Suppose your sleeping bag has to do for both? Then gauge your selection to fit the severest weather to be encountered.

The most effective insulation known is dry, still air. Thus the effectiveness of lining materials in keeping one warm is in direct proportion not to their weight but to the number of dead air cells they can maintain. The thicker a sleeping robe or blanket is and the fluffier its nature, the more inert air it affords.

The most nearly ideal insulating material for use in sleeping bags and in cold-weather clothing is the delicate down of birds. This down varies even among the same species of birds. Generally speaking, the finest grade of down available commercially is the very best white goose down. There is also a lower grade, which is no warmer than the best of gray goose down. Other goose down is next, followed by prime duck down. Still other downs, follow, trailed by a mixture of down and feathers and then by feathers themselves.

Next to downs and feathers in thermal value, and the thing to consider if the family on a budget is going on a backpacking vacation in mild weather, is dacron. This is very satisfactory under such circumstances, and the filler is extremely durable. But you are paying for the difference in cost by taking on added pounds and bulk. For backpacking trips where functional weight is very important, it is not advisable to pick up any of the less expensive sleeping bags, although many are on the market. The bag is so important that it would be advisable to make any necessary savings elsewhere, perhaps by passing up the new lightweight simplicities in the food line and relying, for a while at least, on the old-fashioned staples.

Maximum comfort is attained when one has an air mattress under a good sleeping bag. One of these requires only a minute or so to inflate properly, so that when you stretch out on your side your hip bone just about touches the hard surface beneath. The easiest way to accomplish this is by deliberately overinflating, then lying in position and adjusting the mattress by opening the valve until the desired pressure is reached. For backpacking, where weight and space are primary considerations, a good air mattress to secure is one about four feet long and half as wide. Or you can buy one of the newer rubber or plastic sleeping pads of the same size.

Portable Plastic Shelters

There's nothing quite like overnight camps on backpacking vacations. Along many of the main trails, lean-tos and other shelters are so spaced that difficulties, even in stormy weather, are reduced to a minimum. But the camps made along some of the wilderness ways where a backpacker can set up his own bivouac, are usually the most unforgettable.

Suppose you have a small fire built in front of your tarpaulin or plastic shelter, which is pitched like a lean-to to circulate the heat over your bed, and the weather turns nippier or downright cold. Unless you have already provided for some other reflecting area, when the evening meal is over drive a couple of stout posts about ten inches behind the backlog of the fire, slanting them a little backwards. Pile up a wall of as rugged logs as you can manage, dry or green, against these. Pretty soon quite a blaze will spring up, with the log wall in the rear beating the heat across your bed. By building this fire just before turning in, you may be able to keep it going all night. It will provide warmth while you sleep and in the morning a layer of coals for cooking.

There is no sure formula for keeping a campfire alive all night without attention. Sometimes it will hold. But if heat is necessary for comfortable sleeping, the increasing coldness usually awakens you in a few hours. You grope sleepily for the handy woodpile and toss some sticks into the embers. The pieces flare up quickly, and pretty soon you begin to feel the fresh heat.

You stay hunched up on one elbow. There is a wind high in the trees. Some bird you've never heard before calls in the distance. The smoke smells sweet. An owl hoots. It's good to be awake at such a time. You finally lie back and relax. Almost at once it is morning. After breakfast you're ready to travel again. Put your fire dead out.

The simplest form of shelter is merely a large sheet of plastic which, if it is of light material, will fold and stow handily in a breast pocket. These are so convenient to carry, as a matter of fact, that I always have one with me when I get into the woods. With such protection, even in a downpour you can boil the kettle and have lunch while remaining comfortable and dry. It is easy, too, to improvise a sleeping shelter as by sandwiching the plastic between boughs to form a watertight sanctuary.

The cheapest, and in many ways the handiest, tentage to lug along on the main hiking trails is just a section of large plastic tubing, available from sporting goods stores and outfitters. One such tube, made of polyethylene, is nine feet seven inches long and has a circumference of eight feet. It weighs one pound and costs less than three dollars. The simplest way to erect it is by running a rope through the tube to serve as a ridge and tying this several feet high between two trees. No pegs are necessary. The weight of the occupant anchors the tent.

Tents

Then there are the store tents, the weight of which, although not necessarily the tenting equipment itself, is divided among the hikers. Some such tents big enough to sleep four, with pole assemblies for use in the mountains above timberline, weigh only twelve pounds, which is three pounds per camper. Prices among the big specialists in such equipment run from about $60 to $135, to give you an idea.

Assuring Proper Fit in the Hiking Shoe

The boot, where the hiker and the trail meet, is the most important item of clothing. Poorly fitted and ineptly chosen footwear has taken the edge off far too many hiking sojourns. The vacationist taking to the trails for the first time, on a trip that requires long and difficult foot travel, is apt to discover when it's too late that he is committed to footwear that will handicap or badly cripple him. Thus the grand outing he has been planning, maybe for years, is ruined.

The shoe size you wear in the city—and the one the average salesman there will measure you for—will perhaps do well enough for the several miles of walking which many individuals cover on a usual outing. But beware of this size for a daily tramp of eight to twenty miles over wild countryside, especially if it's hilly country.

One such excursion in city-sized footwear will almost certainly lay you up with blisters and abrasions. After three or four miles of hiking over rugged terrain, your feet swell considerably because of the repeated and varying pressures of walking and because of the increased blood supply that is being pumped into them by the stimulation of exercise. The shoes you select must be large enough to remain comfortable when your feet are in this enlarged condition.

The simple but all-important formula for wilderness walking is heavy socks and big shoes. Regardless of heat or cold, dryness or dampness, only wool socks are suitable for long hikes, although you may like nylon reinforcement at the toes and heels to extend their lives. These socks may vary from thin to medium during the summer, and from medium to heavy through the frosty months.

Taking the thickness of your socks into consideration, here is a general rule you can apply in selecting the ideal size of footwear for hard outdoor wear. With one pair of thin or medium wool socks, have your shoes one full size longer and one full size wider than your proper fit in city shoes. For heavy socks, you have them one and one-half sizes longer and wider. If half-sizes are not available, increase to the next full size.

Breaking in Footwear

It is highly important to break in new footwear well in advance of a trip. Some of us have feet that are shaped differently from normal, probably because of improper fittings in city shoes. The lasts on which good outdoor shoes are made, changing as foot sizes themselves have changed over the generations, are designed for normal proportions.

When shoes are new, even when correctly fitted, they may bring undue pressure on parts of your feet. The new footwear will gradually stretch at those points, however, if broken in slowly and easily.

There are two functional ways of breaking in new leather shoes. One way is to do it gradually by hiking two miles the first day, three miles the second, and so on up to five miles, by which time the process should be completed. The second method consists of standing in four inches of water for fifteen minutes and then hiking until the shoes dry on your feet.

Sneakers

Incidentally, ordinary rubber-soled sneakers and basketball shoes are popular along fairly smooth wilderness ways such as the Appalachian Trail and in comparatively dry country such as that found along stretches on the Sierra Trail. For rugged use, however, don't buy the low ones. Select those with tops about six inches high. The rubber soles should be roughly corrugated or substantially cleated as a safeguard against slipping.

Special Hiking Boots

The proved favorites among most trail veterans, especially in the West, are the special boots, both imported and domestic, stocked by the big catalog-issuing sporting goods dealers for the express purpose of hiking. Equipped with the best of rubber lug soles, these afford high traction and long wear. They are safe, comfortable, and quiet but not inexpensive. With reasonable care they are good for years, particularly as they can be resoled when necessary.

If your sporting goods dealer cannot readily obtain these for you locally, it is practical to order them by mail as a proper fit is guaranteed. To measure your feet, put on the socks you intend to wear on the trail. Then stand on a piece of paper, distributing your weight equally on both feet. Holding a pencil vertically, clearly make the outline of each foot. Send these outlines to the outfitter, along with a notation of the length and width of your normal dress shoes.

Essential Equipment

"It is some advantage to lead a primitive life if only to learn what are the necessaries," an inveterate hiker by the name of Henry Thoreau said over a century ago. "Most of the luxuries and many of the so-called comforts are not only dispensable but positive hindrances."

You'll want a good small compass, an unbreakable waterproof container filled with wooden matches, a few little gauze pads centered on short strips of plastic adhesive tape for use in preventing blisters, an inexpensive watch, some kind of mirror, an extra pair of glasses if you wear them, sunglasses for high altitudes, and maps of the territory, perhaps trimmed to their essentials to cut down on weight and bulk.

Then there are written materials, perhaps a few paperback books, and your toilet kit. Binoculars and camera are not necessities, but the latter in particular can make a lot of difference when you get back home and for years to come. A few yards of nylon cord, strong enough to support your weight in an emergency, will not take up much room.

Having a supply of one of the more effective fly dopes such as the light and compact Cutter's repellent can prevent a lot of annoyance in places and seasons where winged pests are prevalent. A flashlight is always handy in and around camp. If there's any doubt about drinking water, either boil it or use halazone tablets, a small 2-ounce bottle of 100 tablets taking up less room than a 12-gauge shell.

Heavy mineral oil, purchased under that name, is about as good as any of the sunburn preventatives. It is certainly the cheapest.

The odds and ends of a painstakingly selected repair kit will sometimes prove amazingly valuable in comparison with the use they get in civilization. During ultralight travel, it is practical to add a sheath knife for the heavier tasks. Best are those handmade by W. D. Randall, Jr., Box 1988, Orlando, Florida 32502.

290 . . . *One Acre and Security*

Cooking and Eating Utensils

You'll need special cooking and eating paraphernalia. For the lone hiker, the practical minimum is two small kettles with covers and with bails by which they can be hung over a fire, a frypan with a folding or detachable handle, a tablespoon, and a cup. The frying pan will serve as a plate, the cup as a bowl. One's pocket or sheath knife can be used whenever necessary.

Basic Grubstakes

When your appetite is sharpened by the sort of outdoor living for which human beings were made, the mealtimes can include some of the best moments of any vacation—if you take foods that keep well, cook readily, and are easy to handle.

Nothing is more important on a hike than the grub. Most of us go into the farther places to have a good time. If the victuals are poor, unwholesome, and not what we crave, we have a continuous grouch. If they are appetizing and there's plenty of everything, all is rosy. Satisfying food even makes up for rain and hard beds. Good fellowship is at its best around good meals.

To determine quantities, you can experiment at home. If you want oatmeal every morning, for example, find out just how much rolled oats are needed to make the breakfast you will like to eat in the woods. Just as a suggestion, take at least double the amount of sugar and sweets you would use at home, for your desire for them on the trail will be out of all proportion to what you want in the city.

These days you can dine about as easily and well in the wilderness as in a city. Matter of fact, you're likely to find yourself eating considerably better. There may be the disadvantage of not being able to pick up many of the frozen specialties featured in modern markets. But this drawback is more than offset by all the fresh foods that are at hand, free for the taking.

By learning to recognize a reasonable number of these wild edibles, you become like the old prospector who kneels on a lode of silver while he pans gold and platinum from a creek. Whatever your epicurean whim of the moment may be, you can satisfy it.

Dried and Freeze-dried Foods Such words as pemmican, jerky, parched corn, buccan, and pinole are reminders that dehydrated foods were important along the trails of this country even during flintlock days. The basic formula has not changed. It is to remove as much moisture from the edible portion of the particular food as may be practicable. Drying by sun and wind often extracted no more than three-fourths of this water. Modern processes sometimes leave less than 1 percent.

Aside from the usual dried fruits and vegetables, now greatly improved, one of the greatest breakthroughs afforded by freeze-drying—called the greatest innovation in the food field since the invention of the tin can—is the preservation of meat. You can now hike a couple of weeks away from the nearest supply point and each night, farther and farther back of beyond, sit down to tender, juicy beefsteaks.

With new foods forthcoming each year since commercial freeze-dried items were introduced to this country's markets around 1959, well toward one hundred different products are now available at this writing. I have tried many of these. Almost all are faithfully comparable to the fresh products, and I very much like nearly all. Naturally I don't care for a few, just as I personally prefer to pass up their fresh equivalents.

The point is that it is best in general for a hiker to eat on the trail approximately the way he does in day-by-day living. This is to avoid the often unpleasant process of psychological adaptation of physiological conversion. The psychological values of foods are of special importance during the usual short hikes. It's true enough that there is no physical necessity for steaks, vegetables, and fruits if instead, for example, you eat genuine pemmican and vitamin pills exclusively. But if the craving for the former is not satisfied, morale takes a beating. And you're out for pleasure.

Write to the following addresses for information on wide lines of the best dehydrated foods on the market: F. Harmon Saville, Chuck Wagon Foods, Micro Drive, Woburn, Mass. 01801; William B. White, Stow-A-Way Products, Cohasset, Mass. 02025.

In general, foods that freeze well will freeze-dry. Foods high in fats or sugars are difficult to freeze-dry because they freeze poorly.

Produce such as melons and cucumbers freezes, but because of its loose physical structure it will not readily rehydrate back to its original form. But despite these few exceptions, the possibilities are virtually unlimited.

Try out the dehydrated products first. Sampling two or three items from any one company will pretty well determine whether you will like the whole line. Do this testing before you leave home. Tastes differ. A major error is to load up with dehydrated meals for the entire trip, especially some of those dried by older methods, without everyone's doing considerable sampling beforehand.

Breakfast Cereal   Prepare your breakfast cereal according to the instructions on the package. In nearly every case, repack. If the cereal is unnecessarily bulky, reduce in size as much as possible.

A favorite trail cereal of a lot of us is oatmeal. The quickly cooking variety saves time. What I do is ready it the night before by adding one cup of oatmeal and one-half teaspoon of salt to two cups of cold water. A quarter-cup of raisins, more or less, plump out overnight to add flavor.

The next morning I hunch far enough out of the sleeping bag to get the fire going, put on the covered pan, and let the contents come to a boil before setting it to one side for a few minutes. Then I add a liberal spoonful of butter and begin satisfying the inner man.

This, like a lot of things that would be just ordinary experience elsewhere, is a real luxury on a cold, beautiful morning when you're way out in the woods somewhere.

Two nesting aluminum kettles, the larger holding about 1½ quarts, together with an 8-inch frypan with conveniently folding handle, are available from dealers in sporting goods. Weighing less than two pounds, they add no appreciable bulk to a pack, inasmuch as food and other essentials can be stowed within them. Even when there are two or three people in the party, this same outfit can suffice. Just add a plate, cup, and spoon for each individual.

Best of all for camping is a small nested cooking and eating outfit made of a light, tough aluminum compound. Anyone who's ever burned himself on aluminum will agree that the nested cups, and preferably the plates also, could just as well be of stainless steel. The frying pan should be stainless steel, too. I bought an outfit of this sort when I first started going into the real wilderness, and I've used it without replacements or changes ever since. As a matter of fact, many of the components are so handy that even in towns one or another of them is still used almost daily.

Stoves The one-burner primus stove is often the answer for campers who hike beyond the treeline, although if you're in and out without doing any serious climbing, it's often possible to pack wood instead. In any event, these light, efficient little stoves may be obtained in functional units burning kerosene, gasoline, or canned gas. Alcohol is not generally adequate, burning with too cool a flame.

For example, there is a 2½-pound combination selling for about $15 which includes a 3½-pint casserole, a 2½-pint casserole, one lid pan, one upper and lower wind-guard, a potholder, a strap, and a gasoline stove—all nesting in a space 8¼ inches in diameter and 4¾ inches high. Lightweight, leakproof aluminum fuel bottles are also inexpensively available. The big catalog-issuing camp equipment dealers stock a functional variety of these units and combinations.

Fishing Gear If you hike very far, you're apt to be passing through some wonderful fishing country, well back from the roads, where there will be not only great sport but also gourmet food. Fine rods and reels, made expressly for go-light trips, are so compact and comparatively weightless that if your current budget has room for it, you certainly should get a set.

At the very least get a small container, perhaps an aluminum 35-mm film case, and fit in a few hooks, flies, and perhaps either some split shot or a few tiny strips of lead that can later be twisted into place as sinkers. You may want to include some salmon eggs for bait. Don't forget, either, to wind a small quantity of light, durable fishline such as nylon on a piece of cardboard. It can be used with a pole cut on the spot.

CHAPTER FOURTEEN

Eating from Nature's Free Banquet Table

ONE of the advantages of living in the country is the opportunity it affords to gather healthful foods from plants growing wild. Many of these foods can furnish the basis of a profitable business. For instance, many wild teas and preserves made from wild fruit will find ready markets in gourmet food shops. But even if you don't make any money by selling food products made from edible plants growing on your acre, you can enjoy the pleasure and nutritional benefits of consuming them yourself.

With more and more pesticides gradually poisoning too many of the cultivated areas of this continent, it's healthful as well as appetite-sharpening to go into the open places and gather undefiled foods from nature's own pure garden. Too, these wild delicacies have not been contaminated by the dozens of human fingers that handle and rehandle the fruits and vegetables sold in stores.

There's this, too. If you have ever drawn up your chair to a well-prepared meal that included wild vegetables, maybe you've noticed that many of them seem to taste better than their domesticated counterparts. I'll let you in on a trade secret. They are better.

Green leafy vegetables, to give just one example, deteriorate very quickly. Even when purchased as fresh as obtainable from the finest nearby market, they'll already have lost a sizable proportion of vitamins. Some of the food values of greens diminish as much as one-third during the first hour after picking. But gather them free, wild, and fresh and eat them at their tastiest, and you'll enjoy the best they have to offer.

Wild fruits, vegetables, nuts, roots, and teas grow everywhere. If you surely identify as edible everything before you pick it and if you prepare it properly—both of which you can do with the help of such books as my *Free for the Eating* and *More Free-for-the-Eating Wild Foods*—you will never have any trouble. Of course, some of the lichens are bitter in their natural states. But when this acidity is soaked out in water, such a variety as the familiar Iceland moss is so nutritious that it's packaged and widely sold as food and tonic for convalescents—a fact which may give you ideas for a profitable sideline.

Snowberry (Chiogenes)

The longish white fruits with their blueberryish ends, growing on slender branching vines in shady, dry soil as well as in northern muskegs and damp moss woodlands, have a pleasantly tart wintergreen aroma and flavor. Their piquantness adds to the flavor of grouse, which stuff their craws with them in the autumn. The aromatic leaves, dropped into boiling water and set resolutely away from the heat to steep, make a particularly refreshing tea.

"We determined to have some tea made of this," Henry D. Thoreau recorded in his journal when bivouacking in Maine. "It has a slight checkerberry flavor, and we both agreed that it was really better than the black tea which we had brought. We thought it quite a discovery and that it might well be dried and sold in the shops."

Give you a hunch?

Cattail (Typhaceae)

Who does not know these tall strap-leaved plants with their brown sausagelike heads which, growing in large groups from two

Snowberry

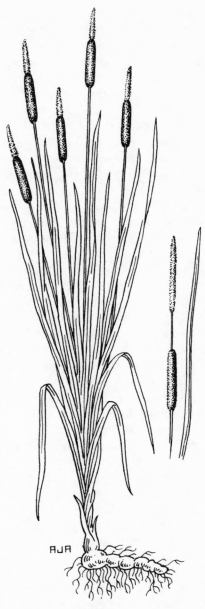

Cattail

to nine feet high, are exclamation points in wet places throughout the temperate and tropical countries of the world?

Although now relatively unused in the United States, where four species thrive, cattails are deliciously edible both raw and cooked from their starchy roots to their cornlike spikes, making them prime sources of nourishment the year around.

Furthermore, the long slender basal leaves, dried and then soaked for a few minutes to make them pliable, provide rush seating for chairs, as well as tough material for handy mats. As for the fluff of the light-colored seeds, which enlivens many a winter wind, this will softly fill your pillows and provide warm stuffing for your comforters.

An easy way to make rush mats and picturesque baskets for your home use or for sale is to tie together the butts of three dried and then briefly soaked long leaves, then to braid them in the usual manner. Once a rush starts to taper, lay in the thicker end of another, continuing the two as one strand. This way the braiding can be continued as long as you want. Rush mats and baskets can then be made by winding and sewing the flat coil together to the size wanted, as suggested by the drawings.

Cattails are also known in different places as rushes, cossack asparagus, cat-of-nine-tails, bulrushes, and flags. Sure signs of fresh or brackish water, they are tall, ruggedly stemmed perennials with stiff, thin, swordlike green leaves up to six feet long. These have round, well-developed rims at their sheathing bases.

The branching rootstocks creep in crossing tangles a few inches below the usually muddy surface. The flowers grow densely at the tops of the plants in spikes which, first plumply green and finally a shriveling yellow, resemble long bottle brushes and eventually produce millions of tiny, wind-wafted seeds.

These seeds, it so happens, are too small and hairy to be very attractive to birds except to a few like the teal. It is the starchy underground stems that attract such wildlife as geese and muskrat. Too, I've seen moose dripping their huge ungainly heads where cattails grow.

Another name for this prolific free edible should be wild corn. Put on boots and have the fun of collecting a few dozen of the greenish yellow flower spikes before they start to become tawny

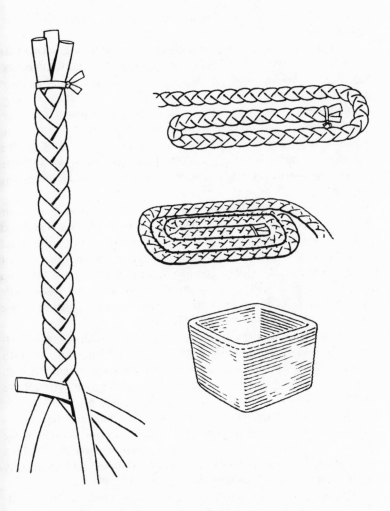

Making Rush Mats and Baskets from Cattail Leaves

with pollen. Husk off the thin sheaths and, just as you would with the domestic vegetable, put while still succulent into rapidly boiling water for a few minutes, until tender. Have plenty of butter or margarine by each plate, as these will probably be somewhat roughly dry, and keep each hot stalk liberally swabbed as you feast on it. Eat like corn. You'll end up with a stack of wiry cobs, feeling deliciously satisfied.

Some people object to eating corn on the cob, too, especially when there is company. This problem can be delectably solved by scraping the boiled flower buds from the cobs, mixing 4 cups of them with 2 cups of buttered bread crumbs, 2 well-beaten eggs, 1 teaspoon salt, ⅛ teaspoon pepper, and a cup of whole milk. Pour into a casserole, sprinkle colorfully with paprika, and heat in a moderate oven 15 minutes.

These flower spikes later grow profusely golden with thick yellow pollen which, easily and quickly rubbed or shaken into pails or onto a cloth, is also very much edible. A common way to take advantage of this gilded substance, which can be handily cleaned by passing it through a sieve, is by mixing it half-and-half with regular flour in breadstuffs.

For example, the way to make pleasingly golden cattail pancakes for four is by sifting together 1 cup pollen, 1 cup flour, 2 teaspoons double-action baking powder, 2 tablespoons sugar, and ½ teaspoon salt. Beat 2 eggs and stir them into 1⅓ cups of milk, adding 2 tablespoons of melted butter or margarine. Then rapidly mix the wet and dry ingredients together. Pour the batter at once in cakes the size of saucers onto a sparingly greased griddle, short of being smoking hot. Turn each flapjack only once, when the hotcake starts showing small bubbles. The second side takes only about half as long to cook. Serve steaming hot with butter and sugar, with some wild syrup perhaps, or with what you will.

It is the tender white insides of about the first 1 or 1½ feet of the peeled young stems that, eaten either raw or cooked, lend this worldwide delicacy its name of cossack asparagus. These highly edible aquatic herbs can thus be an important subsistence food in the spring.

Later on in the fall and winter quantities of the nutritiously starchy roots can be dug and washed, peeled while still wet, dried, and then ground into a highly nutritious meal which you may want to sift to get out any fibers. Too, there is a pithy little tidbit where the new stems sprout out of the rootstocks that can be boiled or roasted like young potatoes. All in all, is it any wonder that the picturesque cattails, now too often neglected except by nesting birds, were once an important Indian standby?

Wild Plum (Prunus)

Some fifteen species of wild plums abound throughout the United States and southern Canada, growing from Alaska and California to the Great Lakes and to the eastern seaboard, where the fragrant white flowers of the prolific beach plum brighten the springtimes.

These free plums are close cousins botanically of the wild cherries. Wildlife does not use the plum so freely, however, foxes being the most avid diners. On the other hand, scattered thickets afford invaluable shelter for birds and small game. The fruit varies considerably, some of it being delicious straight off the twigs. The chief value of much of the rest is in incomparable jellies, jams, and other kitchen delights.

The beach plum, *Prunus maritime,* is a wild native plum which grows in abundance along the beaches, among the sand dunes, and on the coastal plains from Nova Scotia and New Brunswick to Virginia and inland, as around the Great Lakes. It is very abundant in Massachusetts, on Cape Cod, and on the islands of Martha's Vineyard and Nantucket.

Growth and fruiting habits of the beach plum vary, a common trait in seedling plants. It resembles a bush more often than a tree. Some bushes sucker freely from the roots and produce dense thickets. The root systems are coarse, rangy, and deep, as necessitated by the usual bleak and dry habitat.

The fruit, which generally varies between one-half inch and one inch in diameter, ranges in color from red through purple to blue and almost black. Yellow-fruited bushes are occasionally found. The natural home of the beach plum is in sandy, light soils or even the pure sand of wind-sculptured dunes. Most beach plums bloom profusely each year but sport a crop only once every three or four years. One reason for this is that they depend on cross-pollination. The weather, which is often very foggy or rainy, dark, cold, and windy during blooming, may greatly reduce or even stop insect flight so that there is no transfer of pollen among the self-sterile plants. Too, it may slow the growth of the pollen tubes so that fertilization fails.

Specifically, the beach plum is a sprawling shrub up to about six feet in height. It does not have thorns, although the oval leaves are sharp with sawtooth edges. The innumerable white flowers burst out before the leaves start to appear. The fruit, which occupies many thrifty families day after day and finds its way into stores, ripens during the sweltering weather of August and September.

Another wild plum that is often seen in country markets is the *Prunus americana*, a great favorite among the Indians, and a native from Montana to New England, south to New Mexico, Texas, and Florida. Its numerous branches, whose twigs are thornlike, have rough, thick barbs. The oval or oblong leaves, ending in long, tapering points, are sharply saw-toothed like those of the beach plum. The frail white blossoms, again appearing before the leaves in early springtime, are extremely redolent. The red and sometimes yellow plums, appearing in late summer, are about seven-eigths of an inch in diameter, tough-skinned, pulpy, and usually sweet.

In northern California and southern Oregon many families make annual pilgrimages to wild plum orchards in and around the mountains and bring back luscious bushels of richly mottled yellow, red, and purple fruit, especially in the northern part of the range. Here the trees and shrubs are from three to ten feet tall, with ash-gray bark and occasionally spiny branches. The flowers, again appearing before the leaves from March to May, vary from white to rose. By August and September, the branches are often loaded with the handsome fruit, its colors duplicated in the brilliant autumn foliage.

Here is a way to preserve wild plums that does away with the bitterish taste often found in such cooked fruit. Wash the plums and prick the skins with a sharp fork. Pack in hot, sterilized jars and cover with boiling water. Seal and process for 20 minutes in a boiling-water bath. Then cool, label, and store. When you open a jar, pour off the juice for jelly or punch. Pit the fruit and for each quart of plums mix a cup of sugar with a cup of cold water. Pour this over the plums and let stand half an hour. Then enjoy them whatever way your fancy of the moment dictates.

Along Cape Cod there are so many dozens of home stands selling wild plum jelly that many start to enjoy this at an early age. There are

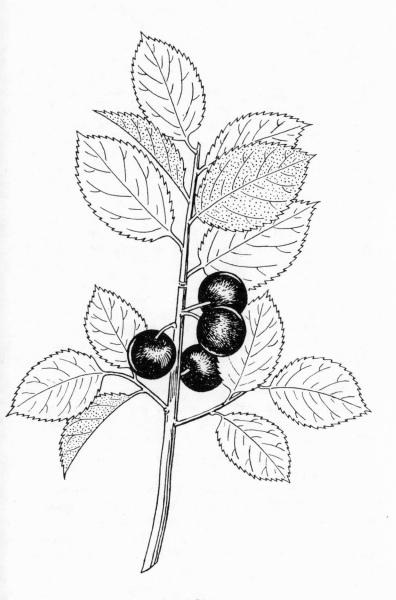

Beach Plum

two secrets of making this delicacy successfully. First, pick the plums while they are still on the unripe side. Second, unless you have special equipment, make only small batches at a time, about three quarts at once being plenty.

Pick over and wash the plums. Barely cover them with water and bring this to a boil. Then drain, cover with boiling water, and cook about 10 minutes or until soft, mashing and stirring every few minutes. Squeeze either through a sieve or a jelly bag. Measure the juice and return to the kettle. Slowly add an equal volume of sugar, all the time stirring. Boil rapidly until 2 drops form on the edge of a metal spoon, then come together to run off in a sheet. This occurs at 220° to 222°.

Pour to within ¼ inch of the tops of hot sterilized glasses. Have paraffin melting over water, and tip a thin layer atop each nearly filled glass, turning and slightly tilting the container so that the edges will be sealed. Cool, add a second thin layer of wax, cool, cover with a lid or aluminum foil, and store in a dark, cool, dry place. This is excellent with game, lamb, poultry, and especially with rare roast beef.

You may also care to experiment by combining plum juice with other wild juices to make your own blend of wild jelly. A particularly successful combination can be achieved by mixing every ⅔ cup of wild plum juice with ⅓ cup of wild apple juice, then proceeding as above to prepare your jelly.

Wild plum jam is also good. Wash and pit a quart of ripe plums, keeping the fruit as intact as feasible. Put in a large saucepan, along with ½ cup of water, and bring to a bubble. Gradually mix in 4 cups of sugar, all the time stirring. Simmer for 15 minutes or until thick, stirring whenever necessary to prevent sticking. Remove the froth.

Spoon into hot, sterilized glasses. Seal immediately with paraffin. Cover to protect from drafts, which might break the glass, and leave to cool. Label and store in dry, cool darkness. Incidentally, any wild jams or jellies that are to be kept in a damp place, or mailed, should be put instead into vacuum-sealed or screw-topped jars.

Maple (Acer)

The maple leaf, emblem of Canada and a principal reason why New England is so colorful in autumn—especially when frost-hazed nights are succeeded by brisk, smoky days—is known to ev-

Leaf and Fruits of the Sugar Maple

eryone. The fruits, too, are very characteristic, being made up of a pair of brown wings with the seeds enclosed in the plump juncture.

Maple seeds are edible by humans, some Indians formerly hulling the larger of them and then boiling them. So are the leaves. The inner bark of the maple is one of the more appetizing sap layers and is eaten in emergencies, either raw or cooked. But it is for the sap that the tree has been famous since Indian days.

Wild turkeys, quail, grouse, and prairie chickens eat maple buds, twigs, and seeds. Black bears, rabbits, beavers, and squirrels dine on flowers, seeds, bark, and twigs. Incidentally, before they store the seeds for winter use, squirrels often thriftily remove the hulls and wings. Deer, moose, elk, and mountain sheep relish twigs and foliage.

The first settlers to venture along the Atlantic seaboard were introduced to the wild sweet by the red men, who caught the sap in birchbark containers and in tightly woven baskets and skin vessels. All the maples have sugar-rich sap. So do other trees, for that matter, such as the birch and hickory. But it is the sugar maple, *Acer saccharum*, that is by far the most famous for this characteristic. Incidentally, the tree is perhaps the most prized of the hardwoods in the lumber industry. It is also a highly desirable shade and ornamental tree; so perhaps you have your own private source of maple sugar growing right by your own home.

Groves of maple trees, with rude sugar houses, are familiar landmarks in many parts of North America, inasmuch as the sugar maple grows from Newfoundland to Ontario and Minnesota, southward as far as Louisiana and Georgia. The trees, often reaching a height of from 60 to almost 100 feet, are tapped in late winter or early spring, before the buds begin to expand. Sharp, frosty nights, followed by mild thawing during the daylight hours, make for the free flow of sap. The sweetness of this varies, but it usually takes between thirty and forty gallons to boil down into a gallon of the high-priced syrup.

Additional boiling makes maple sugar. During early American years, this was about the consistency of present-day brown sugar. In fact, it was used in place of cane sugar by colonists who couldn't afford the then much more expensive sweetening, even when it was available. Maple sugar is still more nourishing than the mass manufactured product, containing the B vitamins, calcium, phosphorus, and enzymes refined from today's sugar beets and sugar cane.

You can buy the necessary spiles and pails for sap gathering. Unless you are going in for sugaring in a big way, though, you can do very well on your own. The Indians used to cut a V-shaped gash in the tree, at the apex of which they drove an elderberry spout. The latter was made by cutting a straight elderberry limb in the spring, drying it with the leaves on, and then poking out the soft pith of the interior with hot sticks.

You may find it less wasteful to drill about a two-inch deep hole with a gimlet, or brace and bit, and to close this with a peg when you're finished. For the spout, just make a single bend in a can top removed by one of the smooth-cutting openers. Don't try to suspend the pail from this, however. Instead, drive a nail into the tree for this purpose. As a precaution, empty the containers often enough so that the sap doesn't hang too long in the sun and sour.

Then it's just a matter of boiling the sap, and spooning off the characteristic scum as it rises, until some thirty-five or so parts of water evaporate, leaving a clear amber syrup. This must be strained very carefully. For sugar, continue boiling until a test portion of the syrup forms a very soft ball in cold water. Then remove from the fire, beat with an egg beater if you're making only a small amount or a regular sugar beater if you have a large quantity, and pour into dry molds.

One's first sugaring-off party is in the same category as that initial seashore clambake—unforgettable! I remember as a small boy riding out to a hillside maple bush behind two glistening horses in a pung. Syrup was already bubbling in the sugar house with an elusive and marvelous odor, and they gave me a small pitcher of it and an old fork.

Everything must have been ready, for when I strung this amber liquid out in a fine line on fresh snow, it hardened. Even before it was cool enough, I twined the string on my fork and transferred it gingerly to my mouth. This I repeated until all the syrup was gone, and then I got some more. The flavor was indescribable, except that there was the aroma of the forest in its sweetness—the fresh wind blowing, the branches swinging overhead, and all the free, rich wildness of the mountains themselves.

You'll get snow in your boots at a sugaring-off party and there'll be an occasional bit of bark in your sweet. But you won't give either a second thought. It's worth it a dozen times over.

CHAPTER FIFTEEN

Where the Hunting and Fishing Are Better

OBVIOUSLY, when venturing from your secure acre in the search for free meat and fish, you won't want to bother any endangered species. All our farming, clearing, road-building, lumbering, industry, spreading cities, and, to a much lesser degree, guns, have wiped out fifty varieties of wildlife and threatened eighty-nine others.

But the fact is that certain animals such as deer, raccoon, beaver, and many of the game birds must be kept thinned out—as they would have been in the past by the now largely decimated predators or by disease—or they'll strip and destroy their ranges by overeating and suffer the more lingering and painful deaths of infection and starvation. Fish, too, must be regularly harvested if the young ones are to continue to grow large and healthy.

The Role of Deer in the Settling of North America

Conditions vary, of course, but North American deer populations in particular are at new heights in numerous areas, so much so that in a number of places their very abundance threatens their existence. Deer in particular have played a major role in our continental development. Whitetails clothed and fed our pioneer ancestors, furnished meat for the Revolutionaries under the command of General George Washington, and were an important means of sustenance for the trappers and adventurers who opened the West.

Some 50 million whitetails bounded among the trees two centuries ago. By the turn of this century, wholesale market killing had nearly exterminated them in most regions. But with conservation measures to give them a foothold, the whitetails quickly repopulated their thinned ranks.

The expansion of our civilization itself has furnished a hand, the cutting of huge stands of timber encouraging the growth of the small woody vegetation on which deer browse in winter. Today there are some 8 million highly adaptable whitetails living almost everywhere. In fact, some of the densest populations are to be found around some of the cities, as in New Jersey, where this is a definite problem, hunting having been outlawed in many of these crowded sections.

Solving the Problem of Deer Malnutrition

When winter loss occurs as a result of overpopulations, it is the greatest among the fawns. Because most of their first summer's food has been used up in growth, fawns do not have the fat reserves of older animals.

Next to fawns the bucks, particularly the older ones, suffer most. Mature bucks have been through the rut and have used up much of their fat reserves before winter began, and this fat supply is vitally important with all deer. First, the fat overlying the back and rump is devoured, then that within the thin tissues surrounding the intestines. Finally, the fat is drawn from the marrow of the very bones. When this occurs, the deer is suffering from severe malnutrition.

The does experience the least mortality. They enter the cold season in good condition, and most of them will survive to produce fawns—nature's way of insuring that the essential productivity of the herd is not destroyed.

Artificial feeding? Most game departments have tried this in the

Whitetail Deer

past and found that it is invariably futile. Artificial feeding, therefore, is not the answer. Keeping the herds to a size that can be supported on the natural winter range is the key to prevention of deer malnutrition; it pays off in less suffering and increased productivity. It has been proved that a smaller, well-fed base herd will produce more deer than a larger, poorly fed herd. You can help, if you are a hunter, by enjoying the vastly better results to be gained by traveling to one of the teeming areas. As a matter of fact, good hunting and fishing in your very own neighborhood may influence your choice of that acre in the first place.

Areas of Game Surpluses

Mule deer hunting remains good to excellent in the continental West. There are bumper crops among the elk. Moose continue to increase and to expand their ranges throughout much of Canada, aided by a substantial nucleus that still inhabit the tall timbers where, as the saying goes, the hand of man has seldom set foot.

Wild turkeys, too, continue to expand. With our technology producing more food on less land these years and with the agricultural experts recommending that marginal farmlands be shifted to other uses, such farm game as pheasant, rabbits, and quail are being given a boost.

Ruffed grouse, whose drumming enlivens the spring woods, are on the increase. Bobwhite quail gunning is rated good to excellent by wildlife biologists in the key southern and southeastern states. These same experts note the huge and underhunted quail crops in such traditional pheasant strongholds as Nebraska, Iowa, and Kansas. Sage grouse, sharptails, and one of the most exciting comers of them all, the chukar partridge, continue to improve in many areas.

Wetlands Conservation and Waterfowl   The increasing support for wetlands conservation is assuring harvestable surpluses of ducks and geese for the present as well as the future, although, of course, waterfowl populations fluctuate over short periods. But the multimillion-dollar federal wetlands program, along with similar efforts of a now acutely concerned citizenry, is making itself felt. Ducks Unlimited, for instance, in 1966 collected more than $1 million for the first time. Only three years later, the conservation unit doubled that amount and took in over $2 million for wetlands management in Canada.

All in all, the sportsman is no longer facing his problems alone. The man on the street, finally, is becoming conscious of his environment and is starting to realize what nimrods have known for years: that the best parts of our world are the easiest to lose. Almost everywhere, wildlife authorities from coast to coast are urging private citizens to take advantage of the bumper crops, for wildlife is one thing that cannot be stockpiled. For the millions of us who hunt, it's reasonable to seek the specific locations where there are overpopulations, for death by gun is more humane than death by starving. There's better hunting, too.

Overpopulations of Deer in British Columbia In British Columbia, for example, deer are so thick on the elongated emerald chain of Queen Charlotte Islands, between the salt waters of Alaska and Washington, that, as Fish and Wildlife Director Dr. Jim Hatter assures me, "There is an open season twelve months of the year, and there is no limit as to the number of deer that may be taken."

This archipelago of 150 islands, prosperous with timber, mines, and fish in addition to game, may in fact be attractive to modern pioneers who would like to live to a certain extent off the land—on sizzling venison steaks, succulent salmon, hearty halibut, and toothsome clams and mussels. You'll see them arising out of the vast Pacific, these wooded isles interlaced with arms of the sea, with mountains and forests to the water's edge, and with endless beaches rimmed with the white and ceaseless surf. But that's another book, my *How to Live in the Woods on Pennies a Day*.

Squirrels, Raccoon, and Small Game

According to the game officials, heavily settled Massachusetts finds that the gray squirrel "would tolerate some additional hunting pressure." As far as this gourmet's delight is concerned, neighboring New Hampshire is having similar difficulties.

Of even more concern in the latter New England state, though, is raccoon overpopulation. The Chief of Game Management and Research there tells me, "The low price for its hide has cut down on trapping pressure. While there are a number of coon hunters with good hounds, there are not enough in New Hampshire to keep the coon population within reasonable bounds. This animal could stand much heavier hunting pressure. As for deer, these are still underharvested in extensive forest lands lacking a network of roads, as in Coos County."

Beaver, although furbearers and not considered a game species, have overpopulated some areas in west Tennessee. According to game authorities, too, the counties along the Tennessee River could stand more deer hunting.

"Raccoon and woodchuck continued to become a problem in scattered local situations throughout Ohio depending on the farming practices and crops involved," the Supervisor of Game Management there told me. And if you've never sat down to a savory feast of these two notable small-game animals, you haven't lived yet. Recipes? For these and many others, see my *Gourmet Cooking for Free.*

Crows, opossum, and raccoon, which when thinned out should be brought to the table and not wasted, are among the species underharvested throughout Wisconsin. Rabbits, when near the tops of their cycles, are problems in Colorado.

That'll give you an idea. Game densities vary, of course, and although at this writing there were numerous other instances of wildlife overpopulations throughout the country, whenever a current local condition of this sort is a matter of personal concern you may well get the up-to-the-minute picture by writing the department of game and fish in the capital city of the state or province in which you are interested.

How to Catch Bigger, Healthier Fish

When we were kids in northern Maine one summer, we portaged a canoe and camped on a remote lake for a week, living largely off the country and mostly on fish which bit avidly and which we grilled on green sticks over small campfires. That portion of New England was famous for its "landlocked salmon," which were new to us. In any event, fish had never tasted sweeter than these, bettered by the tang of birch smoke and helped along by ravenous appetites. We were more than satisfied with the succulencies of "landlocked salm-

Cooking Fish on a Suburban Patio

on," except that when we got back to civilization and described our trophies they turned out to be chub.

In other words, much is in a name and reputation; so don't despise a gleaming string of perch if that's what you catch in place of trout. As for better fishing, it's the same old story. Get back from the traveled thoroughfares.

Speaking of perch, if a pair of one-pound white perch were placed in a pond and only 1 percent of their offspring survived, they could increase to more than 2 million perch in four years. In two or three more years, the numbers would look like those of our national budget. The figure of 2 million may not impress you very much, but can you visualize catching 5,400 perch every day for a year? That would come to just under 2 million. Have you ever seen 54 fishermen catch 100 perch each and every day of the year from your favorite lake? Chances are that most ponds are not fished enough in an entire year to remove 3,700 perch from them.

The Related Problems of Excess Fish and Fish Stunting If a lucky or enterprising fisherman, with a freezer so that nothing will be wasted, happens to be seen with a bushel basket of white perch, a cry of alarm is heard all the way to the state house. Actually, the individual who does remove large quantities of perch from a pond is improving the growth of the millions of small ones waiting for their chance to thrive.

With large numbers of young perch being spawned each year, it's easy to see how the perch in a body of water can become stunted. They literally pile up at a certain size until there is not enough food to go around. The older perch continue to grow because they are large enough to eat the small, stunted perch that few want to keep.

How many times have you heard people say, "We used to catch nice big perch when I was a kid, but now you can't catch one more than four inches long." But how can the small perch grow under conditions so crowded that each one is fortunate if it can find a few insects a day to eat? Unlike many other animals, fish can live for years with very little food, but they do not grow in such situations. Most fish can live for months with no food at all, in contrast to warm-blooded animals, which need a good supply of grub just to maintain their body temperature.

So when people living on the land take the trouble to angle in underfished waters, they are not only going to enjoy more abundant catches, but are also going to be helping the life of that water.

Where to Harvest Excess Fish For example, according to game management authorities, there is "a constant problem in New Hampshire with yellow perch and sunfish. These fish are underharvested wherever they exist in our lakes and streams to the detriment of more valuable game fishes."

"Numerous Rhode Island ponds are overpopulated with fish, and increased fishing would be desirable," says the Division of Fish and Wildlife there. "As an example, Slacks Reservoir in Smithfield produces more than 1,200 pounds of bluegills per day during an annual children's derby."

"Kansas boasts some excellent warm-water sport fishing opportunities but, as is the case in most warm-water fishing areas, over-population of certain species is a continual problem," states the local Forestry, Fish and Game Commission. "As an example, Clark County State Lake, a 300-acres man-made impoundment, has excessive populations of crappie and bullhead and can stand several times the current fishing pressure for these species. Selective fishing pressure seems to be the problem. Fishermen usually exert the most of their efforts on such game species as largemouth bass, walleyes, white bass, and channel catfish. The small panfish species can support much more fishing pressure in almost any of impounded waters of Kansas."

"Overpopulations of panfish exist in many lakes in all regions of Wisconsin," asserts the Supervisor of Big Game Management. "An increased harvest of these species is encouraged with extremely liberal regulations." However, there is still "a lack of interest by fishermen."

"Any of the larger, warm-water lakes in Arizona could stand additional fishing pressures on rough fish, such as carp or bullheads, and panfish, such as green sunfish and bluegill," advises the Game and Fish Department.

"Many lakes in Oregon could receive more pressure," says the Game Commission there. "Our greatest underharvest is with our warm-water game fish such as crappie, sunfish, perch, bullheads, and even the smallmouth and largemouth bass.

"Oregonians are trout, salmon, and steelhead-conscious with only a handful of avid warm-water game fish fishermen. These fishermen go at it energetically, but yet these species are way underharvested. The result is stunting in numerous lakes and ponds. Those waters fished regularly generally produce nice catches and good-sized fish. Owyhee Reservoir is one large reservoir from which anglers take crappie and largemouths out by the tubfull, but generally light fishing pressure barely makes a dent in the populations. We have several other huge impoundments such as Brownlee, Oxbow, and Hells Canyon which are so lightly fished it's almost pathetic."

"Oklahoma fishing is good statewide," avers the Department of Wildlife Conservation. "However, the best sport fishing occurs during the second through fifth year following impoundment of a new reservoir. Upon impoundment, all terrestrial vegetation in the flooded basin dies. Due to the added fertility from the decomposing vegetation, the fish populations skyrocket and sport species grow rapidly in the new lake.

"When this happens, we have a *hot* fishing lake. After a few years, fertility ebbs, conditions become more than optimum for nongame fish, and some forage species become too large for sport species to engorge. Consequently, there is less for them to feed on, and the fishermen catch less which are not as healthy or as large."

Arkansas has its overpopulations of fish, according to the Game and Fish Commission there, but these are mostly composed of the less desirable, though good eating, varieties. The Commission initiated in 1945 "a program of building lakes in areas of high population, or in portions of the state where there is a scarcity of natural fishing water, or in areas where fishing has generally declined despite an abundance of fishable waters." Here you can enjoy fine catches of bass, crappie, big redear and bluegill bream, and the lurking channel catfish.

Among Idaho's 2,000 lakes, many of which sparkle in the high mountains, a scattered number of the more remote have overpopulations of trout which are resulting in stunted growth and the need for additional harvests. Too, there are warm-water fisheries where overpopulations of fish such as bass, crappie, and perch exist. "Brownlee Reservoir would be an example of this kind, on the Snake River in western Idaho, where a large population of small crappie abounds," according to Idaho's Fish and Game Department.

Abundant populations of yellow perch in some Maine lakes are exploited very little by anglers, according to the Department of Inland Fisheries and Game there.

"Additional fishing pressure would be desirable on several of Wyoming's warm-water lakes and reservoirs. These will include Ocean Lake, Boysen Reservoir, and Bighorn Lake," says the Game and Fish Commission in Cheyenne.

"In some of our lakes due to excessive cover and hiding places, forage species such as the bream fishes will overpopulate and become stunted," points out the Louisiana Wild Life and

Fisheries Commission. "For some reason, excessive number of bream will cause the largemouth bass to cease from spawning, resulting in disappearing of a bass population.

"Whether the bass cease to spawn because of overcrowded conditions, or whether the bluegill excretes some type of chemical into the waters which causes the bass to cease spawning, is not certain. However, when the bass-bluegill population reaches this undesired condition, then it is beneficial to fish very heavily the bream species. Fishing bream heavily in lakes usually is always beneficial. Very seldom will the population of bream be decimated to a danger point because of heavy fishing pressure."

QUITTING THE RAT RACE

Admittedly, quitting the rat race before it quits you means more work of a sort: hunting and fishing for your supper, raising your own vegetables, and perhaps building your own home. But it will be work you will enjoy doing. Your money will go five times farther, and you'll look forward to getting up mornings.

Audacity, persistence, courage, and careful planning still win their satisfying and abundant rewards. Why not try it and see for yourself?